Memories of a
Louisiana
Girlhood

http://ulpress.org
University of Louisiana at Lafayette Press
P.O. Box 43558
Lafayette, LA 70504-3558

Printed on acid-free paper in the United States
Library of Congress Cataloging-in-Publication Data

Names: Dubus, Elizabeth Nell, author.
Title: Memories of a Louisiana girlhood : with recipes / Elizabeth Nell
  Dubus.
Description: Lafayette, LA : University of Louisiana at Lafayette Press,
  2023
Identifiers: LCCN 2023007541 | ISBN 9781946160997 (paperback)
Subjects: LCSH: Dubus, Elizabeth Nell,--Childhood and youth. | Lafayette
  (La.)--Biography. | Dubus family. | Burke family. | World War,
  1939-1945--Social aspects--Louisiana. | Acadiana (La.)--Social life and
  customs--20th century. | Cooking, American--Louisiana style.
Classification: LCC F377.L2 D83 2023 | DDC 976.3/4092
  [B]--dc23/eng/20230221
LC record available at https://lccn.loc.gov/2023007541

Cover photo: The author circa 1940 with brother André hiding behind the steps.

Memories of a
Louisiana Girlhood

with Recipes

Elizabeth Nell Dubus

2023
UNIVERSITY OF LOUISIANA AT LAFAYETTE PRESS

Table of Contents

Burke

UNG·ROY·UNG·FOY·UNG·LOY

Ellen Lee
b. 1813, Waterford, Ireland
d. 9/15/1865,
New Orleans, LA

James Lee Burke
b. 2/22/1833, Elizabethtown, NJ
d. 9/13/1886, New Iberia, LA

William Burke
b. 1807, Waterford, Ireland
d. 10/18/1839,
New Iberia, LA

**Walter James Burke
(PaPa)**
b. 10/20/1866, New Iberia, LA
d. 1/22/1941, New Iberia, LA

Mary Pamela Canon
b. 11/8/1838, Natchitoches, LA
d. 9/3/1877, New Iberia, LA

Robert Samuel Perry
b. 12/5/1834, Perry's Bridge, LA
d. 2/24/1900, New Iberia, LA

**Bertha Gary Perry
(MaMa)**
b. July 1871, St. Martinville, LA
d. 12/14/1948, New Iberia, LA

Bertha Gary
b. 4/17/1846, St. Martinville, LA
d. 1878, New Iberia, LA

Burke Family Tree

**André Jules Dubus
(Daddy)**
b. 11/16/1903, Lake Charles, LA
d. 7/14/1963, Lake Charles, LA

Elizabeth (Beth) Nell Dubus
b. 10/26/1933, Lake Charles, LA
d. 8/30/2020, Baton Rouge, LA

**Katherine Bertha Burke
(Mother)**
b. 1/2/1903, New Iberia, LA
d. 12/5/1980, Lake Charles, LA

The Ancient Arms of

Du Bus

Louis Noel Dubus
b. 12/25/1813, Picardie,
France
d. 7/1879, Lafayette, LA

Radegonde Julie Launay
b. c. 1804, France
d. 8/27/1853,
New Orleans, LA

Louis Jules Dubus
b. 3/12/1844, Paris, France
d. 6/18/1896, New Iberia, LA

Louise Henrietta Goujon
b. 4/1/1846, Bretagne, France
d. 5/29/1903, New Orleans, LA

André August (Paw Paw)
b. 12/30/1882, New Iberia, LA
d. 2/9/1935, Abbeville, LA

William Pickens Reames
b. 3/17/1829, St. Helena, LA
d. 9/16/1897, Wilson, LA

Anna Eliza Brooks
b. 9/24/1841, Unknown
d. 2/12/1915, New Orleans, LA

Jessie Ella Reames (Maw Maw)
b. 9/2/1880, Clinton, LA
d. 10/26/1947, Houston, TX

Dubus Family Tree

Katherine Bertha Burke (Mother)
b. 1/2/1903, New Iberia, LA
d. 12/5/1980, Lake Charles, LA

Elizabeth (Beth) Nell Dubus
b. 10/26/1933, Lake Charles, LA
d. 8/30/2020, Baton Rouge, LA

André Jules Dubus (Daddy)
b. 11/16/190,3 Lake Charles, LA
d. 7/14/1963, Lake Charles, LA

CHAPTER ONE

U ntil the flood of 2016, when there was a foot and a half of water in the library/playroom in my home in Prairieville, Louisiana, a dollhouse I had built in the early months of my second marriage as a memory piece stood, its furnishing chosen to mimic rooms I'd grown up with. The house was a replica of a turreted Victorian house, unlike any house I've ever lived in. But it had many elements that transported me back to my childhood, a time of innocence and tranquility.

It had a wide front porch, like the porch of the first house I lived in and the porch that stretched down the side of my maternal Burke grandparents' home in New Iberia. Fireplaces in the living room and gentleman's study reminded me of leaping flames and blackened marshmallows, baby clothes drying on a rack, the scent of pecan wood burning—a montage of sensual memories beginning in early childhood and extending through all the years I've lived since.

There was a sewing room, complete with a Singer sewing machine and dressmaker's mannequin, and a kitchen furnished with copper pots and a German-made miniature of a metal wood-burning stove, reminding me of my paternal grandmother, who starred in both arenas.

A japanned lady's desk, with a blotting pad on which lay a half-finished letter, written in French, brought memories of my maternal grandmother, who spent her mornings sitting at her desk, where she carried on a voluminous correspondence with family and friends from California to New York, sending news of engagements, marriages, births, illnesses, and deaths, writing descriptions of trips to New Orleans or the Gulf Coast, or of teas and literary club meetings, as well as any other bits of family life that might be not only of interest, but also suitable to tell.

The gentleman's study, with a large desk where a pipe rack and a cigar humidor occupied one corner and bookshelves lined the walls, was a replica of my maternal grandfather's study.

A grand piano dominated the music room, just as my Cousin Anna Sartwelle's concert grand dominated her front parlor. In the master bedroom, a wicker tray set for breakfast, with even a tiny pot of orange marmalade (found by my daughter Maggi in Santa Monica), was like the trays brought to my bed during childhood ailments.

The parlor, furnished with a love seat and chairs of carved wood and silk brocade upholstery, had a tea cart drawn up to the fire. Little pastries from Paris were on its tiny china plates and a silver tea service sat on a silver tray, surrounded by minute cups. All the teas of my growing up years, from tête-à-tête's with my mother to formal afternoon affairs, came back as I touched the tea cart with the tip of my finger and felt it move forward, just as though the ladies it served were real.

That dollhouse was a repository of good memories. I acquired it in the first year of my second marriage, to Dick Baldridge, a man who found nothing silly about his wife wanting a dollhouse and took an interest in it that was real.

It was many years later before I faced the reason I wanted a dollhouse. The divorce that ended my first marriage was so destructive that the lawyer handling my side said his law firm, one of the most distinguished in the area, had never handled such a brutal divorce, calling it a war.

In the eleven years after the first marriage ended, the people and places and events of my girlhood had been much more real to me than many of those I dealt with every day. Unable to accept the brutality, the meanness, the sheer waste of the present reality, I fled to a happier time, a time rich in love and laughter, a time that created a kingdom of the mind and heart and spirit, one that, thank heaven, is there for me still.

As is the landscape in which it came into being. The Acadiana I knew is one quite different from the one popularized during the last decades, though the physical setting is the same. Acadiana is bounded on the east by the Atchafalaya Basin; on the west by prairies; on the north by the red clay country of central and north Louisiana; and on the south by Vermilion Bay, which opens into the Gulf of Mexico. It has swamps and woods, bayous and rivers and streams. It has fields of rice and sugarcane and soybeans and winter wheat. It has pastures with grazing cattle and farms where catfish and crawfish grow.

It's famous for its food, its music, and its people, as well as the history that lies in its houses, churches, and cemeteries. Like many places that attract tourists, Acadiana can seem like a theme park, except that its features are real.

The park at St. Martinville has two homes, an Acadian cabin, and a larger home that belonged to the Maraist family before it became a house museum.

The father of one of my best friends, Jeannie Maraist, grew up in that house, and the first time Jeannie and I visited, she said it felt very strange to be in a family home that was now a tourist attraction.

Shadows-on-the-Teche, in New Iberia, is another house museum. It belonged to the Weeks family and is on the National Register of Historic Places. One of its attractions is a door signed by many famous writers, movie stars, and politicians of the early years of the twentieth century, friends of the last heir, William Weeks Hall, who studied art in Paris and lived the life of the creative rich.

Though the family furniture and silver, its china, its linens and paintings are still there, and though guides tell a story about these, and about the house, all the real stories, the ones known only to family and close friends, the stories that change a chair into an artifact, a staircase into a catalyst for tragedy, are left out.

For example, though I have toured the Shadows with visitors seeing it for the first time, I've never heard a story like the one I'm about to tell. My mother's oldest sister, Roberta, and her husband, Francis Voorhies, were close friends of Weeks Hall, as were the rest of the family. (My sister, Kathryn, and I were taken to tea with Mr. Hall on several occasions, though after making our manners, we took our refreshments to a bench overlooking Bayou Teche and left conversation to the grown-ups.)

One evening, my aunt and uncle had been invited to have drinks with Hall. He was in a slow decline and had a manservant in constant attendance. My uncle knocked, and Hall himself opened the door. "And, my dears," Aunt Roberta said when telling this story, "he was absolutely starkers. Not a stitch."

Slight gasp from listeners, followed by, "Good heavens, Roberta, what did you do?"

"I took his hand and told him how delighted we were to see him and kept my eyes fixed on his while your uncle got his manservant, who brought a robe, and then took him off to get dressed." When complimented on her poise, Aunt Roberta said, "One does nothing to embarrass or discommode a friend. No matter what happens, one simply rises above it."

Stories like this bring the people in my interior landscape to life, while remembered sensual perceptions fill it with scents and sounds, textures and tastes: the feel of a humid summer day or the bracing breezes of the first cold spell. And always the sights—the mind's camera capturing them, saving them, and creating settings that make memories real.

One of my earliest memories is the scent of a sweet olive tree that bloomed outside the window of the room my sister and I shared. In other memories, that scent blends with old southern favorites: magnolia frascati, magnolia, gardenia, and confederate jasmine. And roses, the old bourbon and damask roses with intense scents that turned the rose garden into a perfumery.

Other remembered scents are more prosaic. Open kitchen windows blend the aromas of a richly-seasoned gumbo or court bouillon with the outside air, stirring the appetite of anyone who smells it. In summer, there is the unmistakable scent of fig preserves ready to be jarred. Old kitchens have layers of these scents. One enters them and can read the foods that have been cooked there: smothered okra, chicken fricassee, oyster pie. Laced through it is pot after pot after pot of dark roast coffee, dripped tablespoon by tablespoon to make the proper strong brew.

The sounds of my landscape include those rarely heard by people who live behind closed windows in climate-controlled rooms. Not for them the dawn sounds of birds slowly waking or a wagon creaking down a brick street. Voices of neighbors sitting on their back steps drinking the first cup of coffee of the day blend with voices in the house, the lazy morning greetings that, no matter the words, mean, "We're here. We're safe. We made it through the night."

One of the first flavors I remember is pink popcorn, a treat dispensed by a man who drove a box-like wagon through Lake Charles's streets from early spring until winter came. Pink popcorn is sugared, and to this day, one bite and years fall away—I'm standing at the curb with Kathryn while a neighbor child tries to decide between popcorn or a stick of hard candy with stripes of yellow and red.

Everyone has such a landscape. Many resemble battlefields, pockmarked by bombs and shells, littered with the dead and dying. Some resemble prisons, cages in which powerless victims of cruelty or neglect huddle, waiting for rescue. And yet, when I taught Freshman Composition at three Louisiana universities, I learned from my students, in essays written about those landscapes inside, how often memories of someone who loved and supported and encouraged them offset all those who didn't.

This, then, is a story of how my own landscapes were formed, beginning not with my birth on October 26, 1933, in Lake Charles, Louisiana, but with the stories of the family members who came before me and who are still present in my life.

My father, André Jules Dubus, bore one of the names (André) that appeared in family records since the first Dubus arrived in New Orleans in 1793, fleeing the Reign of Terror launched by Maximilian Robespierre and his fellow Jacobins in France. The family fled France with a chest of silver

The Burke family on the porch of their New Iberia home.
Left to right: Donald and Celeste Burke; Mary Pamela Burke; Bertha Burke and
Julian Eves; Clem and Marjorie Burke Binnings; Perry and Darcy Burke, Polly and
James Lee Burke, Peggy and Oran Burke, Roberta Burke and Francis Voorhies.

coins, a few pieces of furniture, some jewelry, and the bayonet my ancestor
had used defending the Bastille.

Once in New Orleans, the silver coins were turned into flat silver by a
silversmith. My nephew, Andre Jules Dubus III, has the spoons and forks, as
well as a mahogany table brought over at the same time. The bayonet was stolen from my brother André's home when he lived in Bradford, Massachusetts.
He always thought the thief must have been someone he knew, though he
never found out who.

The Dubus family remained in New Orleans until the late 1800s. At
that time, there were four brothers. One remained in New Orleans to manage the Dubus Engine Company; one moved to Colorado Springs; one to
Savannah; and the fourth, my grandfather, André August Dubus, to New

Iberia. He opened the first automobile dealership in southwest Louisiana, served as justice of the peace (more like a city court judge today), and headed the Southwestern Louisiana Chapter of the American Red Cross.

He married Jessie Reames, an auburn-haired, blue-eyed woman of Scottish descent who grew up in Clinton, Louisiana, a historic town in East Feliciana Parish not far from St. Francisville. They had four children—my father, and then three daughters, Elsie, Florine, and Annie Mai—and raised the family in nearby Abbeville.

During my father's growing up years, Abbeville had a population of a little over three thousand, but apparently a sufficient number of those adhered to the rules of a civilized society, because, as my father told me, when he and his friends had all the civilization they could take, they would disappear into the swamps with their dogs, their guns, and their knives, emerging after three days "ready to face the ladies again."

He did not remain in Abbeville long. Two months before he turned fifteen, he left for Vanderbilt, planning to major in premed. I have a picture from 1918 of my father with his sisters taken shortly before he left. Their expressions are solemn, affirming the momentous nature of the occasion, as the eldest sibling embarks on his life as an adult. Elsie, the eldest sister, stands on my father's right, with the youngest, Florine, in front of her. Annie Mai, the middle sister, stands to my father's left, her hands on the handle of a wicker doll's buggy, with a long-haired doll in an elaborate dress sitting in it. My aunts' dresses are a style popular in the late teens of the twentieth century, with blouson tops over short, pleated skirts, worn with black stockings.

André Jules Dubus and sisters Elsie Eliza (*top left*), Florine Louise (*bottom left*), and Annie Mai (*right*).

It occurs to me that the solemn expressions of the picture's subjects could also be attributed to two grim events much in the news: World War I and the flu pandemic. Of the two, the pandemic would have been closer to home, particularly for my father, because his father risked his life to visit those stricken with that deadly flu, taking them food and medicine. My grandfather's obituary, which took up the entire front page of the *Abbeville Meridional*, described this act of mercy, stating that, "Mr. Dubus entered homes that even doctors and nurses wouldn't, bringing comfort as well as the necessities of life." That same obituary describes another act of heroism, one that occurred on a train trip to New Orleans. "All of a sudden, a crazed man jumped up, took out a revolver, and began waving it in the air, threatening to shoot, and frightening the women and children on board. Mr. Dubus rose and approached the man. 'You're terrifying these ladies,' he said. 'As well as their children. Now, give me your gun and let's talk.' After a long moment, the man did as Mr. Dubus asked. They sat together and talked in low voices until the train reached New Orleans, where a police officer, called by the conductor, waited."

I never knew this grandfather. He died in 1935, not long after my first birthday. I do have a picture of him carrying me on his shoulder. That and memories told to me by my aunts and my father have made him almost real.

Many times in my life, I've been thankful for the role models my paternal Dubus grandmother and her daughters provided. My maternal Burke grandmother and aunts were also role models, but of a different kind, and between them, I learned how to deal with everything from an unruly guest to a divorce that made legal history.

After her husband died, my grandmother, Jessie, remained in Abbeville as long as her youngest daughter, Florine, was still at home. Florine was a true flapper, with the body to wear the clothes and the temperament to enjoy the lifestyle. She inherited her mother's auburn hair, and whether the golden glints came from Mother Nature or a bottle, her hair was truly a crowning glory.

Like her two older sisters, Florine had gone to what was then called the Normal School, and later became Northwestern State College (and finally, Northwestern State University). There she earned a teacher's certificate, as did Annie Mai before her. Elsie studied business, becoming personal secretary to Mr. Brown, a founder of Brown & Root Company. Many years later, when my car broke down on a lonely stretch of road between Shreveport and Alexandria, I flagged down a Brown & Root truck for help. When the young men inside told me the company didn't allow them to pick up passengers—I needed a ride to the Dodge dealer in Alexandria—I told them my aunt had been Mr. Brown's secretary, that she always described him as a perfect gentleman, and that I was sure any company with his name would allow its employees to rescue a lady in distress. Young, southern men raised by southern mommas know when they're beaten. To a chorus of "Yes, ma'ams," the door opened, and I got my ride.

Florine married Ed VanHart Hardaway, a quiet, gentle man, who, my father said, needed no spirit of his own as Florine had enough for them both. When they moved to Shreveport, where both Elsie and Annie Mai lived, my grandmother followed, and so though I have memories of the big house in Abbeville, I have far more of the Shreveport homes of my aunts.

At that time, Elsie was married to Rupert Peyton, a brilliant political reporter who made a name for himself during the Huey Long years. Elsie and Rupert had sadly lost two young children, André Dubus and Rupert Rudolph Jr. My only memory of Rupert is being taken, along with Kathryn, André, and Rupert and Elsie's only surviving child, Patricia—born, as it happened, one day before my brother—to the *Shreveport Times*, where he worked. In those days, the papers were still set in type. The typesetter set our names for us and gave us the slugs, and I kept that memento for many years, holding it against an ink pad and printing out my name.

My father and the other men in the family spoke highly of Rupert's writing, but when the truth about his marriage to Elsie came out, people no longer mentioned his name. Like many brilliant people, Rupert had a volatile nature and an addiction to alcohol. He had apparently taken his drunken anger out on Elsie for years, but Elsie, with the kind of courage all my Dubus aunts had, put her daughter's welfare ahead of her own and tried to keep an impossible marriage alive. By the time she finally divorced him, he was so far gone that he spent time in a mental hospital and then emerged like the proverbial phoenix to marry a rich widow and have, I suppose, a good life.

Annie Mai's husband, W. P. Miller, died of cancer when their two girls were eight and six. My father used to tell the story about the Caddo Parish sheriff calling Annie Mai not long after W. P. died and asking her to come down to the station to get a present he had for her. Annie Mai drove down, and he handed her a huge pistol with a belt and holster to strap around her waist. Then, he told her he wanted her to walk home wearing that gun, so that every vagrant in Shreveport would know Mrs. Miller might be little, and she might be alone, but she packed a big gun.

My Dubus aunts were the sort of women whom life could never defeat. They all had a great deal of energy, both psychic and physical, and thank heaven I inherited those genes, because even on days when what I really want to do is lie in bed and stare at the ceiling—read "give up"—those Dubus genes get me up and into the kitchen to make coffee and act on my father's advice: "If you really are at the worst place you'll ever be, then keep going, because it's bound to get better."

They were living examples of how to survive, no matter how hard life gets. I never saw any of these aunts less than perfectly turned out, whether it was Aunt Elsie dressed in one of the softly tailored suits she wore to work, or Aunt Annie Mai in a summer cotton print, or Aunt Florine in a silk dress with clinging bodice and swirling skirt.

And always, I remember laughter. They adored my father, whom they called Ade—pronounced "Ah-day"—and when one or more of them visited us, or we went to Shreveport, they couldn't get enough of him, entertaining him with stories of life in the "north," bringing up childhood memories, adding more threads to the fabric of family life.

I say life in the north because north and south Louisiana are so different, they may as well be different states. The equivalent of the Mason-Dixon line is drawn at Alexandria. Some French families live there, but not enough to add more than a soupçon of French sensibility to an essentially Anglo-Saxon place. The Felicianas, where Jessie Reames grew up, are also essentially Anglo-Saxon. Thus, south Louisiana was mostly Catholic, the Felicianas and north Louisiana were mostly Protestant, with Episcopalians at one end and Baptists at the other.

Although she married a Catholic and lived in Abbeville, the heart of Catholic Acadiana, my grandmother Jessie insisted that the four children born to her and André be christened Methodists. At that time, any Catholic whose children were not brought up in the faith could not receive the sacraments, nor be buried from the church.

When my grandfather André died, his funeral was a Requiem High Mass, and his grave was in his family's plot in the cemetery next to St. Peter's Roman Catholic Church in New Iberia. One of the little old ladies who make it their business to question priests' decisions, as well as keep them abreast of details of their parishioners' lives, called on the pastor of St. Peter's not long after my grandfather's funeral. "I want to know why André Dubus was buried from the church, and buried in the cemetery, when every one of his children goes to the Methodist Church," she told him.

"Well, it's none of your business, but since I want people to know the truth, and I'm sure you'll tell them what I say—André and I had a talk about that a long time ago. He said the good Lord sent him Jessie, and He had to know what kind of woman she is."

This is what I love about the French Catholicism I grew up with. It has a kind of humanity, a sensibility that allows it to accept human foibles and follies, recognizing that a man who risked his life to comfort dying flu victims or disarm a raging stranger should not be judged by narrow-minded neighbors who couldn't see true virtue when it stood in front of them.

My cousin Patricia told me a story about our great-grandmother Liza Brooks Reames that shows where grandmother Jessie got her backbone. She played the organ for the Methodist Church in Clinton on Sunday mornings, but on Saturday nights her children invited friends over and she played the piano for them to dance. One Sunday, the Methodist minister preached a rousing sermon on the evils of dancing, whereupon our great-grandmother, long skirt swishing, marched out of the church, followed by the entire choir. She did not return until the minister made an apology from the pulpit.

Thinking about this story makes me believe there must have been French genes somewhere in that Scottish blood.

During his year at Vanderbilt, my father had the good fortune to have classes with both John Crowe Ransom and Allen Tate, and listening to him relate their views on both literature and language instilled a reverence for the written word in me at a very young age.

My father's life course changed from medicine to engineering when he spent the summer with an uncle in Colorado, a mining engineer who convinced his nephew to switch to the Colorado School of Mines and pursue that career. Which my father did, until he realized that mining engineers had little future in below-sea-level Louisiana, switched to Tulane, and earned his civil engineering degree there. Had he become a doctor, I would not be here, because he met my mother only because of his choice of careers.

Katherine Bertha Burke was the seventh child of Walter James and Bertha Gary Perry Burke. She had two older sisters and four elder brothers, as well as two younger sisters and one younger brother. Every time I think about my grandmother Burke, I wonder that her slender figure could produce ten children but show none of the effects.

The Burkes came from Waterford County, Ireland, where William Burke's father had been mayor, landing first in Canada, then moving to New Jersey and later Texas, settling on land where Spindletop, the first big oil field in Texas, was later discovered. But due to "hostile Indians," as the family records state, they left Texas and moved to New Iberia. They retained the Texas property until Reconstruction, when they had to sell it to pay taxes on property they owned in Louisiana.

William and Ellen Lee Burke were still British citizens when the Civil War broke out. Their three sons, James Lee, Patrick Edward (P. E.), and William Richard, served in the Confederate army, and when, after the war, they asked the federal government for reparations promised when Burke property was appropriated by federal troops, they were told that because they fought for the South, no payment would be forthcoming. The lawyers in the family still argue that though the three heirs might have been in the Rebel army, the federal government owed the estate—a noncombatant—reparations, and every once in a while, in an idle moment, someone in the family figures up what we are still owed.

Residents of Acadiana had long depended on water transportation to get to New Orleans, and after the war, packets that were, as one observer noted, "veritable floating palaces, and the last word in luxury," carried passengers from New Iberia to the city. An ancestor of mine, Captain P. E. Burke, owned one of these, the *Ingomar*, celebrated as one of the largest and most richly outfitted boats. In addition to sleeping quarters, a dining room, and a lounge, the *Ingomar* provided its passengers with a ballroom, an extra attraction. The captain himself was another attraction. The family papers describe him as tall and handsome. He was also a skilled boatman, which drew the admiration of male passengers, while his charm and gallantry drew the admiration of the ladies.

My mother's father, Walter James Burke, and his brother Porteus both graduated from Tulane Law School. My grandfather is still considered one of their notable graduates because of his service to the state. A member of the state senate, he introduced the first bill to reform education in Louisiana in 1912 and introduced the first worker's compensation bill in 1918. PaPa, as we called my grandfather (pronounced pa-PAH), also served as a delegate to three Louisiana constitutional conventions. A leading opponent of Huey Long, he was asked to run against Long but refused on the grounds that a man's good name is one of his most valuable legacies to his children and that though he was well-known in south Louisiana, he was not known in north Louisiana, and he didn't want the first time people there heard his name to be from Huey Long's mouth. He was instrumental in founding Southwestern Louisiana Institute, a college designed to provide education to the sons and daughters of rural families who needed to stay at home to help their parents, but who would benefit from a college education. One of the buildings on what is now the University of Louisiana at Lafayette campus was named for him. Coincidentally, the Speech and Music departments were in that building, and because I majored in Speech and English when I attended, I spent a great deal of time in a building that would be named for him years later. It is now called Burke-Hawthorne Hall, honoring both Walter James Burke and an additional benefactor.

Burke Hall named for my grandfather, Walter James Burke.
Courtesy of the University of Louisiana at Lafayette Special Collections.

***

My maternal grandmother, Bertha Perry Burke, counted among her ancestors Captain Robert Samuel Perry, who fought in the American Revolution,
as well as Commander Matthew Perry, who opened Japan to the West in
1854, and her great-uncle Admiral Oliver Hazard Perry, a hero of the war
of 1812. Two of her sons were named Oliver and Perry after these ancestors.

Not long ago, in sorting through family papers, I found a journal written by Corporal Owen Perry, a member of an Ohio regiment, in which he
described his service in the Civil War. My Burke ancestors fought in Virginia,
and his unit was part of the siege of Vicksburg, so they never fought each
other, though all too many times in that war brother fought against brother
and friend against friend.

Robert S. Perry, my grandmother's father, was born in Lafayette Parish. He
attended the Kentucky Military Institute, then studied law at the University
of Louisville, and, after practicing law in Texas, moved to Vermilion Parish.
He served in the Eighth Louisiana Regiment and fought in Virginia until he
was taken as a prisoner of war.

That may have been the same battle in which one of my Burke ancestors was captured. Offered his freedom if he would take an oath of loyalty, he refused, and wrote home requesting a jacket "in that shade known as Confederate gray." That letter, along with many other papers, is in the Tilton Library at Tulane. Another large collection is in the Louisiana Room at the University of Louisiana in Lafayette.

When the war ended, Robert took his law practice to St. Martinville and married Bertha Gary, the eldest of the three children. Perry became a circuit judge in 1888. There is a small community near Abbeville called Perry's Bridge, after Judge Perry, and in one of those strange coincidences so difficult to believe in fiction, one of my Aunt Annie Mai's daughters, Dollie, and her husband, Dennis Gibson, bought the old Perry house.

Dennis, a librarian, headed the Louisiana Room at the University of Louisiana at Lafayette, and it was there he and my Uncle Perry met. Uncle Perry (my mother's brother) was looking for documents to use in his efforts to get the old cemetery on the property put on the National Register of Historic Places. They worked together and succeeded, though, unfortunately, a lack of funds has prevented much restoration from being done, and though the graves are still there, going back to the American Revolution, the cemetery, like so many others, is in disrepair.

Walter and Bertha Burke's first home was on Main Street, on property that stretched back some three city blocks to the banks of Bayou Teche. A typical Queen Anne-style, turn-of-the-century house, its wide galleries and spacious rooms provided a comfortable home for the ten children born to them.

But one cold winter night, when everyone in New Iberia had left their taps running to prevent frozen pipes, the house caught fire—the fire chief said probably because of a faulty electric wire—and burned to the ground while the firemen and family watched. My grandfather forbade anyone to enter the blazing house, saying nothing material was worth a man risking his life.

His personal library, all but a few bits of furniture, and everything else turned to ashes. Though workers sifted through the ruins hoping to find jewelry, none survived except a ring my mother had with her in New Orleans. The rest had been driven into the sodden mud by the falling beams.

A mahogany rocking chair with dogs' heads at the end of the arms, which now stands in my library, was one of the few things saved, and when I tell children the dogs' names, Peter and Paul, and watch them stroke the heads just as four generations of children have done, I remember when Kathryn and I were small enough to sit together in that chair, rocking in the great central hall of the Tudor-style house my grandparents built to replace the one lost in the fire.

At the time my parents met, my mother, Katherine Bertha Burke, had finished college at the Academy of the Sacred Heart in New Orleans, a school still operating but no longer a college. She taught seventh grade and spent her summers visiting friends and relatives on the Mississippi Gulf Coast (where New Orleanians went to escape the heat) or having friends visit her.

My father graduated at a time when utility companies in Louisiana were expanding, with a Massachusetts-based firm, Stone & Webster, providing a good portion of the engineering services. He went to work for them and ended up in New Iberia, where he met my mother's brother Perry, a widower who lost both wife and baby when Caroline died in childbirth.

Perry was my mother's favorite brother, and she his favorite sister. She had beaux, but none who suited her. A man named E. J. Carsten was her mother's choice. His family and the Burke family had been friends for many years and, like the Burkes, active in New Iberia's civic and social life. Whether my mother ever would have married him, I don't know, though years later, his sister, a close friend of mother's, told me that once André Dubus entered the scene, no man on earth stood a chance.

Uncle Perry told my mother about this young man, how good-looking and smart he was, and suggested they meet. She turned up her nose and said she had no interest in meeting a "Tulane jelly bean." To this day, I've no idea what that phrase meant, though I gather it meant someone without a brain or serious thought in his head, which never applied to my father.

At any rate, Uncle Perry drummed up a reason to get mother to his office when my father happened to be there. And the rest, as the saying goes, is history. They were passionately in love with each other until the day my father died, proving, I suppose, that big brothers (as well as fathers) sometimes know best.

A close friend of my mother's, who had been at Sacred Heart with her, told me that when she visited mother that summer, every morning at six my mother would wake her, look out the window at my father, and say the same thing: "Oh, Florence, isn't he gorgeous."

Florence had made a name for herself at Sacred Heart, climbing over the wall when she missed curfew and reading *The Sheik* with a flashlight under her blankets. "Which your mother never did," Florence told me. "Of course, after she met your father, she didn't have to."

My Burke grandmother, who we called MaMa (pronounced ma-MAH), proved to be as stubborn as my Dubus grandmother, though in ways that caused pain, which Jessie's stubbornness never did. When she learned that her daughter would marry a man she hadn't chosen, she arranged a small wedding to be held on Monday, November 26, 1928, in the Burke home in New Iberia.

When my Uncle James Lee Burke became engaged to Polly Benbow, a girl he met in Houston (where he worked with an oil company), the wedding was held at my parents' home in Lake Charles, and later, when as a grown woman I reassessed the dynamics in that family, I realized that the only daughter-in-law my grandmother truly liked was Celeste Dimitry, wife of my Uncle Donald. Celeste's charm, wit and beauty would have won over any mother-in-law, but it was her family name that won MaMa. Actually, the Benbows were well-known and respected in Texas, but they weren't French, they weren't Catholic, and my grandmother knew no one who knew them, meaning that the network through which southern mothers learn about their children's prospective spouses was of no help.

My Uncle Oliver married Jacqueline Webster, from another old family, who lived in Jeanerette. I imagine my grandmother approved of that marriage, because when it ended in divorce, she showed a wisdom and compassion that, looking back, surprises me, given what a martinet she could be. Her family often gathered for the noon-day meal, and after his divorce, my grandmother told Oliver he was welcome to dine with the family during the week, but that on Sundays and holidays, his ex-wife and children would be there, and he would not. "They are part of this family and will be treated as such," she said.

My grandfather respected and liked my father, and they developed a close friendship. Later, when she came to know him, my grandmother's attitude changed, but by then the damage was done. Being the gentleman he was, my father treated her with the courtesy his wife's mother should have, and when I'm channel surfing and light for a few moments on a "reality" show featuring warring families, I wish the civility that maintained family amity still ruled.

I think my grandmother's coldness could be attributed to her mother's death when she was six. Her father remarried five years later, only to have that wife die that same year. My first husband's mother, Josephine, whom we called "JoJo," another cold and controlling woman, had the same experience, except that her mother died in childbirth having her, and three years later, her stepmother died giving birth to her half sister. In the only really personal conversation she and I ever had, she told me that her father closed down, not allowing himself to become attached to anyone ever again. "We had charge accounts all over New Orleans, even at the corner candy store, and nurses to take care of us. But when it came time to make our debuts, none of our aunts lifted a finger to help us, because we were competition for their daughters.

When I met Walter [my first husband's father], I met the first person in my life I believed loved me."

Years later, I found a letter my father had written to my mother before their marriage, expressing his concern that marrying him might cause her life-long regret. Written in his elegant hand, with a use of language that conveyed the honor so characteristic of my father, it is one of the most heartbreaking letters I have ever read, in which a man who was truly one of nature's no-blemen offers to release his beloved from their engagement because, by her mother's standards, he fell short.

Fortunately, my mother's heart and head—as well as the encourage-ment of her older sisters—prevailed, and so, they married and set up house in Lake Charles.

My mother knew little about running a house and nothing about cook-ing when she and my father married. Her mother had a staff of six: a house-keeper, a cook, a maid to assist the housekeeper, a laundress, a gardener, and, for many years, a man to look after the horses she and my grandfather rode every favorable day. I have a picture of them on horseback, he in jodhpurs and boots, she in a long skirt, because, of course, she would never use anything but a side saddle.

Mother did have someone to help her with the housework. A friend suggested Rosanna, the sister of a woman who worked for her. The friend brought Rosanna to our house, and after asking Rosanna a few questions, my mother hired her to come three days a week. Later, when Kathryn was born, Rosanna came five days a week.

Despite Rosanna's thoroughness in household duties, there was one flaw. She didn't know how to cook anything but the simplest staples like grits, eggs in many forms, and vegetable soup. She didn't attempt gumbo, because it needed a roux, which can be challenging for a cook. My mother had seen a stove, of course, but she had never used one. Now, she had to use her stove, but even with several recipe books to guide her, her cooking was barely edible.

After eating my mother's mistakes and mishaps for a month, my father asked her if she minded his mother coming for a visit and teaching her to cook. By this time, my mother knew that, despite the best will in the world and a cookbook to guide her, she needed lessons from someone who had mastered the not-so-simple culinary arts. I imagine, remembering my own later experiences with lessons from my Dubus grandmother, that mother wel-comed her mother-in-law with mixed feelings. She couldn't have had a better instructor, however, because MawMaw, as we called her, had an instinctive feel for ingredients and how to handle them that lifted her from the ranks of an excellent cook to a superb one.

Mother later taught me the basics she learned in the early days of her marriage. "First," she told me, "your grandmother insisted I learn to judge seasoning with my sense of smell, not taste, because once you've tasted something, the sharpness of the taste buds is affected. And second, there are four procedures that, once you master them, will give you the skill to make any dish in the world."

The four are: a perfect salad dressing, a perfect roux, a perfect pastry, and a perfect cream sauce. If you think about these, you will realize that the salad dressing requires a balance between the oil and the lemon juice or vinegar mixed with it; the roux requires the ability to slowly cook the flour and shortening to the right degree of brown while maintaining a consistency into which liquid will blend well; the cream sauce also requires a balance of doneness and texture upon which the success of the sauce depends; and pastry depends on knowing how to cut shortening into the flour so that the mixture has the proper consistency. The next step is more difficult, because the cook must know precisely how much cold liquid to add, and, most important of all, to blend the liquid with the flour mixture with as few strokes as possible, because too many strokes result in tough pastry. Many cooks consider a dish like a soufflé to be too difficult to make. But, actually, it's the cream sauce, the base for so many soufflés (not the whipped egg whites that make it light), that's tricky.

At any rate, my mother learned to cook, and, at the same time, learned to love this peppery, stubborn, and very disciplined woman who had lost her husband at such a young age, had survived the death of a son-in-law, the madness of another, and fought a battle with asthma every day of her long life.

Eleven months after my parents married, the stock market crash of 1929 brought an end to the Jazz Age and opened the door to ten years of anger and despair that reached the point of violence in the early 1930s, with jobless men marching on Washington, crime rates rising, and the hungry homeless becoming more aggressive in their search for food. When someone found a house whose inhabitants handed out a meal, he would put a blue chalk mark on the gate or porch post, signaling others that here they could get help.

Though householders erased these marks as soon as they discovered them, still they reappeared, constant reminders that famine, one of the four horsemen of the apocalypse, rode through our town. No wonder the birth rate

Mother (Katherine Bertha Burke) with my sister Kathryn (*left*) and me (*right*).

dropped. It took courage and faith to bring another mouth to feed into the
world, which, thank heaven, my parents had.

My earliest memory is of my mother rocking me and singing a lullaby. At
some point, I began "singing" with her. Then, a voice said, "Those aren't the
words, she's just making sounds." It was Kathryn, three years older and well
able to sing the right words herself.

"She's just a baby," my mother said. "She can sing how she wants."

Daddy (André Jules Dubus Sr.) with
my brother, André Jules Dubus Jr.

This memory, like the next one, is set to music. *The Merry Widow* was one of my parents' favorite records. In the memory, my mother is wearing a summer evening gown, pale yellow with a print of wildflowers. The sleeves are puffed, the neckline is one called "sweetheart" because its lines mimic the shape of the top of a heart. Both neckline and sleeves are edged with eyelet, through which dark green ribbon is threaded, and a wide sash of the same green circles my mother's waist. Her black hair, with a silken sheen, is in waves that frame her face, and her green eyes, fixed on my father's blue ones, are soft. They're ready to go to a summer dance, but before they leave, they dance for my sister and me, my father whirling my mother around our living room, the music from the record player closing the four of us in one of those moments in which time does not stand still, because it no longer exists.

My next memory is the day of André's birth. My father came home from St. Patrick's Hospital in midafternoon on August 11, 1936, to tell Kathryn and me that we had a baby brother. He had come to take us to meet him, whereupon I threw what might have been the only tantrum of my childhood, stamping my foot and saying I wouldn't go. My father asked me why. And I, having heard insensitive adults tell my mother for months that if the baby were a boy, Beth's nose would be cut off, said, "Because I won't be the baby anymore."

My father knelt down and looked me in the eye. "I tell you what. André is the baby boy, but you will always be my baby girl." Which, until the day he died, I was.

When we got to the hospital and entered our mother's room, I saw a small, white crib in the corner, from which issued the most pitiful sound I had ever heard. I approached the crib and saw a baby, not as big as my own baby doll, face red and scrunched up, crying his little heart out. At that moment, I told myself, "He needs help." So devoted to André did I become that when he got whooping cough in his first year of life, and Dr. Tom Watkins, our family doctor, wanted to send Kathryn and me to stay with our cousins, Pack and Anna Sartwelle, I made such a fuss that he decided it would be worse for me to be away from André, and so we stayed.

That fall, a puppy we named Buttons came into my life. My father found her when he got home from work and came into the house carrying a small ball of fur that looked very much like the stuffed animals piled in my crib. There is a picture of me and Buttons in a family album, showing me in a wool outfit—jacket, leggings, cap—knit by MawMaw (who not only excelled in the kitchen, but who also never met a needlework project she couldn't conquer). Buttons is playing on the sidewalk in front of our house, a chubby ball of fur. I'm staring at Buttons as if I'm not quite sure what to make of this new small thing. I didn't have much time to figure it out, because despite our care, it soon became apparent that Buttons was one sick puppy. There came a day when my father drove away with Buttons in his lap and returned alone. He sought me out, carrying me out to the grape arbor where there was a swing.

"I'm not going to lie to you," he said. One of my father's strong suits was that he did not lie, and that characteristic caused me a lot of pain later, because of course I thought that everyone I met would tell the truth, too. "Buttons is really sick, and in a lot of pain. The vet wants to put her to sleep." He held me closer. "She won't wake up again, do you understand?"

Then he gave me a standard that couldn't have meant much then, because of my pain, but in later years, when I more fully understood the lesson, it meant a lot. "We love Buttons, and we care about her. We really need to let her go, be free of pain. Is that okay?"

I think I nodded yes. My father's arms around me convinced me that what he said was right. I trusted him utterly, and until the day he died, I never had a reason not to.

Recipes for a New Cook

These are recipes my mother wrote down when my grandmother Jessie came to introduce her to the culinary arts.

CREOLE MEAT LOAF

2 lb. lean ground meat
½ lb. ground pork
2 tablespoons hot vegetable oil
1 teaspoon salt
1 cup cold milk
1 teaspoon black pepper
1 cup seasoned breadcrumbs
3 teaspoons chopped parsley
1 egg, beaten
1 cup chopped celery
1 teaspoon Worcestershire sauce
2 medium white onions, chopped
Dash of Tabasco
3 tablespoons flour

Mix the parsley, celery, and onions into the meat. Stir the flour into the hot oil, stirring until slightly browned. Add the milk slowly, stirring constantly so that the flour doesn't lump. Bring this to a boil, then add the seasoned meat. Cook for 1 minute, then mix in the breadcrumbs. Remove from heat, stir in the beaten egg, Worcestershire sauce, and Tabasco. Form into a loaf and lay in a well-greased pan. Dot the top with butter. Cook for about 1.5 hours in a preheated 350° oven, basting several times. Serve hot with tomato sauce or cold accompanied by stuffed tomatoes on lettuce.

Yield: Serves 8 to 12, depending on appetites.

Note: Cold meat loaf sandwiches with plain or Creole mustard are incredible!

SHRIMP CREOLE

1 generous tablespoon shortening
½ teaspoon cayenne pepper
1 generous tablespoon flour
1 teaspoon salt
2 medium white onions, chopped
1 bay leaf
2 cloves of garlic, minced
⅓ teaspoon celery seeds
1 large green bell pepper, chopped
¼ teaspoon powdered thyme
2 teaspoons parsley, chopped
2 lb. raw shelled shrimp
No. 2-size can chopped tomatoes
2 teaspoons Worcestershire sauce

Melt shortening in a cast iron pot over moderate heat. Stir in the flour and brown slowly. Add the white onions, minced garlic, and bell pepper and cook slowly, stirring to keep roux from sticking, until vegetables are wilted. Add the tomatoes, parsley, salt, pepper, bay leaf, celery seeds, and powdered thyme. Now add the shrimp and cover. Let all cook slowly for an hour. Half an hour before serving, add the Worcestershire sauce.

Yield: Serves 6 to 8.

Note: It is wise to simmer the shrimp shells in a small amount of water and reserve to be used in case the juice from the tomatoes and shrimp is not enough. The sauce should not be "soupy"; it is more like a gravy. Serve over rice.

CREOLE COURT BOUILLON WITH REDFISH

4 to 5 lb. redfish fillets, cut in 2-inch pieces
4 cups fish stock (fresh)
½ cup cooking oil
1 teaspoon Worcestershire sauce
2 tablespoons flour
Salt and black pepper, to taste
3 cups white onion, finely chopped
⅓ cup parsley, minced
1 large green bell pepper, chopped
1 cup white wine (or a light red)
1 large can tomatoes
1 lemon, thinly sliced
1 cup celery, chopped
3 cloves garlic, minced

Heat oil in heavy pot, add flour and cook to medium brown. Add onions and cook until transparent. Add tomatoes, green pepper, celery, and garlic and cook slowly for about 25 minutes. Add about 1 cup of stock and allow it to cook down again. Then add remaining stock, fish, Worcestershire sauce, salt, pepper, and parsley. Let simmer about 20–25 minutes. In the last 5 minutes of cooking, add the wine and sliced lemons. Serve over bowls of cooked rice.

Yield: 6 to 8 servings.

Note: This is one of the most delicious soups you will ever eat and a longtime favorite of south Louisiana cooks. If you can't get redfish, substitute a firm-fleshed fish, as you want chunks of meat.

PERFECT BOILED RICE

1 cup long-grain rice
1½ cups water
½ teaspoon salt

Put rice, water, and salt in a heavy pot, either cast iron or cast aluminum. Bring to a fast boil, uncovered, then *immediately* cut to lowest heat setting and cover. Let cook covered for 20–25 minutes, check after 20 minutes. If almost all of the water has been absorbed, turn off the heat and let the rice finish cooking. You will get perfect rice every time.

Yield: 4 servings.

Note: Formerly, rice needed to be washed in several waters to get the starch from the rice, which is why red beans and rice became a Monday (wash day) staple, as the rice water could be used to starch clothes, and the rice eaten. Now, one doesn't need to do this. Do not leave the rice in the pot in which it was cooked for more than 5 or 10 minutes, as it will pack. You may refrigerate rice, covered, no longer than a week, but it may be frozen for up to six months. Heat it in a colander over boiling water. Last, *never* stir rice while it is cooking, or it will become gummy.

TOMATO SAUCE

4 tablespoons butter
2 tablespoons chopped celery
3 tablespoons flour
2 sprigs parsley
2 tablespoons chopped green onion
1 teaspoon salt
1 cup prepared tomato sauce
1½ cups meat stock

Cook celery, onions, and parsley in butter until brown. Add flour and tomato sauce and stir until smooth. Add the stock and seasoning. Cook over a low heat for 30 minutes. Strain before serving.

FLOATING ISLAND

This is an old French dessert that was always made for people whose appetites needed tempting, and in strawberry, peach, and berry season, fresh fruit was placed in the bottom of each dessert dish with the Floating Island served over it. One does not have to be ailing to enjoy it!

Custard:
4 egg yolks
¼ cup sugar
Pinch of salt
2 cups milk (not skim or low-fat)
1 teaspoon vanilla

Using a heat-proof glass bowl, beat the egg yolks slightly, then add sugar and salt. Scald the milk. (This means heating the milk over a *moderate* heat, watching carefully until a skin begins to form. Turn the heat down immediately and remove the skin before continuing.) Add the milk *very slowly* to the egg mixture, whisking to prevent yolks from curdling. Place the bowl over boiling water, stirring constantly until custard begins to thicken and coat the back of a wooden spoon. Add vanilla. This will not be a firm custard but will have the consistency of a sauce.
Yield: 2 ½ cups.

MERINGUE:
4 egg whites
¾ cup sugar
Pinch of salt

Beat egg whites and salt until they form soft peaks. Slowly add the sugar and beat mixture until very stiff. When the custard is done, spoon egg whites onto the top of it. Let poach for about 2 minutes. Using a slotted spoon, turn and poach the other side.
Refrigerate before serving.
Note: I find it simpler to spoon the meringue onto a baking sheet and run it into a 325° oven until the meringues have a glossy surface but are not brown. Then, place them on top of the custard.

Lagniappe

(That Little Something Extra)

PAIN PERDU

8 slices stale French bread, cut on bias, about 1¼-inch thick
1 cup half-and-half or whole milk
4 large eggs, well-beaten
¼ cup sugar
2 teaspoons vanilla extract
A few gratings of fresh nutmeg, to taste
4 tablespoons butter
4 tablespoons vegetable oil
1 teaspoon powdered sugar, mixed with ½ teaspoon cinnamon

Combine half-and-half or milk, eggs, sugar, vanilla, and nutmeg in a large bowl and mix thoroughly. Soak the slices of stale French bread in the mixture until they are soaked through. Melt the butter in a heavy-bottomed skillet and add the oil. When the butter/oil mixture is very hot—put a drop or two of water into it and if that sizzles, it is hot enough—fry the soaked bread slices one or two at a time on each side, until golden brown. Drain on paper towels and hold in a warm oven until all the slices are cooked.

Sprinkle cinnamon/powdered sugar mixture on slices just before serving. May be served with Louisiana cane syrup, honey, or real maple or fruit syrups.

Note: Pain perdu means "lost bread," referring to the French bread left over from a meal. Though regular bread may be used, it is best when made with French bread. Never use sourdough bread.

CHAPTER TWO

I don't know the precise dimensions of our backyard. It couldn't have been as large as I remember it, but in my memory's eye, it contained everything from Flash Gordon's spaceship to Tarzan's jungle home. A massive live oak provided shade, as well as roots that protruded above the ground, making a sort of natural dollhouse carpeted with the green moss that grew between them. Here, I brought my dolls and tea sets and spent hours giving my dolls lives, some drawn from the stories my mother read to me, some I created myself.

My mother made bed linens for our dolls from the survey maps our father used. These were made of linen, and when he had finished with one, Mother bleached the lines out and made sheets and pillowcases trimmed with lace crocheted by MawMaw for the dolls' cradles and beds. She made clothes, too, and until the 2016 flood, I still had a doll's slip made from fine batiste and trimmed with crocheted lace.

Along with the usual baby dolls, I remember some special ones. One wore a ski outfit and had real skis, and lo and behold, the week after the Christmas Day I received her, it snowed, and she could actually ski down the "slopes" of the snowy ditch. The Dionne quintuplets, born in 1934, were much in the news, and MaMa gave Kathryn and me a wonderful toy, a wide wooden cradle, large enough to hold five babies, with a drawer at the end that opened to reveal tiny plates and cups and saucers and cutlery, with a hinged piece that came up over the cradle footboard to make a table.

Also at that time, Colleen Moore's famous fairy castle toured the country to raise money for children's charities. A top star of the silent movie era, Colleen Moore had always loved dollhouses. When her father suggested she design her dream castle, she proceeded to do so, enlisting the aid of skilled craftsmen from Disney to create what is still one of the most spectacular miniatures in any museum. (It is exhibited in the Museum of Science and Industry in Chicago.) The fairy castle came to Lake Charles, displayed at Muller's Department Store. Mother took Kathryn and me, and I still remember the awe with which we studied each detail, a memory that made

Katherine Mansfield's story, "The Doll's House," resonate with me when I read it years later.

I have two other memories of Muller's Department Store. One is about the machine used in the shoe department to determine the fit of your shoes. You stood with your feet under the machine, and an X-ray image of your feet showed the bones and whether your toes had enough room.

The other memory is not so benign. Although a water fountain that provided cold water was readily available, our mother never allowed us to drink from it, not because she feared germs, but because next to it was a rust-stained china water fountain with a faucet from which flowed water blacks were expected to catch in their hands. Signs hung above each of these designating who could drink from which fountain, and my mother would not allow her children to drink from a fountain forbidden to others.

On one of our trips to downtown Lake Charles, I met with an accident that could have caused serious injury or death had the brick street not had a slight downward slope to the curb. My father and mother sat in the front seat of the car, Mother holding André, with Kathryn and me in the back. I sat behind my father, and when my door suddenly swung open, I fell out. I still remember rolling under the car, looking up and seeing pipes above me, hearing the screech of brakes, and then coming to a stop at the curb. Then, a montage of my father's face as he picked me up, my mother's as she followed my father into a nearby drug store, carrying André and holding Kathryn by the hand, where the pharmacist determined I had nothing more serious than scrapes and bruises. He put iodine on the scrapes, ointment on the bruises, and then offered ice cream all around.

I don't remember if that ice cream came in waxed cardboard cups with movie stars' or sports figures' pictures on the underside of the top, but it probably did, as such containers had come into use in 1930 and proved extremely popular. I do remember the eagerness with which I pulled up the top, hoping to see the face of my favorite star, Nelson Eddy. Kathryn and I had mad crushes on him. Our parents had recordings of him and Jeannette MacDonald singing, and Mother had taken Kathryn and me to see at least one of their movies, perhaps *The Student Prince* or *Maytime*. Our father and Nelson Eddy had a strong resemblance—both blond with blue eyes, both handsome in much the same way, and both with beautiful tenor voices.

I remember my father singing songs like "Ah, Sweet Mystery of Life," "The Sweetheart of Sigma Chi," and "I'm Falling in Love with Someone," especially on hot summer nights when he took us for rides, the breeze stirred by the moving car cooling us, and his voice singing love songs to our mother, soothing us to sleep. Those summer evening drives imbued me with a romanticism that, while it has led to much happiness, has also occasionally led me astray.

In a time when wonder drugs lay in the future, serious illnesses killed many children during their early years. Typhoid was especially virulent, sweeping through a community, perhaps carried by someone who didn't manifest symptoms but was nevertheless highly contagious. The infamous "Typhoid Mary," though apparently healthy herself, infected fifty-three people, three of whom died, during the time she worked as a cook.

When typhoid fever was found in a local dairy worker, our family switched from drinking raw milk to pasteurized. This took a while to become accustomed to; since the cream rose to the top of raw milk, most women skimmed off some of it to use in cooking or to make cream cheese. The milk left was still nutritious, but not as rich-tasting as pasteurized, nor was the cream cheese bought from a dairy as good as that my mother made.

I remember those mornings I would enter the kitchen to see a cheese-cloth bag tied to the sink faucet, whey dripping slowly as the cream clotted. I learned then that for a summer breakfast there is nothing better than freshly made cream cheese and just-picked figs. I don't make my own cream cheese, but I do have fig trees, and a local producer's cream cheese tastes just the way I remember that of my childhood.

I escaped the diseases that afflicted many children at the time I grew up, nor did I ever break any bones. Still, one episode had lifelong effects. Kathryn and I often joined neighborhood children in a late afternoon game of hide-and-seek. Being timid by nature, I always tried to hide where none of the bigger boys could find me, as I knew how they teased their "captives."

A large clump of tiger lilies grew at the corner of our front yard. In late summer, the blooms reached their full height, and the broad leaves made a fine hiding place for a small child. Unhappily, something else hid there: a nest of yellow jackets that attacked me, stinging me all over my bare arms and legs, as well as any other skin not covered by clothing. I ran screaming to the house, where my mother poured baking soda into my bath and then, after dabbing me dry, put calamine lotion on the stings. I recovered in a day or so, but unknown to anyone, that amount of histamine from the stings altered my body chemistry, so that years later, by a sheer stroke of luck, my family doctor determined that I was fatally allergic to all antihistamines and would go into anaphylactic shock if I ever took any—which, in a place where seasonal pollen has people sneezing and coughing as allergies react, is not a good thing. Still, better to fight allergies with few allies than die.

Yellow jackets, wasps, and bees attack only when disturbed. Mosquitoes never quit. Mosquito bites, if they became infected in those pre-antibiotic days, could pose severe health threats, including carrying malaria, one severe enough to cause death. My brother had so many infected mosquito bites one summer that, when calamine lotion and other standard remedies had no success, Dr. Tom Watkins, who not only delivered us but cared for the whole family, recommended we take him to the Mississippi Gulf Coast, where immersion in the brackish salt water could provide nature's own healing powers.

My father contracted malaria while leading survey crews through the swamps. His youth and good health, along with doses of quinine, brought him through, but after that, every unexplained fever—and there were a great many—got treated with Febriline, a quinine medicine that was advertised as tasteless, but was instead sickly sweet. Small white dots of quinine were suspended in a colloid solution so nauseating only the promise of a treat to overpower the taste made me open my mouth.

It's no wonder we rubbed mosquito repellent, containing a large proportion of citronella oil, over every inch of bare skin in the daytime and slept under mosquito nets at night. I have never forgotten those summer nights when the scent of sweet olive and gardenias came in through open windows and the objects in the room, so familiar by day, became strange and mysterious seen through a thin gauze veil.

***

Though strange men often came to the back door and asked for food, a request always granted, I had never given them much thought, nor had anyone else seemed to. My father began having to make business trips, which kept him away overnight. (Later, I would understand that these trips were preparation for his eventual transfer to the Gulf States Utilities headquarters in Baton Rouge, where he would leave the field for an administrative position.) Worried about leaving his wife alone with three small children while hobos roamed the streets, he enlisted the aid of our neighbor, a Frenchman I will call Monsieur Rene LeBlanc, as I don't remember his name.

Monsieur LeBlanc and his wife had come to Lake Charles for reasons I don't remember, but they may have been among the people drawn by the new industries growing up in the area, due largely to a bold enterprise undertaken by the citizens of Lake Charles: to build a port for ocean-going ships. Refused any governmental aid, the citizenry raised the required funds and in 1924 opened the third deepwater port in the state and the one closest to the Gulf of Mexico.

Though Monsieur LeBlanc dressed like any other man when leaving home in the morning, in a business suit and tie, when he arrived home in the evening he changed into a soft shirt with a wide collar and one of a collection of smoking jackets, garments made from brocade, heavy silk, and light wools in a paisley design. These smoking jackets had the de rigueur black satin collars, as well as fringed sashes, and he wore one of these the evening he came over to watch my father install the signal system my mother would use to call Monsieur LeBlanc if she needed help.

He also carried a large handgun, displaying it to my parents and assuring them that any miscreant would be sorry indeed if he dared disturb the sleep of Madame Dubus. My father examined the gun, determined that it didn't work, and asked Monsieur LeBlanc if he would be comfortable carrying his own Colt .45. Monsieur LeBlanc agreed to carry it, adding that he would, however, show the marauder his own weapon. "It is, as you can see, a most formidable piece. I assure you, one look at it and any sane man runs." After Monsieur LeBlanc left, my father told my mother he imagined the sight of the Frenchman in his smoking jacket, waving that huge gun around, would indeed put the fear of the Lord or the devil, whichever one scared him most, in any vagrant.

The signal was simple. My father ran a wire from their bedroom through the window and into the LeBlancs' bedroom. The wire there ended in a bell. If Mother needed help, she would pull on her end of the wire and the bell would ring, bringing her knight in brocade armor to the rescue. If she ever did ring the bell, I never knew it. But just knowing it was there made all of us sleep better.

I have what is almost a slideshow of memories of those early years. One memory centers on a daily radio program in Lake Charles that accepted requests from its listeners. At the time, Kathryn's favorite song was "I Love You Truly" and mine was "Red Sails in the Sunset," perhaps because I saw so many sailboats on Lake Charles when Dr. Watkins had to give us a shot and told us to pick out a sailboat and watch it.

Mother felt that one call a day requesting our favorites was more than enough—in fact, too much. Rosanna proved more amenable. On the afternoons when Mother was out playing bridge or at a tea, we would ask Rosanna to call the station several times. Each time she would make the request, using our names, and each time the announcer would play the songs, for "little Miss Kathryn Dubus" or "little Miss Beth Dubus." Finally, even that patient announcer had had enough and asked Rosanna if we could please be satisfied with one song per day. Later, I understood that, in such a small town, the announcer of course knew our parents, and, as is usual in small towns, wanted to be agreeable.

In the fall of 1938, I began kindergarten. My mother walked me there the first day, and when she came to get me at noon, asked the question most parents ask a child on the first day of school: "How did you like it?"

"It's quite the silliest place I've ever been."

"Really? Why?"

"In the first place, a boy played the piano, and everyone clapped even though he got the notes all wrong."

"What else?"

"The teacher wanted to teach us to tell time, so twelve children stood in a circle to make the numbers and two others lay on the floor to be the hands. Then, the teacher would tell them where to move and we told her what time it was, which was really silly because there was a perfectly good clock on the wall."

"Do you want to go back?"

"No." And I didn't. This serious streak, which manifested itself so early, has been either a major flaw or a great asset all through my life, depending on the situation. While I believe I have a good sense of humor, and take great pleasure in many things, I have never been able to be silly, which doesn't mean I can't laugh at myself.

Perhaps I felt the teacher ignored the innate dignity of children, something many adults do, unwittingly I hope. Certainly, none of the adults in my life ever treated me in a way that made me feel insignificant. Nor did they give me an undue sense of my own importance. They never forgot their role as adults: to guide, to mentor, to help a child attain the self-discipline so necessary if one is to live effectively in the world.

All too many children born in those Depression years didn't have a secure start in life. My siblings and I were among the lucky ones who did. When I think of my early childhood, one of the most striking memories is of firelight flickering on the deep amethyst glasses on the dining room table and the smell of vegetable soup rising from the bowl in front of me. Warmth and nourishment—no wonder that scene stayed in my mind.

Another memory is sitting at the kitchen table watching Mother prepare my father's lunch. She used an entire loaf of bread every morning, putting the sandwiches back into the bag the bread came in while I watched, big-eyed, as she fixed the rest. A few hard-boiled eggs, apples or oranges, a large thermos of coffee to keep him going all day, plus homemade cookies, usually oatmeal with raisins, as those were nourishing, too.

I still have a clear image of my father as he was at that time. Blond, blue-eyed, he was a handsome man and, in his "work clothes," an imposing figure. He wore leather, knee-high lace-up boots over jodhpurs, with a khaki long-sleeved shirt, a bandanna around his neck, and a broad-brimmed hat similar to those worn by the Canadian Royal Mounties. A Colt .45 revolver in a holster attached to a Sam Browne belt completed his outfit. The boots and revolver protected him against snakes that infested the properties on which his crew surveyed rights-of-way for Stone & Webster. He used to practice shooting on the weekends, driving to a right-of-way and setting tin cans up on a fence rail, where he picked them off one by one while my siblings and I watched.

He shot snakes on many occasions. In a subtropical climate, snakes are always part of the outdoor equation. Children learn very young to tell the difference between a harmless king snake or corn snake and the poisonous cottonmouths, copperheads, rattlers, and coral snakes. Since the chicken snake has markings very similar to those of a coral snake, wise parents made sure their children could tell the difference from a distance far enough to provide time for escape. But the best protection is sturdy leather shoes, thick socks, and a strong stick.

From not knowing how to boil water, my mother had become an excellent cook, an achievement my father never failed to praise. Listening to him, I decided I wanted to cook for him, too. I had received a little electric stove the previous Christmas, one that actually cooked. Stubborn even at age five, I refused any help from my mother, which resulted in biscuits hard as rocks because I'd forgotten to put in the shortening. My father, however, announced that he loved hard biscuits because they didn't fall apart when you dunked them in coffee, and heroically ate half the batch. It would be years before I realized that empathy for others formed a large part of my father's character, revealing itself in things as small as eating a daughter's baking mishap to showing compassion for his employees, earning the kind of devotion and respect only a wise and fair employer can.

One of the stories that most poignantly illustrates this—in my view—I learned the night before my father's funeral. The room in which my father's casket lay had been crowded from the moment visiting hours began. You could get through the crowd only by pushing your way. At one point, my mother beckoned me over and asked me to go speak to a man who had come in and taken a seat at the very back of the room. "Please find out who he is and make him welcome." Though my father's death broke her heart, she never lost her manners, which dictated making others comfortable, no matter one's own state.

I introduced myself to the man, and heard this story:

"I met your father when I came out of the army in 1946," he said. "Got a job working on a line crew at Gulf States in Lafayette. Had a wife and two kids—and memories I didn't want to tell anyone. Gnawed at me, I guess. Anyway, I acted like a wild man, showing up late, goofing off. Finally, the foreman told me I had an appointment with Mr. Dubus that afternoon. 'And after that, I won't have to put up with you anymore,' he said. That woke me up, and I realized what I'd done. More men than jobs—now how could I take care of my family? I went to your father's office feeling like I was about to face a firing squad. I walked in, and this is what he said: 'Close the door and sit down, son. Then, tell me why you insist on making a damn fool of yourself.' Well, I sat there and all the memories poured out. Your father never had a question or a comment. He just sat and listened. At the end, we sat a while and looked at each other. And then your father said—and I'll never forget it—he said, 'Son, you think you're ready to go to work now?' I couldn't believe my ears. 'Yes, sir,' I said. 'Good,' he said. 'But, son—you ever need to talk again, you just come see me.'"

By that time, we were both in tears. "I still work for Gulf States in Houston. Heard about your father's death on the grapevine yesterday. Got in my car and headed over. See a lot of men here worked for your father. Not many like him around anymore."

He was right.

CHAPTER THREE

We usually spent several weeks in July visiting family in New Iberia. My mother's two youngest sisters, Bertha and Pamela, lived at home, and their presence made visits to our grandparents magical. Young, beautiful, full of fun, they greeted us with hugs and kisses the minute we entered the door, telling us, "The house is yours," and leading my sister and me to the bedroom they shared. They opened their closets and told us to play dress-up in anything we chose, showed us where they kept their costume jewelry, and indulged every wish our mother and grandmother allowed.

They shopped in New Orleans, and I still remember some of their clothes. Aunt Bertha had a "golfing" dress of gabardine in a shade of light aqua with enamel buttons, perfect replicas of the various popular cigarette brands of the day, all the way down the front. Aunt Pamela had a silk shirtwaist dress with a printed design that began with a cloud-studded blue sky at the shoulders and became a border of green hills, ending in a meadow filled with flowers and grazing sheep. Other dresses had wide, floating skirts of cotton voile with halter-neck bodices, or silk organdy with sweetheart necklines. When we watched our aunts dress to go out with any of the number of beaux they each had, we got a glimpse of glamorous, sophisticated lives that set a standard I hoped one day to meet.

Our aunts spoiled us in every way they could. They made fudge for us to "sell" to various relatives, buying several pieces themselves at the absurd sum of twenty-five cents each. Since relatives gathered every evening at our grandparents' home, sitting on the sun porch that stretched along the eastern side of the house in summer or in the big central hall in winter, selling the rest proved no problem.

On one visit, we met Carol Dupree, who lived on a sugar plantation in Martinique and spent time with her grandparents every summer. Kathryn and I were very well-behaved little girls. Carol was not. She was an only child, and her parents allowed her the run of the plantation, the only stricture that she had to have lessons from tutors brought from the States. Knowing their daughter well, her parents told her that if having tutors did not work, she would be sent to a boarding school noted for its strict rules. Though Carol displayed perfect manners when with adults, when not with them, she searched for ways to release her high spirits, which often led Kathryn and me into mischief neither of us would have thought of by ourselves.

The family who lived across the street from my grandparents had a daughter a year younger than Carol and Kathryn and two years older than me. Her name was Suzette, but she was called SuSu. Kathryn and I didn't like her because she put on airs and clearly thought herself superior to us. When Carol met her, and proclaimed her a stuck-up prig, we felt justified—so much so that when Carol proposed we play a trick on SuSu, we went along.

SuSu had been invited, either by my mother or grandmother, to come have lemonade and cookies one afternoon. We helped Carol pull one of the long hoses with a sprinkler attached close to the sidewalk leading up to the house so that anyone walking by it would be drenched. When the time for SuSu's visit approached, we hid near the faucet so we could turn it on at just the right moment.

SuSu wore a white piqué dress and a big white bow in her dark hair. She looked as though she'd been starched from head to foot, and I remember the instant the sprinkler began whirling, sending a shower of water over her that turned her into a dripping mess. She gave one outraged cry, and then ran home, while we, suddenly subdued by what we'd done, waited for our punishment—which, because Carol took the blame, didn't happen. She turned off the water, walked up to the front door, and rang the bell. When our mother answered, she began her confession, insisting that not only had the drenching been her idea, but that she alone had set it up. Since our mother could see Kathryn and me standing at the foot of the steps, our faces betraying our culpability, I know she didn't believe a word Carol said. But she accepted the apology, and said that since lemonade and cookies were waiting, we might as well come in and have some.

Later, I learned that SuSu's mother had never been a favorite of my mother, which explains her reaction to what was, at the least, a terrible breach of manners and, at worst, an act of childish meanness.

Our next escapade had more serious consequences. Carol, Kathryn, and I decided we would have a Festival of Flowers. We got a pen, ink, and paper from our grandfather's study to write the invitations, but in carrying these supplies outside we managed to leave a trail of black ink, requiring much scrubbing to get the stain out of the summer rugs. (Wool rugs were taken up in summer and much lighter ones put down.) As if that weren't enough, when we gathered the flowers for our festival, we literally denuded my grand-mother's cutting bed, and these two acts could not be ignored. Carol's grand-parents would deal with her, our grandfather with us.

PaPa didn't have his brother's fierce look. We had never seen anything but a genial expression on his face, nor had he ever been anything but loving and kind. Still, when we were called to his study, I felt an emotion I had never before felt: dread. We listened while he recounted the "charges" against us. When he finished, he asked if we were sorry for what we had done. Of course we were, to the point of tears I could no longer hold back. "I have consulted the judge, and he says there is only one thing to do: cut off your heads."

We knew he couldn't mean this—could he? "Close your eyes and hold out your hands," he said. We did—and felt rounds of metal drop into our palms. We opened our eyes to see he had given us two quarters each. "It's too hot for an execution. Why don't you go to the movies instead?"

And that was the end of that. The lesson I learned that afternoon didn't become clear until I had children of my own: Elizabeth, Pamela, Maggi, Aimée, and DeLauné. Putting it into practice, I came up with a method of child-rearing that ended up in a little book, *When a Parent Imposes Limits: Discipline, Authority and Freedom in Today's Family*, published by Abbey Press in St. Meinrad, Indiana, that stayed in print for ten years. The basic premise is that with privilege goes responsibility, and it is a system in which children learn that their actions have consequences—some good, some bad, but al-ways as a result of their own choice.

The long, leisurely midday meals at my grandparents' house provided the adults with an opportunity for relaxation and the kind of conversation that promotes good digestion. But for Kathryn and me, those long meals became a test of our patience as well as our manners. The adage, "Children should be seen and not heard," was alive and well during my childhood, and nowhere was it in force as strongly as at my grandmother's table.

As the meal dragged on, my sister and I became increasingly restless. André, too young to dine with the family, had his meal first. Not for him the enforced silence, the tedium of having to wait until the grown-ups had their coffee before asking to be dismissed.

And so, we found diversions, the most daring involving the bell under the rug beneath our grandmother's feet. MaMa used this bell to summon the helper from the kitchen to remove plates. At times, she pushed it twice, meaning she wished to see the cook. My sister and I thought Louisa an im-posing and mysterious figure. We saw her every morning when she knocked on our grandmother's door, and when the door opened, told MaMa what the local grocer, Mr. Disch, had fresh that day. MaMa then decided what the cook should order, and how it should be cooked. But once the kitchen door closed behind her, no one in that household, even my grandmother, ventured inside. Louisa's power came from the fact that she was one of the best cooks for miles around and that even close friends had been known to try to bribe her away. Cutting Louisa some slack would have been a small price to pay to keep her happy.

Using a signal that we thought no one else saw, my sister and I would decide which of us would slip under the table, negotiate the legs, both wooden and human, to arrive at the bell, which the perpetrator pushed twice, then scuttled back to safety, emerging from under the tablecloth to the usual buzz of laughter and conversations, waiting for the pantry door to open and for Louisa to emerge.

"You rang, Ms. Burke?" Louisa would say.

"Why, no," MaMa would say.

"Somebody did."

"Are you sure you're not hearing things?"

By this time, my sister and I would be racked with silent convulsions of laughter, so consumed by our own cleverness that it never occurred to us that Louisa, our grandmother, and the entire table of adults, were allowing us this guilty pleasure, probably remembering just how long and boring a meal with grown-ups can be.

Except for our late morning visits to our grandmother in her boudoir, we had little direct contact with MaMa. She led an ordered life, having her petit déjeuner served in her boudoir, where she began the day with prayers and a rosary, followed by spiritual reading. Then, after consulting with Louisa about the noon meal and giving the housekeeper instructions, she went to her desk, where she responded to invitations and letters, reviewed her engagement calendar, and managed the details of a life that included not only her concerns and those of her immediate family, but also extended family, numerous friends, and various organizations in which she had an active role.

A longtime member of the Daughters of the American Revolution, she was grand regent of her district and began the New Iberia Little Theater, a feat which, when my fourth daughter decided to become a theater director, affirmed that theatrical genes were part of her heritage. I have a picture of one of the productions MaMa directed. My uncle Donald, his wife Celeste, and my mother are on stage, and though I've no idea what the play is, the attitudes of the actors, and the set imply it must have been one of the drawing room comedies so popular at that time.

New Iberia Little Theater

This week's old photographic memory comes from the I.A. & Carroll Martin Photo Collection, courtesy of the Iberia Parish Library. The picture, taken in 1923, shows the cast of New Iberia Little Theater's first play, "Belinda," held at the Old Elks Theater, located on Main Street in downtown New Iberia, where Bouligny Plaza stands today. According to records those pictured include F.J. Carstens, Catherine Burke, Mrs. Donald Burke, Donald Burke and Annie Archer. The play was directed by mrs. Walter Burke. If you have an old photo you would like to share with our readers, please contact Jennifer E. May or Jerri Carlson, family section, The Daily Iberian, P. O. Box 9190, New Iberia, La. 70562 or call 365-6773. We can only use actual photographs, no newspaper clippings or photo copies, however, all pictures will be returned after publication.

Burke family's theatrical roots. *Courtesy of the* Daily Iberian *(New Iberia, LA).*

Perhaps this skill could be attributed to MaMa's lineage, which included one of the Booths of Virginia. She claimed Edmund Booth, a noted actor, as a forebear, but not his brother John Wilkes, Lincoln's assassin. When asked how this could be, she replied, "We are connected to Edmund through marriage, which does not include his unfortunate kin."

I think this flair for the theatrical gave MaMa an élan that touched everything she did. The way she dressed, the way she ran her home and family, she was the "auteur," holding the script and making sure everyone knew their lines.

My godmother, whom we called Aunt Nell—my middle name is after her—and her husband, Uncle Ed Estorge, lived in a big white house on Main Street, catty-corner from the Shadows-on-the-Teche. Their house is now a bed and breakfast inn. My daughter Pamela and her husband, Vic Chavez, gave me a walk down memory's path for my eightieth birthday, a tour of familiar places in Acadiana with an overnight stay at my godmother's old house. The furnishings were different, but the structure of the house and the placement of the rooms was the same, and as I went to bed that night, I felt the deep connection to a past that sustains me still.

Aunt Nell gave a party for Kathryn and me on the Fourth of July, 1939; I still have the write-up from the *Daily Iberian* with the headline, "Mrs. Edward Estorge Honors the Little Misses Dubus." Dotted Swiss was a favorite fabric for both children's and adult dresses. Kathryn and I wore white dotted Swiss frocks with rosettes of red, white, and blue ribbons on our shoulders.

We had at least met most of the children who came that afternoon, though the only ones I remember are Carol Dupree, our cousin Elizabeth Voorhies (a few years older than Kathryn), and our cousins Claire and Sue Mire, both older than us. I also do not remember any of the games except pin the tail on the donkey, which I have always hated. I have never understood why children enjoyed being blindfolded, spun around until they lost their sense of direction, and then made to find an elusive donkey and pin the tail at the appropriate spot.

The games were held outside, and I stoically waited for my turn, resigned to the fact that I would come nowhere near the donkey. My godmother tied the bandanna over my eyes and spun me around, and I began walking, feeling in front of me for something solid that might be the tree with the donkey mounted on it. Either heat or excitement or apprehension or a combination of all three had put me in a kind of daze, and when I finally touched something solid, I drove the pin anchoring the tail in as hard as I could.

Greeted by shouts of laughter, I jerked off my blindfold and saw what I had pinned: the rear tire on my godmother's chauffeur's roadster, a vehicle Charlie prized above anything else. My godmother and Charlie assured me it would take more than a pin to hurt the tire, but in my embarrassed misery, I only wanted to get away, turning and running across the lawn, not looking where I was going—until I fell into the fishpond. Memory draws a gentle veil, as lady memoirists of the nineteenth century wrote, over the rest of the afternoon. And, thank heaven, journalists in New Iberia knew better than to record that incident in the write-up about the party.

Uncle Ed owned Estorge Wholesale Drugs and also Estorge's Drug Store in the business district of Main Street. PaPa had the generous custom of giving Kathryn and me money for the movies whenever the theaters changed shows. We would walk down Main Street, passing Aunt Roberta and Uncle Francis's house first, and then, just before we reached Shadows-on-the-Teche, the house belonging to Great-Uncle Porteus and his wife Mabel.

After the movie, we crossed the street and entered Uncle Ed's store. Air-conditioned like the movie theater, it offered an oasis of coolness in the midst of summer heat. The air smelled of a combination of powders and perfumes from the cosmetic counter, mixtures for tonics and syrups from the prescription area in back, and the scent of hot fudge rising from behind the marble soda fountain counter that ran along one entire side of the store. A few round marble-topped tables with ice cream chairs provided seating for grown-ups, mostly ladies stopping by for a treat. Kathryn and I sat at the counter, lifted onto the tall stools by Uncle Ed, who always told the soda jerk on duty the same thing: "These are my little princesses, and they may have anything they want."

Though we both longed to try a banana split, we never did because we had been brought up to observe moderation in all things. We doubted we could ever finish an entire banana split, and thus would prove that "our eyes were bigger than our stomachs." So, we stuck to ice cream sodas and sundaes, my favorite being marshmallow with chocolate ice cream.

Thinking about ice cream brings a memory of a summer day when Aunt Nell planned a trip to St. Martinville, some fifteen miles away, to visit the old Maraist house, now a museum. Charlie brought her Buick limousine up to the porte cochere, and Aunt Nell, Kathryn, and I got in. (André, still too young for such long adventures, remained at our grand-parents' home.) A large picnic hamper had been loaded onto the luggage rack on the back of the Buick, and next to it Charlie had lashed an ice cream freezer. I saw him remove his livery coat as we walked toward the museum, and I remember wishing Aunt Nell would tell him not to put it back on, as a coat of any fabric on such a hot and humid day must have been very uncomfortable.

What I didn't know was that even if she had made this suggestion, Charlie would not have heeded it. He was a stickler for doing things as they should be done, and when, on occasion, a young relative of his came to help with weeding or some other chore, a constant stream of correction came from Charlie's lips.

The museum was a dim, rather dusty place, but I remember seeing an old bedstead with the "springs" made of rope woven from one side of the frame to the other, while a moss-filled mattress sat on top. At that time, and for a few decades more, factories cured moss for mattresses, making good use of a parasite so readily available.

We finished our tour and returned to the car. Aunt Nell directed Charlie to a table under a giant oak, and we helped her set out the picnic: chicken sandwiches made with white meat only on buttered bread, deviled eggs, grapes, and for dessert, ice cream freshly-churned. Charlie turned the handle on the freezer, and when the ice cream had reached the right degree of firmness, he took out the paddle and asked if we wanted to lick it. Of course we did, but did not expect Aunt Nell to allow it. To our surprise, she did.

"Charlie and I will have our ice cream like civilized adults," she said. "But you children may lick the paddle first. Only you have to turn away from me to do it."

I can hear exclamations ranging from "What idiocy," to "Imagine children being repressed like that." However, I have to say that being brought up in such a way that licking the paddle of an ice cream freezer was considered an indulgence certainly put far more dangerous behavior way down the list of things we would think of doing. If you've never read F. Scott Fitzgerald's short story, "Bernice Bobs Her Hair," read it sometime. It emphasizes my point, which is that when children grow up with reasonable limits, it can take a very long time, and perhaps never, for them to cross the line from behavior that is merely unacceptable to behavior that ends with prison, permanent injury, or death.

On that same day, Aunt Nell presented Kathryn and me with gifts "for no reason." She gave me a necklace and bracelet of clear cut-crystal beads, which I kept until at some point, years after I'd stopped wearing them, the strings broke, the beads scattered, and they exist now only in memory. I don't remember Kathryn's gift, but I'm sure it was as pretty as mine.

When my daughters first heard these stories of our visits to New Iberia, they exclaimed, just as they did when they heard other stories of growing up in the time and places I did: "You were the luckiest thing!" Looking back, I see that I was. Part of a large extended family—I had twenty-one first cousins and second and third cousins too many to count—full of interesting and loving adults who saw rearing children and giving them the guidance to become mature, productive people as one of life's most solemn duties, I realize how very lucky I was.

I remember a lesson I learned from Mother on an Easter visit. When Kathryn, André, and I came downstairs on Easter morning, I am not exaggerating when I say that the bottom six steps of the big staircase were filled with Easter baskets, brimming with stuffed rabbits, lambs, and chicks, and, of course, with candy. Our aunts and uncles provided enough treats for a dozen children, a situation Mother soon remedied. After we had examined the contents of our baskets, she told us to choose the things we liked best and put them all in one basket. "The rest will go to children who have none. This day is a celebration of our Lord's resurrection, and of all days, this is one on which we should follow in his footsteps."

Trying to teach children to be charitable by telling them to give away their gifts seems harsh. But in a country where homeless people lived in cardboard boxes, where families subsisted on corn meal mush, where people had lost their life savings, their homes, and their possessions, sharing with others was instilled in children at a very young age.

And I'm glad it was. My generation, born in the Great Depression, growing up during World War II, doesn't feel entitled to anything. We know all too well the cost of economic disasters and war and how very fortunate we were if we only paid a small part of it. Our generation also learned that the only standard by which we should measure ourselves is character. To quote my father: "Don't ever tie your sense of self to anything you can lose or that can be taken from you. That leaves education and the character to use it."

Those words came to mind when I read Bernard Malmud's *The Fixer*. At the end, he faces torture and death, but realizes that no matter what his enemies do to him, they can have his spirit only if he gives it to them.

In one way or another, I have met and interacted with a number of "celebrities" in my life, but the only ones who truly impressed me—not that it mattered to them!—were the ones who had character.

MaMa, the very model of a well-brought up lady, had a sister-in-law, Gabriele (called Gabe, pronounced Gah-bee) who was the very model of an idiosyncratic French woman who did as she damn well pleased. Gabe married PaPa's brother William, who had an export-import business, which, along with thousands of others, didn't survive the crash of 1929. Like many other ruined men, William died of a stroke not long afterward, leaving Aunt Gabe with a Buick touring car, contacts on the docks, and a host of friends and relatives stretching from New Orleans to New Iberia.

I have a picture of Aunt Gabe in her New Orleans home, pre-crash. She wears a long glittering gown, carries an ostrich feather fan, has a band around her forehead surmounted by another plume, and a look in her eyes that hints at inner fortitude as well as wit. Aunt Gabe solved her many problems by driving the Buick to the docks, loading it up with green bananas and wooden boxes of ant poison, and then setting out on the old Spanish Trail to visit friends and relatives. She always extended her trip to Lake Charles, but by the time she reached us, the remaining bananas were black, though she insisted still edible. "Gabe, no wonder you sell so much ant poison," my father told her. "You bring the ants yourself." She adored him, and he adored her, humoring her eccentricities until the day she decided to take us for a drive.

Daddy sat in front with Aunt Gabe, Mother, Kathryn, André, and I in the capacious back. The roads were rutted and so rough that they were called "corduroy," and, finally, tired of bouncing, Aunt Gabe drove up a railroad crossing and turned on the track. "At least," she said, "the bouncing is regular." Daddy ordered her to get off the track immediately, but she refused.

"Why would a train come, André?"

"Because it's a damn track. Gabe, you get my wife and children off this track or I'll—"

"If you insist. But don't blame me for the rough road."

Aunt Gabe is still famous in a family known for fine conversationalists as the only member who, as a houseguest, would come down for breakfast in the morning, with these opening words: "Now, as I was saying."

Great-Uncle Porteus, like his brother Walter, had graduated from Tulane Law School, but the resemblance between the two ended there. For one thing, Porteus had left the Roman Catholic Church to become an Episcopalian, for reasons I never knew. Worse than that in the eyes of the more conservative members of the family, he had become a Mason, an organization whose anti-Catholic sentiments were well-known.

Tall, handsome, with a white goatee and mustache, he walked down Main Street to the law office he shared with his brother twirling his gold-headed walking stick, nodding to those he passed with an air that proclaimed him the master of all he surveyed. Except when he was with his wife, Mabel, probably the quietest, gentlest, woman I have ever known. He worshipped her, though their only child, Nina, ran a close second. Looking back, I realize that Uncle Porteus was made in the mold of a nineteenth-century southern gentleman, powerful and domineering in the outside world, a protector and generous husband at home.

We saw little of Porteus; Nina was much older than us, and Aunt Mabel's fragile health meant we visited her only occasionally and never stayed very long. So, when our mother told us that Uncle Porteus had organized an outing for the children in the family, and included others in the right age groups, we felt first surprised and then faintly alarmed; what sort of outing would a curmudgeon devise?

A perfect one, as it turned out. He hired a large horse-drawn wagon with a striped awning to keep out the sun and escorted us, riding his own horse, to Charenton, a shell-covered beach on a waterway in the Atchafalaya Basin. Originally settled by the Chitimacha tribe, Parisian Alexandre Frere named it Charenton on his deathbed when he said, "Anyone choosing to move to that part of Louisiana belonged in Charenton," a notorious insane asylum outside of Paris. Considering malaria-carrying mosquitoes, humid heat, snakes, and alligators, he might not have been far wrong.

But when we drove to Charenton, there remained only vestiges of the community. I remember a small shop where the women sold hand-woven baskets made from split river cane. I have one of these baskets on my desk, a small one with a top, and friends who collect baskets regard those made by the Chitimacha's among the very best. Like many ancient crafts, this one almost became extinct until preservation efforts brought it back. The increasing difficulty of obtaining river cane from the wetlands and the lack of interest among younger tribe members give this effort a high priority as both the public and private sector recognize how important these artifacts are. However, at that age, I considered the small basket only a souvenir of a pleasant summer day.

Live oaks draped in moss hung over the shallow water lapping at the shell beach. We wore rubber bathing shoes so as not to cut our feet on the sharp oyster shells, left there by centuries of Native Americans who caught oysters in the waters nearby. Such shell mounds exist all along the Gulf Coast, and there is a large one on Dauphin Island that my birding partner and I visit frequently, almost always seeing a marvelous variety of birds.

Because the beach sloped gently, increasing in depth not by feet but by inches, the water near shore, never warmed by the sun because of the thick leaved oaks, felt almost cold until I splashed and kicked enough to get my blood circulating. The older children walked out far enough to reach water deep enough to swim in, and I watched them surface dive and race each other well past the end of the pier.

Uncle Porteus sat in a folding canvas chair far enough from the water to avoid getting splashes on his white linen suit. He smoked cigars, and though at home he only smoked in his own study (like my grandfather), here he lit up, sending smoke billowing upward, its sweet scent carried to us by the breeze. The smoke also served to keep mosquitoes away from him, while the rest of us depended on insect repellents.

The picnic lunch, with perishable items kept cold in Westinghouse ice chests and large thermos jugs, was served on long wooden tables set under the oaks. Aunt Mabel had sent cloths to cover them, with napkins to match, as well as the "kitchen" china and cutlery. The menu was typical of summer picnics in the South: lemonade, fried chicken, ham sandwiches on white bread, cabbage slaw, potato salad, sliced Creole tomatoes marinated in a vinaigrette dressing, and, to top it off, pound cake and fig ice cream.

Fig ice cream tops my list of favorites. More delicate than peach or strawberry, it is difficult to find now that fig trees are less common. Louisiana figs don't last long off the tree, stores don't carry them, and if a roadside produce stand does, they go quickly. Fortunately, I have fig trees myself, and as I write this, a colander-full sits in the refrigerator ready to be turned into ice cream or preserves.

Riding home through the late afternoon, drowsy with sun and good food, we were surprised to hear Uncle Porteus singing, followed by an invitation for us to join in. Whether in gratitude for a lovely day or because we dared not refuse, or more probably a combination of both, we did as he asked, singing songs learned from hearing the grown-ups in the family playing them, or, in my sister's and my case, hearing our father sing them to our mother in his beautiful tenor voice. "Shine On Harvest Moon," "Beautiful Dreamer," "Annie Laurie," and other such old standards, sung in young voices of various tones and pitch, may not fall gently on any ears but those of loving family, but when we drove up in front of Uncle Porteus's house, and Aunt Mabel stood on the front porch clapping, we felt—or at least I did—that this was indeed, as another song says, "the end of a perfect day."

Two events happened in our last year in Lake Charles that would mark significant changes in Louisiana, and in the world at large. On September 1, 1939, Hitler's armies marched into Poland, and in May 1940, Sam Jones was elected governor of Louisiana, breaking the hold of the Long machine and giving hope that graft and corruption would end.

I sat on my father's lap while he listened to the news that day in September, and though I couldn't understand the words, his face told me that something bad had happened. And, months later, I stood beside him, with Mother, Kathryn, and André, watching Sam Jones's victory parade through his hometown. In a picture taken that day, I'm wearing a bandanna around my neck, a straw cowboy hat on my head, and carrying a cap pistol poised to shoot. It contrasts with another picture taken around that time, in which I'm wearing an embroidered piqué jumper over a pale green organdy blouse, standing in a row of children at a birthday party, turned away from the boy next to me with my nose very definitely in the air. It's easy to read these as two sides of my developing personality: the extrovert interested in the world around her; the introvert withdrawing from anyone who tried to get too close.

Recipes from Two Picnics

BAKED HAM WITH BROWN SUGAR MUSTARD GLAZE

1 large ready-to-cook smoked ham, about 12–16 lbs.
1 cup light brown sugar, packed
1 tablespoon light corn syrup
2 tablespoons flour
¼ teaspoon cinnamon
1 tablespoon prepared Dijon or gourmet mustard
1 tablespoon cider vinegar
2 tablespoons water

Heat oven to 325°. Line roasting pan with foil. Wrap the ham in foil, keeping the fat side up, place in pan. Bake for 18–20 minutes per pound, or until meat thermometer reaches 145°.

For glaze, combine all ingredients in a saucepan, stir over medium heat until smooth. Then simmer, stirring, for 1 minute.

Remove foil from ham and cut off excess fat. Score the ham's surface in a diamond pattern. Pour the glaze over the ham, return to oven, and bake at about 155°, basting frequently with glaze, for another 30 minutes.

Let cool, slice.

POACHED CHICKEN BREASTS

6 boneless, skinless chicken breasts
Celery stalks and leaves
Salt and black pepper to taste
Green onions

You do not have to chop either the celery or the green onions. Wash them well and cut the celery stalks and onions into pieces so as to release the juices. Put these with the chicken breasts and salt and pepper to taste in a pot with water to cover. Simmer until the breasts are cooked through. Cool and slice for sandwiches.

24-HOUR COLESLAW

1 medium head cabbage, shredded
2 medium white onions, cut in thin rings
½ cup sugar

Dressing:
1 teaspoon celery seed
1 teaspoon sugar
1½ teaspoons salt
1 teaspoon dry mustard
1 cup cider vinegar
1 cup vegetable oil

Stir ½ cup of sugar into cabbage and place half of amount in large bowl. Cover with onion rings. Cover with remaining cabbage. Combine dressing ingredients except oil. Bring to a roaring boil. Stir in oil. Bring to boil again. Pour over cabbage and onions. Do not stir. Cover and refrigerate for 24 hours. Keeps indefinitely.

Yield: Serves 6 to 8.

DEVILED EGGS

12 eggs
Mayonnaise
Chopped parsley
Sweet pickle relish
Dry mustard to taste
Salt and black pepper to taste
Paprika

To boil eggs: Bring the eggs to room temperature. Place them in a pot and cover them at least halfway with tap water. Put heat on high and bring the water to a rolling boil. Then, turn the heat off and cover the pot. Let the eggs stand for 12 minutes. (Once you have found the length of time it takes for the eggs to fully cook while standing in the hot water, you can adjust the time.) Putting the eggs in a colander that still allows them to be in water can keep them from cracking while cooking. When I am boiling many eggs, I often put the carton or part of it in the pot, so the eggs don't touch each other. Note: Week-old eggs peel better than very fresh ones.

Shell the eggs. Cut lengthwise and scoop out the yolks into a bowl. Mash with a fork. Now mix mayonnaise, parsley, sweet pickle relish, dry mustard, and salt and black pepper to taste in a bowl. Amounts depend on your choice. Stir the egg yolks into this mixture until it all blends. Spoon into the egg whites, sprinkle paprika on top. I have found that a muffin tin makes a good substitute for an egg tray to keep the stuffed halves neat.

HERBED BUTTER

Soften a stick (½ cup) of butter
Use any of these herbs to flavor the butter:
Tarragon
Marjoram
Parsley
Thyme

If using fresh, chop finely. The normal proportions are 2 tablespoons of herbs to 1 stick butter. Blend herbs and softened butter, let stand for at least an hour so butter can absorb the flavors.

ANOTHER FLAVORED BUTTER

1 stick butter, softened
Ground rosemary
2 tablespoons chopped black olives

Blend together, let stand for at least an hour so butter can absorb the flavors.

POUND CAKE

1 cup vegetable shortening
3 teaspoons baking powder
2 cups sugar
1 teaspoon lemon extract
5 eggs, beaten one at a time
Salt to taste
3 cups cake flour, sifted with other dry ingredients
1 cup sweet milk

Mix shortening and sugar well, beat until creamy. Add eggs, one at a time. Add flour mixture and milk alternately, beating slowly. Add lemon extract and mix well. Either grease a Bundt or angel food cake pan or use baking spray. Put batter in the cake pan and bake in a preheated 300° oven for 1 hour or until a straw inserted comes out clean.

FIG ICE CREAM

½ cup milk
1 tablespoon lemon juice
2 egg yolks
½ cup sugar
1½ cups heavy cream, lightly whipped
1 teaspoon vanilla
1 quart ripe figs, peeled and pressed through a sieve

Scald ½ cup milk and stir it slowly into well-beaten egg yolks. Cook the mixture in a double boiler or in a bowl over boiling water, stirring constantly, until the custard is thick enough to coat a wooden spoon. Cool; then fold the custard into the lightly whipped heavy cream. Sprinkle the fig purée with the lemon juice, stir in the ½ cup sugar and vanilla, and add to the custard. Blend ingredients thoroughly and freeze in an ice cream maker according to the manufacturer's directions.

Lagniappe

OLD-FASHIONED LEMONADE

1½ tablespoons lemon juice
3-4 tablespoons sugar
1 cup water

Boil the sugar and water together for 2 minutes. Chill, then add lemon juice and water. Serve over ice in a tall glass garnished with mint and/or a maraschino cherry.

Yield: 1 serving. Multiply this recipe according to the number of people to be served.

CHAPTER FOUR

Had we lived anywhere in Louisiana but Lake Charles, I would have begun first grade the fall of 1939. But at that time, Lake Charles had two school systems: the Lake Charles City Schools and the Calcasieu Parish Schools. To enter a City School's first grade in the fall, one had to turn six by June 30th. After that date, one began in January. With a November birthday, my sister had begun school in January 1937 instead of September 1936. Born in October 1933, my formal education began in January 1940, and since we moved to Baton Rouge in April, I ended up skipping the first half of first grade.

The only lasting effect is that I have one of the world's worst handwritings, though in an age when many children learn to use a computer before they go to school, and taking notes by hand went out with typewriters and dial telephones, increasingly the elegant handwriting of the past is gone, replaced by emails, text messages, and other forms of communication that, I suppose, make up in efficiency what they lack in grace.

My naivete lasted well beyond childhood: I say this because I must have been well into my teens before I realized that a conversation I "overheard" between the principal of my new school in Baton Rouge and my mother was intended for my ears. This came sometime in May, after I had been at Bernard Terrace—then the newest elementary school in Baton Rouge—a little over a month. I was working away at something when I heard my mother's voice, and turning to look out the open door, saw her and Mrs. Evelyn Daniels, one of the most outstanding educators I have ever known, standing in the hall.

"Beth is ready for second grade in reading, spelling, and arithmetic," Mrs. Daniels said. "But whereas all the children in her class can print the entire alphabet, as well as writing it in script, she can only print up to H. So, I'm afraid if she doesn't learn the rest of the letters, she'll have to be held back."

Of course, this conversation produced the desired result. I spent every spare moment mastering both the printed and the script alphabet. Though some of the letters could hardly have been called legible, with the assurance from my mother that we would practice during the summer break, Mrs. Daniels sent me on to second grade.

We stayed in Baton Rouge until I was in fifth grade, and then Gulf States Utilities transferred my father to head a new district in Lafayette. I view those years in Baton Rouge as a time of transition in many ways, perhaps the greatest one being that my world expanded from a very narrow one to one that encompassed the globe.

We arrived in Baton Rouge before America entered the Second World War, but at a time when the country had begun preparing for it. Standard Oil had established a refinery as well as administrative offices in Baton Rouge in 1909, choosing it because it was the first high ground with soil that, unlike the sponge around New Orleans and its environs, could stand the weight of storage tanks. It was growing in both size and importance, as were other soon-to-be war industries.

Thus, housing was literally impossible to find, and had we not been able to stay the first six weeks with the Johnsons, friends of my parents, I've no idea where we'd have lived. Hester Harrop Johnson was a friend from Lake Charles. An artist, she concentrated not on the domestic arts, but on the fine ones. Even had Hester been a proficient housekeeper and cook, my parents wouldn't have wanted to impose five extra people on her, and so, during those six weeks, we ate in a restaurant every single night.

At that time, Baton Rouge had, essentially, three restaurants: the flagship of what would become the Piccadilly Cafeteria chain on Third Street downtown; Italian Gardens on North Boulevard; and Mike and Tony's Steak House on Plank Road near the Standard Oil plant. The Piccadilly was the most usual choice, because then, as now, it served "regular" food, meaning a wide variety of vegetables, salads, and side dishes, with beef, pork, chicken, and Louisiana seafood cooked in the standard ways. They also had—and still do—great cornbread and rolls and excellent desserts. Italian Gardens served southern Italian food: spaghetti and meatballs or sausage in a traditional red sauce and other pasta dishes that I don't remember because spaghetti and meatballs was the only one I was familiar with and the only one I wanted to try.

Later, when meat was rationed, Mike and Tony's didn't have nearly the range of cuts it had when we began going there. I could eat a small T-bone chop and a baked potato, with a vegetable (usually spinach) on the side, but my brother André, only three years old, found eating out an increasingly difficult trial. He had become a favorite at the Piccadilly, which had white-jacketed waiters with black bow ties who carried patrons' trays to their tables. They all knew him by name, and if he couldn't finish the food on his plate, they would assure him that he didn't have to, the cooks always served too much. One night as we stood in line and the women serving the food waited for him to tell them what he wanted, he burst into tears. "Couldn't I just have a peanut butter and jelly sandwich?"

Not long after that, Daddy came home from work to say that Harold Leonard Sr., the vice president of this region of Gulf States Utilities, who lived directly behind the Johnsons, had talked an LSU professor who was building a house one street over from the Leonard's into staying where he was so we could rent it. We moved in and were immediately "welcomed" into the neighborhood with pranks that began with tin cans tied to the screen door handle and progressed from there. But not very far. Most parents were aware that their children were not perfect—they could commit acts that at the very least annoyed the neighbors, and at the worst enraged them—and if a neighbor reported such an act, lo and behold, he was believed.

My father spoke with Mr. Leonard, whose two sons, along with a few other boys, were part of the welcome committee. Confronted with their deeds, the boys said that since our last name was Dubus, they had been sure we were German spies and wanted to let us know they were on to us. (One of those boys grew up to marry a woman who became a best friend of mine, and, to this day, Ned Clark and I laugh about the logic that convinced a bunch of kids that anyone with a French name had to be a spy for the Germans.)

The boys apologized, watched by their fathers and mine, and though I thought surely none of them would ever speak to us again, the opposite happened. My sister and I were initiated into the Victory Club, and Dick Hearin, whose family lived behind us, became a playmate to my brother André and me. As the only girl, I played Aleta to their Princes Valiant and Gawain, the brave battlefield nurse to their wounded heroes. The summer afternoons might seem to stretch into infinity, but they were never long enough to match our imaginations, and when our fathers built a tree house supported by four oak trees, the games became more elaborate, as the boys flew dangerous missions over Germany and I, the radio operator, guided them home.

Children's radio programs were extremely popular, supported by advertisements from companies like Wheaties, which sponsored *Jack Armstrong, the All-American Boy*, and Ralston's Cereal, the sponsor of *Tom Mix*. These ran every weekday: *Jack Armstrong* first, followed by *Tom Mix*. A new story began on Monday, with another chapter following each day, climaxing on Friday. As if this format weren't enough to guarantee faithful audiences, the sponsors, advised by a burgeoning Madison Avenue, soon offered premiums ranging from magic rings to toy guns to bandannas to code-breakers in return for box tops from their products.

Though I never became a big fan of *Jack Armstrong*, I did like *Tom Mix*. For one thing, since the radio character was named for the character in the Tom Mix westerns, I could picture him and the terrain through which he rode. For some strange reason, I still remember one episode, titled "The Ghost Train," and can still hear the whistle, muffled by the distance between the real and the supernatural, as the train hurtles toward our hero, trapped on the tracks. We knew that, like any mystery series with heroes who have to live to sleuth another day, neither Jack nor Tom would ever get into a fatal fix. But still, it was exciting to see how the villains would entrap them and how they would outwit them and escape.

Like many other children, my favorite program was *Let's Pretend*, a long-running (1934–1954) children's show produced on CBS radio and sponsored by Cream of Wheat. Centered on fairy tales, the hour-long show presented well-written, well-acted dramatizations, and many a birthday party was scheduled to avoid that hour on Saturday morning when most children were glued to the radio. As well as entertaining us, these shows inspired Dick and André and me to enact at least parts of them, even if we had to assume more than one role.

The summer passed quickly. We spent our usual two weeks in New Iberia, and Grandmother Jessie visited us, staying a month because the trip from Shreveport was a long one in those days of dirt roads and, besides, the longer visit gave her opportunities to spend a few days with Dubus relatives in New Orleans.

I remember visiting my grandmother's sister, Anne, there on a few occasions, but not until my novel *Cajun* came out and I was signing books at a store in New Orleans did I meet Aimée, one of my Dubus cousins, my great-aunt's granddaughter. "I knew you had to be a cousin," Aimée said. "There just aren't that many Dubus out there." I also met a cousin from the branch that settled in Savannah—they're still there—when I appeared on a television station in Pensacola, Florida, also promoting the book. A final bit of Jungian synchronicity occurred when I ordered a gift for a son-in-law from a liquor store in Albuquerque, using a credit card in my maiden name. When the clerk heard "Dubus," he said he'd dated a girl with that last name. I asked where, and he said Colorado Springs. I said she had to be a descendant from the uncle my father visited the summer after he began Vanderbilt, as that is where that uncle lived.

I knew nothing about any of these Dubus relatives until an enterprising cousin, Marie Dubus Garrett, began searching for Dubus and not only organized the first Dubus family reunion in New Orleans in 2012, but found a French genealogist who traced the family in France back to the mid-seventeenth century. Marie arrived at the reunion with wall charts showing how relatives were connected, and from which branch they came, as well as smaller, but complete, charts for everyone to take home. She also prepared a book for those who had contributed to pay the French genealogist, which contains photos and information I know I would never have without this wonderful cousin! To date, over one hundred present-day Dubus have been located, all descendants of the four brothers who lived in New Orleans in the nineteenth century, until one went to New Iberia, one to Savannah, and one to Colorado Springs. Only one stayed in New Orleans continuing to run the Dubus Engine Company, whose location was announced by blue and white tiles set in the sidewalk on the corner of a side street and Tchoupitoulas Street.

MawMaw, my Dubus grandmother Jessie, was the complete opposite of my Burke grandmother, MaMa. She was a doer, a woman of spirit and self-discipline, who had met many obstacles in her life, and, if she hadn't overcome all of them, had learned to survive despite them. Her arrival was special for a number of reasons. For one, we rarely had family visitors, as it was easier for us to visit them. Second, she traveled with a steamer trunk, and watching her unpack it provided us children with an afternoon of surprises. After removing the clothes on hangers from the trunk and placing them in the closet, she would tackle the drawers, though not the ones with her undergarments. As she lifted a stack of handkerchiefs, we might spy a small metal car or a tiny doll or a minute tea set, which she would present to the child for whom she had chosen it. Treats had been hidden all through the trunk, the fruit of one or more of her tours of Woolworth's, where she could find treasures that would delight any child's heart.

Yet another fascinating thing about our grandmother was that she smoked. Not tobacco cigarettes, but medicated ones for the asthma that plagued her all her life. These cigarettes contained alkaloids of belladonna, derived from the dried leaves and flower tops of Datura stramonium. They had a bronchodilator effect, thus helping the coughing spasms that asthma victims suffered.

(Since belladonna drops dilate pupils, some women used them to enhance the size of their pupils on special occasions. My mother reported that one of her classmates, invited to a party where she would meet Enrico Caruso after his concert in New Orleans the summer of 1920, put belladonna drops in her eyes, only to have her pupils dilated for so long that she was, quite literally, unable to see the great man's face and could only grope blindly for his hand. Caruso had been scheduled to sing at the French Opera House, which, after a cessation of performances during World War I, had staged its first post-war opera on November 11, 1919, after the Armistice had been signed. Not a month later, it burned to the ground, and not until February, 1943, when a group of opera loving New Orleanians, under the leadership of Walter Loubat, formed the New Orleans Opera Association, did New Orleans once more have a permanent company and a fixed season, replacing the touring companies that had provided the only opera in the city since the French Opera House burned.)

And the final difference grandmother Jessie made in our household was her industrious application of her wide knowledge of domestic arts. A superb cook, she made the dishes my father had grown up with, including her famous crab stew. I have seen this dish on only one restaurant menu, a café attached to a gas station in Morgan City, Louisiana. I had been in Morgan City for personal reasons and drove from there to New Orleans the next day for professional ones. I stopped to get gas, went in to get a Coke, and had I not had an appointment in New Orleans, would have stayed for lunch: I would have had my choice of two versions of crab stew, one red, one brown, but since Jessie always made brown, that's what I would have chosen.

This dish, prepared properly, takes a long time to make. You begin with live crabs, which you boil in seasoned water—without red pepper, which is added later. That alone is a problem, as salted water thrown out on grass kills it, so there always had to be a place available where the water could be disposed of without harm. When the crabs are cool enough to work with, you first remove the claws and set these aside. Then you crack the shells and after getting rid of the lungs, which we called "dead man's fingers," you extract the lump crabmeat and set it aside. Shelling crabs one by one to eat yourself is worth doing. Shelling several dozen crabs for crab stew is an act of love. (I learned some years ago that inventive Cajuns realized that the wringers of old-fashioned washing machines would make perfect crab crushers, because the wringers could be set at varying heights, resulting in the right pressure to crack the shells without mangling the meat.)

Once the crabmeat is ready, the next step is to chop the "Holy Trinity" of south Louisiana cooking: white onions, celery, and green bell pepper. When I make crab stew, or indeed any dish with crabmeat, even if the recipe calls for green bell pepper, I either use it very lightly or not at all, because I think the bell pepper can overpower the delicate taste that makes jumbo lump crabmeat such a treat. (Note: There is a vast difference between what many Louisiana restaurants and even seafood markets call "lump crabmeat" and "jumbo lump crabmeat." By lump, they simply mean white crabmeat which is not in lumps, but in bits and pieces. "Jumbo lump crabmeat" is just what the name implies: lovely, succulent lumps of crabmeat that need very little done to them to make an amazing meal.)

I learned to cook many dishes, particularly seafood, without measuring by watching my grandmother Jessie at work. The amount of onions, celery, and bell pepper depended on how much crabmeat she had, and the amount of roux required to make the gravy depended on the total bulk of all those ingredients.

Once the roux had been made, the vegetables, along with other seasonings of her choice—thyme, lemon peel, salt, and both red and black pepper to taste, were added, as well as the claws, all in a heavy pot, with water sufficient to cover the contents. Then, the stew simmered on low until the gravy thickened to the right consistency, and only then would the crabmeat be added, stirred gently so as not to break up the lumps.

While the stew cooked, Jessie or my mother prepared the rest of the meal. Corn is a good accompaniment for crab, so often, while the stew simmered on one burner, maque choux cooked slowly on another. (This is a smothered corn, fresh tomato, onion, and bell pepper dish that is a summer favorite, as it should be made only with truly fresh corn.) Sliced summer squash might be another choice, but no vegetable with too distinctive a taste would ever be served with crab stew.

Finally, the noon hour would arrive, and we would gather at the table. After allowing my father just enough time to say grace, my grandmother would lift a spoon of stew to her mouth, and not giving anyone, even her son, time to get in a compliment first, she would say, "Jessie, this is the best crab stew I have ever had in my life." And it always was.

Jessie also sewed. Before her visits, at her request, my mother would find patterns and fabric for garments for my sister and me, and, once in a while, for herself. Our grandmother sewed beautifully, both by hand and machine, and seeing that I seemed interested, decided that I should learn to do both. The embroidery lessons began with cross-stitch, the simplest one, because all you had to do was make row after row of little crosses, following the stamped pattern on the tea cloth or pillowcase.

But learning to use a sewing machine proved frustrating, not because Singer sewing machines in the forties presented complicated programs, but because my grandmother, herself gifted with the ability to master any form of handwork within a few hours and also the ability to make a garment in one day, found my early efforts completely unacceptable.

I had been given the task of hemming the tea towels I embroidered. After learning to fill the bobbin with thread and successfully thread the needle, as well as maneuver the bobbin thread through the proper space, I started my first hem. I snipped the thread and handed the tea towel to my grandmother, who said, "Rip it out and do it again. It's crooked."

Some eight tries later, when told one more time to rip out the hem, I rebelled. "It's only a tea towel," I said.

My grandmother fixed me with a fierce eye. "Only?" she said. Joan Crawford and Bette Davis would have envied the cold disdain she put into that word. "If that's the way you feel, why do anything at all?"

I ripped out the hem and finally paid attention to what I was doing. And as straight hem after straight hem rolled smoothly under the needle, I realized what a truly remarkable woman this grandmother was. Kind and giving most of the time, she knew that one of the worst things we can do to children is to fail to help them develop a work ethic and a standard by which to judge the results.

***

Summer ended, and I began second grade. There were two classes for each of the six grades at Bernard Terrace. I was in Mrs. Hamilton's room, a motherly looking lady with a kind, gentle way of instructing I found very pleasant, and since most of the classmates from first grade were also in that class, I felt at home.

I have four memories of second grade year, two of which were written up in the Tatler column of the *Terrace Tattler*, Bernard Terrace's school paper, put out by students in the two sixth grades. The first instance created an immediate stir when, after morning recess, I did not return to class. The building and school grounds were searched, neighbors were queried, but I was nowhere to be found. Meanwhile, I was sitting on the front steps of a mom-and-pop grocery store on Government Street, a few blocks away, waiting for my father to pick me up to go home to lunch. (That store became Calandro's, still operated by the same family, with two sites. It is one of Baton Rouge's best and most accommodating stores, carrying any item its customers suggest, even things that only a few people might want.)

Eventually, Mrs. Calandro came out to ask me if there was anything wrong. I said there wasn't, and she went back inside. But as time went on, she decided she would have to find out why I sat there alone, and so I told her my father should have been there long ago to take me home for lunch. She immediately understood my mistake, but instead of telling me that it wasn't even eleven o'clock, she asked for our home number and called my mother. My mother called the school and came to get me, suggesting I have lunch at home with her, and then, since there would only be a few hours of school left, not go back. I am still grateful for two understanding women—make it three, including Mrs. Daniels—who knew that a shy seven-year-old child would rather any punishment than having to face her class after creating such a fuss. By the time the item appeared in the school paper, it had been turned into what could be viewed as a charming story, though at recess I did get offers of help finding my way back to class.

The second event that got the *Tattler* column's attention centered around a boy named Wesley Brummett, who even in second grade had what used to be called "bedroom eyes," with a dashing shock of black hair over them. Just after the bell ending recess rang one day, he pulled me behind an azalea bush and gave me a kiss square on my mouth. He came down with red measles within days, I came down with them the next week. This small scandal was duly reported, and the teasing we both got lasted much longer than my "lost" adventure.

Years later, a close and dear friend happened to be sitting next to Wesley at a local watering hole and told him he'd heard Wesley went around kissing girls and giving them the measles.

"Beth Dubus, second grade," Wesley said. "Does she still have long brown curls?"

"Short brown curls."

"Does she still not know how pretty she is?"

"Despite my best efforts, she still doesn't."

The two other events introduced me to performing in public, first at one of the monthly programs featuring books and the second as a sunbeam in the Christmas pageant.

Mrs. Daniels believed that reading and mathematics formed the two legs on which a strong education would stand, and as part of the school's emphasis on reading, each month a program was held in which twelve students, one from each class, gave reports on a book they had recently read. To add interest to the program, the presenters dressed like a character from their book.

First and second graders participated, but our reports weren't expected to be more than the briefest summary of our book's plot. I either chose or had *Rebecca of Sunnybrook Farm* chosen for me, but since I liked the book and found the idea of dressing up as Rebecca appealing, I put aside my qualms at appearing in public and prepared for my turn.

The costume, a blue cotton dress with a white ruffled pinafore, topped by a broad-brimmed hat, was easy to assemble, and I rehearsed what I would say to willing family members until I felt certain I knew every word by heart.

I hadn't counted on how I would feel when I looked out over what seemed to be a vast number of rows and saw all those faces gazing up at me. Fortunately, when I reached my place on stage, all I saw were blurs. Since much of the world appeared blurred to me, I didn't mention this to anyone, and since I always sat in the first row, I could read the board.

At some point that year, my parents realized I had a vision problem, and I was fitted with glasses, which opened a world of clarity I had never known. I was near-sighted, so had seen objects up close very well, which was, of course, the main reason my problem went unnoticed for so long. But to actually see separate leaves on trees, or the details of a bird perched on a high branch, was a source of constant pleasurable surprise.

The details of that Christmas pageant have long disappeared from my mind. I only remember my part and the costume I wore. Along with other second grade girls, I had been cast as a sunbeam. We wore tutus of deep gold tarlatan, a stiff net-like fabric, trimmed with gold tinsel like that used on Christmas trees. We had a song and a dance, and I had one line. Given the line, the sunbeams must have been instrumental in solving whatever problem prevented Santa from delivering toys on Christmas Eve, though I can't imagine what we might have done, unless we gathered in force and melted the villain.

My stage instructions were to step out of line, approach Santa, and ask, "Did we do wrong, Santa Claus?" Which got one of the biggest laughs of the night, and I still don't know why. I may have asked my parents, but probably not. Later, when I acted in plays, I realized how disconcerting an unexpected laugh can be, so maybe even at that age, I decided the audience had simply not understood the significance of what I said, and I should not let it bother me one bit.

I caught bronchitis from getting chilled when waiting in a drafty room to go on stage and so spent that Christmas in bed. I would catch bronchitis again the next year, when I played a candle in the Christmas pageant, because we wore long flannel gowns and I got too hot. However, I did seem more prone to bronchitis and tonsillitis than my siblings, so perhaps I would have gotten sick anyway.

Not long after Christmas, Mother came down with pneumonia. That early in 1941, the United States still wasn't at war, but as I said earlier, preparations were being made. The two hospitals in Baton Rouge, Our Lady of the Lake near the state capitol and Baton Rouge General on Government Street, were overcrowded, and though Dr. Roy Wallace, our family doctor, would have preferred putting Mother in the hospital, faced with those conditions she had to be cared for at home.

The woman who helped in the house had just quit to work in the kitchen at Harding Field, where fighter pilots would be trained. Kathryn and I took turns staying home from school to be with her. When Mrs. Leonard learned of Mother's illness, she assured Daddy that she would send the kind of delicate meals Mother could enjoy at noon every day. She had a particular affection for my mother. She always called her, "That lovely young girl." True to her promise, she sent her butler bearing a silver tray with silver domes covering plates of light and delicate food every day. This is the sort of gracious gesture that marked Mary Leonard's life, and watching our mother spoon up chicken broth or eat the meringue from Floating Island cheered me as nothing else could.

With Mother taken care of, Kathryn and I concentrated on fixing meals for the rest of us. To make life easier, Daddy stayed downtown for lunch, and whichever one of us had KP (kitchen patrol) duty that day packed one for André. Thanks to watching Grandmother Jessie cook, I had some vague ideas about how to proceed, and with a cookbook as guidance, I managed to produce simple main dishes with even simpler vegetables when it was my turn to cook.

I remember carrying a pot of something or other into the bedroom, and Mother lifting herself off her pillows to inspect it while I asked if it looked all right. I also remember her laughing one day, telling me the story of how my father had had to get his mother to come teach her to cook. "I suppose it runs in the family," she said, "having to learn to cook with the equivalent of a gun at your head."

During that year, Mother enrolled my sister and me in catechism classes taught by Sister Mary Frances, a St. Joseph nun, and Father William Borders, a newly ordained priest. The classes were held in a room at Bernard Terrace on Saturday morning, and there I mastered the lessons in the Baltimore Catechism in preparation for my First Communion in May. (Later, all five of my daughters would be students at St. Joseph's Academy, founded and maintained by the St. Joseph Sisters of Calais, and my early favorable impression of that order created by Sister Mary Frances grew even stronger the day I met Sister Claire Germaine, principal when I enrolled my eldest daughter, Elizabeth, in her future first grade class at age fourteen months.)

In Lake Charles, my mother, Kathryn, André, and I went to Mass at the Church of the Immaculate Conception of Mary while my father went to Good Shepherd, the small Episcopal Church some blocks away. Now, in Baton Rouge, he dropped us off at Sacred Heart, a wooden combination chapel and church hall, before driving downtown to St. James, where

Clockwise from center: Mother, André, Kathryn, and me
dressed for Kathryn's Confirmation.

he served on the vestry. Both Good Shepherd and St. James, as well as the Episcopal church in New Iberia and Grace Church in St. Francisville, resembled the Anglican churches I'd seen in books, giving them an air of distinctive antiquity, no matter their age. The Immaculate Conception in Lake Charles was and is an imposing brick structure with a bell tower, column-framed doors, and other fine architectural details.

So, the small wooden church seemed to lack the solemnity and grandeur I always thought of when I thought of church, and since I knew none of the other candidates for First Communion, nothing about the coming event seemed real, a view reinforced by the daylong retreat at Sacred Heart Church. I remember very little of that day. We spent part of it rehearsing going up to the altar, kneeling, and opening our mouths to receive the wafer. Small rounds of thin bread substituted for the real thing, and I do remember how they stuck to the roof of my mouth and how difficult it was for my tongue to loosen them.

Monsignor Blasco, the pastor, questioned us, not going through the entire Baltimore Catechism, but selecting those questions most central to the church's beliefs. We answered these in a group, developing a sing-song rhythm that must have told the monsignor how little any of us understood what we said. However, understanding would come later. At that point, rote learning would serve.

We also made our first confessions. I had practiced this at catechism class, with Sister Mary Frances playing the part of the priest. Of course, I didn't actually confess anything. She just wanted me to know what to expect. Until I entered the confessional and felt the heavy curtain fall behind me, I hadn't been nervous. But now, as I knelt and heard the sound of the door covering the grate open and knew that Father Borders sat on the other side waiting for me to speak, my mind went blank.

"My child, shall I help you?" he said.

"Please, father."

"Then let's say it together—'Bless me father, for I have sinned.'"

"I remember it now," I said and continued the rest by myself. And then, I stopped. I had thought of sins I could confess. Now, they seemed foolish—I had eaten the last piece of cake without asking my brother if he wanted some; I had used one of my sister's handkerchiefs to make a skirt for a doll without her permission—and I wished I had some grander sin to confess.

The wish was not, thank heaven, the father to the act. I hurriedly told Father Borders my sins and received my penance, one Our Father and three Hail Mary's, which, forever after that, would always seem to be a signal that my sins barely made it across the line from white to pale gray.

Father Borders, who later became a bishop, was not only a very kind young priest, he was movie-star handsome, and I had heard adult women compare him favorably to Robert Taylor and Tyrone Power, not at all an exaggeration. When war came, he entered the army as a chaplain, and I heard speculation that he had either chosen or been sent to a male-dominated environment because a priest with such looks attracts the kind of attention from women that would make his job difficult. Years later, in 1958, when my first husband and I moved to Baton Rouge, Father Borders served as the chaplain at Christ the King, the Catholic chapel on the LSU campus, and so we met again in the river of connection that life creates.

My grandmother Jessie had made my dress, white dotted Swiss trimmed with lace. I wore a veil and carried a mother-of-pearl prayer book my godfather, Tommy Kieller, sent—one I carried later at my first wedding. I have that book in my office and start my morning prayers reading from it.

A First Communion is a very special event in a Catholic child's life, an event that one hopes to look back on with a particular kind of joy. Unfortunately, the child who sat in front of me had long, dark, heavily perfumed hair, which wouldn't have mattered if she had knelt when everyone else did. But she didn't. Complaining of a stomachache, she sat for the entire Mass, and every time I knelt, I had a face full of her hair, with that cloyingly sweet scent seeming to get worse with every breath.

I went to Communion feeling I had much more to confess than I had the previous day, for the thoughts I entertained about that child were not only not Christian, they were downright mean. I confided my feelings to my father. "Well, Beth, there're times when we can't help what we feel or think. The main thing is you didn't let her know." An early initiation into the wise advice that if you don't have anything nice to say, don't say it.

A new church, a splendid new church, large and faintly Byzantine in design, was in the process of being built on the other side of the street from the wooden one, and a Belgian monk, Dom Gregory deWit, had been engaged to paint its murals. He had painted the ones for St. Benedict's Abbey in Covington, as well as St. Meinrad Abbey in Indiana—whose Abbey Press later published the book I wrote on child-rearing—but I doubt that many of Sacred Heart's parishioners had seen his work until the unveiling the day the church was consecrated. The murals over the main and side altars created a huge stir among the very traditional, mostly Italian parishioners. They were Expressionistic rather than realistic, and the portrait of Christ, filling the space above the altar, had eyes which not only seemed to follow you everywhere, but also to be questioning what they saw. Parishioners became used to Him, but never to the hair of the two angels flanking the altar. "It looks like they've been electrocuted," was the kindest comment, and I must admit, I have never before nor since seen angels with hair that looks like a bright yellow explosion and bears no resemblance to a halo.

Because I remember my own irreverent thoughts in church as a child—and, if the truth be told, later—I don't take children's boredom, inattention, or interest in some completely extraneous thing as a sign of anything but youth. I say this because the Mass I remember the most during the time we went to Sacred Heart Church was the day a little girl stole my ring and my sister's godmother got it back.

Aunt Pamela had brought me a silver ring from Mexico. It had a silver filigree sombrero on top and immediately became a cherished treasure. Though I had been told not to, I played with the ring during Mass, taking it off and putting it on other fingers until, while rising for the Gospel, I dropped it. And saw the little girl in front of me, who had been watching, dart under the pew, retrieve the ring, put it in her pocket, and fasten her eyes on the priest, all in a move so quick I wasn't sure I'd seen what I thought I had. I kept thinking she would turn and give me the ring but dared not attract attention by asking her.

Then, when Mass ended and the final prayers had been said, I saw her following her mother out of their pew and burst into tears. One question, and I revealed the theft. Aunt Louise, a courteous title because she was my mother's close friend, stepped forward, put her hand on the little girl's shoulder, and said, in tones that I would have feared to deny, "You have my niece's ring."

The little girl started to shake her head, the mother turned and opened her mouth, either to question or defend her daughter, but Aunt Louise was too quick for them both. "It's in your pocket. If you return it right now, I won't tell the priest."

The child handed the ring over, her mother led her off in a huff, and when Mother asked Aunt Louise if she really would have told the priest, Aunt Louise laughed. "Katherine, you know damn well all you have to do is *look* like you could talk to the priest to be listened to. You don't have to actually do it."

Another lesson in survival that served me well!

***

In July, a large number of uncles, aunts, and cousins, including our family, visited cousins who lived in New Orleans, but who, like so many families from that city, migrated in summer to the cooler and easier life on the Mississippi Gulf Coast. A commuter train took businessmen from New Orleans to their summer homes in the various small towns stretched across the coast: Bay St. Louis, Pass Christian, Long Beach, Gulfport, Biloxi, and Ocean Springs. The houses remained until first Hurricane Camille, and later Katrina, destroyed most of them, but they still stand in my memory: large, two-story wooden houses with screen porches front and back, wide lawns shaded by live oaks, moss-covered cisterns standing like truncated towers from a fairy tale.

The waters of the Mississippi Sound are shallow for quite a distance at low tide. Because of the sharp-edged shells covering the mud bottom near shore, we wore rubber bathing shoes. Each big house had its own pier. At low tide, I could see the barnacles attached to the posts, though by high tide, water covered them within a few feet of the deck. Thus, small children like me went into the water only at low tide, where, under the eyes of older cousins sworn to watch us, we splashed and played. Most of my first cousins are boys. The four Binnings boys from New Orleans—Clem, Walter, David, and Rob, sons of my Aunt Marjorie and Uncle Clem—were my favorites, probably because we saw so much of them. My third daughter, Marjorie (who goes by Maggi), was named for this much-loved aunt. I really didn't know the two

Voorhies boys, Robert and James, whose parents were my Aunt Roberta and
Uncle Francis. But I got to know one of them too well.

He was about twelve, and whether to show off or just to tease me,
he picked me up and said that if I didn't give him a kiss, he would throw
me in water over my head. Despite being a very shy child, I had an inner
standard of justice and saw nothing just about an older cousin using his
size and age to embarrass me. I refused to kiss him, and he dropped me
into the water, which was not over my head if I had stood up. But I didn't.
I lay there until one of the Binnings snatched me up, while another let the
villain know just what would happen if he ever did something like that
again. As he carried me back to the house, my rescuer asked why I hadn't
stood up. "Because he deserved for me to drown," I said. My cousin's silence confirmed that view.

The following summer, I would say those same words, but this time to
my oppressor's face. LSU had summer camps for children, and I had been enrolled in one for children between ages six and eight. I enjoyed the crafts, the
picnics, and the games, but dreaded the daily swimming lesson, first because
they took place in an Olympic-size pool at the old Field House, with very
little water that wasn't over my head, and second because LSU's swimming
coach, Coach Higginbotham, was the teacher.

At first, the lessons went fairly well, as we clung to the side of the pool
and kicked, or stood on a three-foot ledge of shallow water and practiced
strokes. But then came the day when Coach said we were ready to put it all
together. This would be done by lying across his arms in deeper water, strok-
ing and kicking until we told him we were ready to be let go.

When my turn came, I told him I wouldn't even let him pick me up if he
didn't promise that he wouldn't let me go. He made the promise, and so I lay
across his arms and began to stroke and kick. After a bit of this, he let me go,
and I plummeted to the bottom of the pool. Where I stayed until, just as my
cousin had, he snatched me up.

"Why didn't you try to swim?"

"Because you lied to me and deserved for me to drown."

I reported this to my father, who drove me to camp the next day. He had
a word with Coach Higginbotham and that was the end of my swimming
lessons. In Coach Higginbotham's defense, he was an excellent swimming
coach, and it isn't surprising that the techniques that produced winning teams
didn't adapt well when used with children.

Many of our meals came from the waters of the Mississippi Sound, with
the men gigging for flounder or catching Spanish mackerel off the end of the

pier and all of us, except the very smallest children, setting lines for crabs. This is done by tying bait—usually chicken necks—to the end of a string and then tying the string to nails that have been placed along both sides of the pier. Nets are used to take the crabs off the line.

When I lived in Lake Charles, both as a child and an adult, crabbing provided not only a pleasant way to spend an afternoon but also a succulent meal. The Lake Charles Country Club, when still in its old building, allowed members to take their crabs to the kitchen to be boiled. We ate them on the big, screened porch that overlooked the golf course.

So, between the bounty of the Mississippi Sound and the bounty provided by produce stands along the beach road, even the large number of people those summer homes held could be easily and deliciously fed.

Recipes from Summers on the Gulf Coast

CRABMEAT IMPERIAL

2 lb. jumbo lump crabmeat
½ cup unsalted butter
2 bunches of celery, chop only the tender stalks
6 green onions (including green tops), chopped
5 eggs
1½ tablespoons herb-flavored vinegar
1 tablespoon Dijon mustard
2 teaspoons fresh lemon juice
⅔ cup bottled chili sauce
2 teaspoons Worcestershire sauce
1 teaspoon Tabasco sauce
2¼ tablespoons good quality olive oil
Minced parsley, preferably flat-leaf

Carefully pick through crabmeat and remove any bits of shell and cartilage, being careful not to break up lumps of meat. Set aside. Melt butter in a heavy 12-inch skillet over medium heat, add chopped celery and green onions. Cook, stirring often, until vegetables are slightly wilted (5–6 minutes). Add crabmeat and stir just to blend, again taking care not to break up the lumps. Divide into 6–8 individual ramekins or au gratin dishes. Set aside.

Position oven rack 6 inches below heat source and preheat broiler.

Meanwhile, prepare topping: In a food processor fitted with a steel blade, combine eggs, vinegar, mustard, lemon juice, chili sauce, Worcestershire sauce, and Tabasco sauce. Process until smooth, and then process 60 seconds longer. With machine running, pour oil through feed tube in a slow, steady stream, processing to form a smooth emulsion. Spoon an equal portion of topping over each serving of crab and place under preheated broiler. Broil until lightly browned and bubbly (about 5 minutes).

Sprinkle parsley over each serving; serve hot.

Yield: 6 to 8 servings.

Note: Regarding celery stalks, I boil all the greenery and the tough stalks in water, to cover, for about 45 minutes. The resulting stock can be frozen in ice cube trays or refrigerated for more immediate use in soups, gumbo, and gravies.

CRAB CAKES

1 egg, beaten
1 teaspoon salt
½ teaspoon white pepper
½ teaspoon paprika
1 tablespoon Dijon mustard
1 teaspoon Worcestershire sauce
1 tablespoon mayonnaise
1 tablespoon chopped parsley
½ cup minced green onion tops
1 tablespoon butter, melted
1 lb. jumbo lump crab, picked over for shells and cartilage
Breadcrumbs, as needed
Butter or olive oil for frying

Combine all ingredients except crabmeat in a large bowl and mix lightly. Fold in the crabmeat, being very careful not to break up the lumps. Add breadcrumbs very gradually. You only need enough to make the mixture stick together. Shape into 3-inch crab cakes. Coat lightly with breadcrumbs and chill, covered, for 2–3 hours.

Heat a nonstick 12-inch skillet over medium heat. Place enough butter or olive oil in the hot skillet for frying. Add the crab cakes and fry until brown on both sides and cooked through.

Yield: Serves 4.

Note: Instead of frying crab cakes, I place them on a cookie sheet sprayed with baking spray, spray the crab cakes, and then bake them in a preheated 350° oven until they are cooked through, 20 or so minutes. At this point, they may either be served or the cookie sheet can be covered with freezer-proof wrap. After the crab cakes are frozen, place them in a Ziploc bag and use as needed by reheating them in a 350° oven, *not* in a microwave. Also, I use the rings that are meant for perfect fried eggs to help mold the crab cakes. Or, one can fold aluminum foil into rings.

JUMBO LUMP CRABMEAT AND MUSHROOMS

1 lb. jumbo lump crabmeat, picked over for bits of shell and cartilage
½ lb. fresh mushrooms, stems removed
2 tablespoons butter
2 tablespoons fresh lemon juice
Salt and white pepper to taste

Melt the butter in a heavy saucepan over medium heat. Add the lemon juice and mushrooms, cook until mushrooms are done. Add the crabmeat very carefully and stir just until mixed in with the mushrooms. Cover and let simmer until crabmeat is hot, 5–10 minutes. Serve immediately in warmed individual ramekins.

Yield: Serves 4 as an appetizer, 3 as a main course.

Note: This is a recipe from Broussard's, which was one of my father's favorite New Orleans restaurants for lunch. It is one of the easiest ways to fix crabmeat that I know of, and despite—or because of—its simplicity, it is also one of the best.

DEVILED CRABS

1 cup freshly chopped parsley
1 whole green bell pepper, seeded and chopped
2 cups chopped celery
3 or 4 green onions with top, chopped
Pinch of ground sweet basil
Pinch of ground marjoram
Dash of Tabasco sauce
Pinch of white pepper
Salt to taste
Whipped butter, as needed
2 lb. white crabmeat (jumbo lump not required)
2 eggs, beaten
Breadcrumbs, as needed

Sauté all above ingredients except crabmeat, eggs, and breadcrumbs in a generous amount of whipped butter. Cook until onions are clear and bell pepper and celery still crunchy—do not brown. Remove from heat. Stir in the eggs and crabmeat, then add breadcrumbs only sufficient to bind the mixture. Put into individual ramekins or shells, place on cookie sheet, and bake in a preheated 350° oven for 20–25 minutes. May be frozen, but not for more than two weeks.

Yield: Serves 6.

BOILED SHRIMP IN BEER

1 lb. unpeeled shrimp, with heads
1 can beer or more as needed to cover shrimp
1 clove garlic
1½ teaspoon salt
1 dried red chili pepper
1 medium white onion, chopped
Sprig parsley or celery leaves
Juice of 1 large lemon
1 teaspoon red pepper

Combine all ingredients except shrimp. Bring to a boil. Add shrimp to liquid, making sure all are covered with liquid (add beer or water to cover). Bring to quick boil and then simmer for 15–20 minutes. Drain and peel shrimp. Return shrimp to liquid, chill in refrigerator, then drain thoroughly and serve.

Yield: 1 lb. serves one person.

Note: Except when shrimp are boiled in a seasoned liquid as above, they should be steamed, so they don't lose their juices as they do in boiling water. If you don't have a steamer, use a colander or bowl-type strainer set over a pot of boiling water, and covered so that the steam will be confined. Do not let the container reach the water.

When I steam shrimp, I use either peeled or unpeeled, layering fresh lemon slices in with the shrimp. They are done when they have all turned pink.

BAKED SHRIMP

3–5 lb. medium-large or large unpeeled shrimp, with heads
1½ sticks melted butter
Salt, black, and red peppers to taste

Place washed shrimp in a large baking pan. Pour melted butter over shrimp. Sprinkle seasoning freely over all shrimp. Bake in a preheated 350° oven until shrimp are done. Serve in large soup plates so diners can dip up the sauce with French bread.

Yield: Serves 2 to 4.

Note: You may use your favorite barbecue sauce instead of the melted butter and seasonings listed here.

BEER-FRIED SHRIMP

Raw shrimp, peeled and deveined
Prepared biscuit mix
Beer (any brand)
Vegetable cooking oil

Prepare batter by mixing biscuit mix and beer—the batter should not be too thin. The amount of batter depends on the amount of shrimp to be fried. Dip shrimp in batter and drop into hot deep fat and fry until golden brown. Drain on paper towels and serve.

Yield: 2 servings per pound or, more likely, 1 serving per pound.

DEVILED EGGPLANT

1 eggplant
1 medium white onion, chopped
2 cloves garlic, chopped
2 tablespoons vegetable oil
4 slices dry bread
2 cups raw, peeled shrimp (if frozen, thaw first)
Salt and black pepper to taste
Breadcrumbs

Boil peeled eggplant in salted water until tender. Sauté onions and garlic in vegetable oil. Remove from heat. Drain the eggplant and mash with a fork; add to onions and garlic. Soak the bread in water, squeeze out the excess water, and add to eggplant mixture. Mix in shrimp. Place mixture in a casserole dish. Sprinkle with breadcrumbs and bake at 350° in a preheated oven for 30 minutes.

Yield: Serves 4 to 6.

Note: This is a classic south Louisiana dish. Crabmeat may be substituted for or used with the shrimp. To make sure any bitterness is out of the eggplant, before cooking cut it into chunks, put in a bowl, and salt the cut surfaces. Let stand until moisture forms all over the cut surfaces. Rinse well, pat dry, and cook as usual.

OVEN-CRISP FISH

6 firm white fish fillets
Salt and black pepper to taste
6 tablespoons butter
1½ tablespoons Worcestershire sauce
½ cup seasoned breadcrumbs
⅓ cup white wine

Season the fish. Melt the butter in a 9 x 13 oven-proof dish in a 400° preheated oven. Stir in the Worcestershire sauce. Coat fish with butter mixture on both sides, place in dish, and bake until fish flakes easily. Remove from oven and turn on the broiler. Sprinkle the fish with breadcrumbs. Add the wine to pan juices. Put under broiler until the fillets are brown and crisp—watch to prevent burning. Serve immediately.

Yield: Serves 6.

FLOUNDER

2 large flounder
½ lemon, sliced thin
1 stick butter, melted
¾ tablespoon poultry seasoning
Salt and pepper to taste
Juice of 1 large lemon
1 tablespoon parsley, minced
3 green onions, tops and bottoms, diced

Score flounder. Lay lemon slices into the slits. Melt butter; add the seasonings. Broil flounder in center of oven, basting with the sauce. Broil until fish is done—moist and flaky.

Yield: Serves 2 to 4, depending on size of flounder.

Note: Flounder gigging used to be a popular nighttime activity along the Gulf Coast and in some places is still allowed. Equipment consists of three-tined fork-like spears and lights to attract the fish. Low tide is best for flounder gigging. Flounder are also found in the brackish water of the marshes, bayous, and inlets flowing out to the Gulf. While some flounder fishermen go out on boats, many wade along the shoreline, and if you are sitting on a beach house deck at night, the flickering lights in the water reflect the stars overhead.

SPANISH FISH FILLETS

6 fish fillets, any firm white fish will do
4 tablespoons vegetable oil, divided
4 tablespoons flour
1 medium white onion, diced
2 cans (8 ounces each) tomato sauce
½ cup chopped green olives
Salt and black pepper to taste

Brown the fillets in 2 tablespoons of the oil and place in a shallow baking dish. Heat remaining oil in saucepan. Add flour and blend. Add the remaining ingredients; stir well. Pour over fish. Bake in a preheated 400° oven for 30 minutes or until fish flakes easily with fork.

Yield: Serves 6.

Lagniappe

Lazy Days Ice Creams

LEMON ICE CREAM

Juice and grated rind of 1 large lemon
1 cup sugar
1 cup milk
1 cup whipping cream
2 teaspoons gelatin dissolved in as little cold water as possible

Add sugar to lemon juice and rind and mix well. Add milk and whipping cream. Add dissolved gelatin. Mix in a *very* small amount of hot water until gelatin disappears. Mix well, pour into an ice tray with dividers removed, cover with plastic wrap or aluminum foil and freeze. Check to see when it begins to freeze and then stir back and forth. Return to freezer until it is frozen.
Yield: 1 quart.

BANANA ICE CREAM

6 very ripe bananas
Juice of 2 lemons
Juice of 2 oranges
3 large cans evaporated milk
1 cup sugar (or more to taste)
½ cup homogenized milk

Mash bananas. Add sugar and juices. Let stand for 30 minutes. Add evaporated and homogenized milk. Stir well; freeze in ice tray. Stir often while freezing.
Yield: 1 quart.
Note: Stirring while these mixtures freeze keeps them from getting "icy" and results in a creamy ice cream. While it is not as creamy as that made in a churn-type freezer, it is still a good and very easy summer dessert, especially when on vacation.

CHAPTER FIVE

S ummer ended, and I began third grade in the fall of 1941, and the usual after-school routine of games with André and Dick continued. We also listened to the adventures of Jack Armstrong and Tom Mix. A new element had entered these programs. Jack and Tom began to be involved with spies and traitors, and this darker tone seemed to escape from the radio and shadow what had been a bright world.

Still, the greater reality was here and now. Third grade brought new classmates, including Alice Lewis and Mary Stiles, both of whose fathers had been transferred from Standard Oil's New Jersey operations to the plant at Baton Rouge. Alice's family found an upstairs apartment on Government Street, only a few blocks from Calandro's. Mary's family settled in a house in Old Goodwood, a neighborhood with many trees and lovely old houses that is still, in my view, one of the prettiest in Baton Rouge.

Alice Lewis's father soon got transferred back north, but not until my manners had been tested in a most unpleasant way. I had been invited to Alice's home, not only for the afternoon, but also for dinner, after which her father would drive me home. I sat down and stared at the plate in front of me, seeing only one thing: liver. I couldn't stand liver, and my mother, understanding that not only its taste but its texture put many people off, never made me eat it, though she cooked it for my father often. I knew I had to eat it, but I had no idea how I would manage. Then, I spotted the bottle of catsup and had my answer.

I cut the liver into the smallest imaginable pieces, slathered catsup over them, and then ate them one by one, barely chewing, letting the catsup help them slide down my throat. "My goodness," Mrs. Lewis said, "I suppose that's a southern custom, to put so much catsup on meat?"

I said it was.

A further test of manners came when I spent a Friday night at Mary's house. Once again, I saw meat on my plate: not liver, but a small T-bone chop that I would have enjoyed very much. But not on a Friday. I knew I couldn't eat everything else and not the meat. I could think of only one thing to do:

say I wasn't hungry and not eat at all. Which I didn't, not even the hot fudge sundae that Mrs. Stiles had prepared as a special treat.

Later, I did wonder why Mrs. Stiles, who was a nurse, hadn't asked me why I wasn't eating. Not until I moved to Lafayette, which at the time was 95 percent Catholic, did I understand that since the majority of church-goers in Baton Rouge, like the people in Mrs. Stiles's native Midwest, were Protestant, it never occurred to her that I would be anything else.

These two experiences had a lasting effect on me, so much so that when I invite people who have never dined at my home to a meal, I always ask if there's anything they're allergic to or anything that, if they saw it on their plate, would make their hearts sink.

***

Fall progressed in its usual way, climaxing, as always, with the LSU-Tulane football game on the Saturday after Thanksgiving, November 29, 1941. That year, Tulane hosted the game, and so we spent Thanksgiving with Uncle Clem, Aunt Marjorie, and their boys in their New Orleans house on Broadway. The rivalry between LSU and Tulane goes back to 1893. Tulane, a much smaller university, had few football players, but this changed when the Navy ROTC was established at Tulane in 1938. Many of the members were football players, and they helped lead Tulane's teams to victories that would have been impossible without them.

My father was an avid Tulane fan, and living in the middle of Tiger land, he had to be staunch indeed to defend the Green Wave against LSU fans who, alongside the Alabama Crimson Tide's supporters, rank as some of the most fanatical in the nation.

In 1941, however, Tulane defeated LSU in an afternoon game held at the Tulane Stadium, and so joy reigned in New Orleans. My parents had gone to the game with my aunt and uncle, leaving Kathryn, 11, André, 5, and me, 8, to stay home with our much older cousins David, 20, and Bob, 15. (Our cousins Clem Jr. and Walter were already out of college and not living at home.) I remember the intensity of our attention as we listened to the game on the radio, and when Tulane won, we cheered as loudly as we could, proud that our team had vanquished such a formidable foe.

When I entered my teens, however, I often accompanied my parents to games in Tulane Stadium and, later, went with dates. I have always thought there is no better preparation for a night in the French Quarter than a sunny fall afternoon in that open-air stadium where fans, resigned to losing, but hopeful of winning, cheered their team with appropriate enthusiasm but without the madness that prevails in "Deaf Valley," as the LSU Stadium used to be called. The name came from the roar of the crowd as the teams run onto the field, which was so deafening that coaches of teams playing there for the first time warned them about it as part of their training. In fact, Tiger Stadium has been called the most dreaded site for away games, so it's not surprising that "Deaf Valley" eventually became "Death Valley," a nomenclature all too many teams find to be true.

One of Tulane's most memorable victories over LSU, in my mind, came in 1981, the year after my mother died. Tulane defeated LSU in basketball, and then, that fall, defeated them in football. When dismayed Tiger fans questioned how these upsets could have happened, I told them that I imagined my father had told God that since these were the first Tulane games he and his beloved wife would see together since 1962, he felt victories would be appropriate. And yes, I know that sounds either totally daft or cutesy whimsical, but if belief in a collective unconscious was good enough for Jung, it's good enough for me. As Shakespeare says in *Hamlet*, "There are more things in heaven and earth, Horatio, than are dreamt of in your philosophy." Since I have had experiences that can be explained only by a ghostly presence, I agree!

Our cousin David, with whom I listened to that illustrious Tulane victory in 1941, was a genius. But like many geniuses, he became a recluse, living at home and working at night as a dispatcher for a truck line. After he died many years later, it turned out that this "recluse" had a wife and two children who lived within walking distance of his parents' final home on Second Street. I've no idea how anyone else in the family felt about this, but I thought it absolutely splendid that David had managed to keep such a secret for so many years, thus guaranteeing that he and his family would not be forced to attend the kinds of family celebrations he could only stand for perhaps thirty minutes before fleeing back to his den.

David and I formed an affinity, based initially on books but later expanding to include the many subjects that interested us both. One day while cleaning out a folder I found a letter from him written on the occasion of the *North American Review* publishing a short story of mine. He chides me for not letting "people who love you and are interested in your work know that you have appeared in print," and after that I made sure that he received copies of any published work.

***

A week and a day after the Tulane victory in 1941, on Sunday, December 7, as André and I played with his lead soldiers, and my parents listened to the NBC Symphony's Sunday afternoon program, a voice broke in with the words that no one who heard them would ever forget: "The Japanese have just bombed Pearl Harbor."

My father's face had the same expression it had on September 1, 1939, when I sat on his lap while he listened to the news that Germany had invaded Poland, but this time, given the long hours he'd been spending at work and talk of air raid wardens and blackouts, I knew a faraway war had just entered our living room.

My sister and I were due at the Hearins' to rehearse Christmas carols with the other neighborhood children, and after a quick phone call to Mrs. Hearin, our mother told us rehearsal was still on. We joined Frank and Bobby Leonard, Ned Clark and his sister, Nancy, Don and Dick Hearin, and some of the Frey children, whose father served as Dean of Arts and Sciences at LSU, around the grand piano in the Hearins' living room, where Ned's mother, Sally, was already playing.

Mothers in the forties looked nothing like mothers today. We never saw them in anything but complete dress, rarely without makeup, and certainly not with curlers in their hair. Hazel Hearin was a beautiful and glamorous woman. She wore clothes like those of Barbara Stanwyck, Gene Tierney, and Joan Crawford, and jewelry chosen to complement the color and design of her costumes. Sally Clark, while not beautiful, had compelling blue eyes, silver blond hair that framed an expressive face, and since she was quite tall, wore simply cut clothes in tailored styles.

Mary Leonard left the weekly rehearsals to Sally and Hazel. A descendant of a First Family of Virginia, she was an Episcopal minister's daughter, and one of the most loving, gentlest women it has ever been my privilege to know. Her husband kept from her the many scrapes their two younger boys got into, and even now, when Dick and Ned and I are together, we laugh at our memories of Mary and her innocent delusions.

Within days of Pearl Harbor, life in Baton Rouge changed. High on the enemy's target list would be a city on a river emptying into the Gulf of Mexico and also the site of the Esso Laboratory and Standard Oil Refinery, which would manufacture almost half of the 100-octane aviation fuel produced during the war, as well as its Baton Rouge Chemical Plant, which produced synthetic rubber to replace the loss of rubber from the plantations in the Japanese-held territories in the Dutch East Indies.

Just days before the attack on Pearl Harbor, the Civil Air Patrol (CAP) had been created, commissioning civilian pilots to patrol the coast and borders and engage in search and rescue missions as needed. German submarines, the small two-man ones that could be dropped from a larger vessel, prowled the Gulf of Mexico even before the U.S. declared war on both Germany and Japan, and the very real fear that they would come up the Mississippi River and shell the Standard Oil plants made CAP a vital element in Baton Rouge's civil defense system. (Years later, through mutual friends, I met a couple, both of whom had been in the CAP during World War II and were credited with spotting many subs in the Gulf.)

In order to prevent any subs reaching Baton Rouge from identifying its location by lights, blackouts went into effect almost immediately, with air raid wardens walking their beats to make sure not the smallest glow showed through the black curtains. By spring of 1942, rationing of a long list of items, including sugar, coffee, butter, chocolate, nylons, meat, shoes, cigarettes, gasoline, liquor, cheese, fats, tires, cars, stoves, typewriters, and farm machinery began. Housewives had to learn an intricate system of rationing: uniform coupon rationing, in which all consumers received an equal share of a single commodity (sugar is an example); point rationing, which provided equivalent shares of commodities by coupons issued for points, which could be spent for any combination of items in the group (processed foods, meats, fats, cheese); differential coupon rationing, which provided shares of a single product, such as gasoline or fuel oil, according to varying needs; and certificate rationing, which allowed individuals products only after an application proved need—these might be tires, cars, typewriters, and the like. Actually, gas rationing's main purpose was to save tires. Anyone owning more than five tires had to turn the rest in, and a 35-mph speed limit was set for the duration.

There are always those who think a system doesn't apply to them, and many people, either by buying coupons from others or by more devious means, became hoarders. I don't think it was punishable by law, but it earned the scorn of anyone finding out about it, particularly those with family and friends in the armed services.

One would truly have had to live through those times to understand the national mood after Pearl Harbor. Though the worst of the Great Depression was behind us, as a nation we had been through a dark passage that shook our faith in many of the institutions we had thought invulnerable. The fact that misery from all over the country could be spread through radio and newsreels at movie theaters, as well as in newspapers and magazines, meant that no one could be unaware of the destitution and tragedy that economic disaster caused. Worst of all, there was no hope for better days until Franklin Delano Roosevelt's New Deal began. A major force for recovering from the Depression was the Works Progress Administration, which gave work to everyone from Saul Bellow and Ralph Ellison, who were among the writers who put together the state guides published during those years, to out-of-work men who helped build roads, cabins at state parks, hospitals, and other such public works.

Now, the country had something to rally around, and every citizen, no matter how young or old, could make significant contributions to a nation gearing up for war. Thus, though the task of shopping might be complicated by the rationing system, though the four gallons of gasoline per week allowed to drivers with the lowest priority might cause inconvenience, though housewives found themselves using soybeans and other meat substitutes to provide protein lacking in meatless meals, still, if anyone complained, they did so very seldom and never to anyone but a close family member or friend.

Our neighborhood Victory Club, which prior to Pearl Harbor had been mostly a gesture of support to the European nations already under Hitler's heel, became active, as we joined children and adults across the nation collecting the scrap needed to make up for raw materials now controlled by the Germans and Japanese. We collected rubber, everything from worn-out tires to rubber boots and raincoats. We collected metal, begging housewives for pots they could do without, scouring empty lots for metal junk. I still remember our excitement when Dick Hearin and I asked the owner of a metal airplane mounted on the roof of his toy store if he would give it to the war effort. Maybe six feet long, it had been a fixture for years, and we had no expectation that he would say yes. But he did. Between them, Harold Leonard and Don Hearin got a crew to take the airplane down and haul it to the scrap-metal yard.

Bernard Terrace, like other schools, set up centers for newspapers, tin foil, and bacon grease. The foil liners of our fathers' cigarette packages were the usual source for tin foil; bacon grease came from our mothers' kitchens. Many years later, I heard my youngest daughter, DeLauné, explain to her sisters why I made such a fuss if any of them used aluminum foil to wrap something in. "It's because they saved tin foil during the war," she said. Until that moment, I had never seen the connection.

Even before Pearl Harbor, President Roosevelt had been discussing how to finance the war if the United States entered it. In 1940, the federal government issued defense bonds that would mature in ten years, with denominations beginning as low as $18.75; these paid $25.00 at maturity. After Pearl Harbor, defense bonds became war bonds, and a nationwide campaign to encourage their purchase began. Norman Rockwell, known to Americans as the painter whose work graced so many covers of the popular *Saturday Evening*

Post, created four paintings titled *The Four Freedoms*. They toured the country, raising $132 million in war bond sales, and before the war ended, 85 million Americans bought $185.7 billion worth of bonds.

Every Tuesday morning, students at Bernard Terrace had the opportunity to buy Victory stamps. These cost ten cents each and were mounted in government issued stamp albums. A large poster in the main hall of the school building showed the rising total of the school's purchases, with the picture of an item the goal would purchase at the top. During my time at Bernard Terrace, which ended in May of 1944, our school purchased enough Victory stamps to buy a Jeep, an ambulance, and, most exciting of all, a B-25 bomber. And we had photos of each of these items with a driver or pilot waving to us from the front seat or cockpit to prove it.

My father, employed by an industry considered part of the war effort, didn't enter the military. But five first cousins, one uncle, and the husbands of two first cousins did. Theirs were typical wartime weddings, hurried up because the grooms were headed overseas, simple and quiet because the elaborate celebrations of peacetime seemed in very poor taste. My Aunt Roberta, whose two sons and two sons-in-law were overseas, kept a large map of both the European and Pacific theaters, marking with colored pins the last known whereabouts of family members.

In the first year of the war, the news from overseas was rarely good. Mail was censored; signs reminding us that "a slip of the lip can sink a ship" kept rumors and gossip to a minimum; and I have long thought that the strength the families of our fighting men and women had to have to get through months of not knowing where a loved one was or if he or she were alive helped form the non-military segment of what we call, and rightfully I think, the Greatest Generation.

Gold stars began to appear in windows where blue stars had hung, signaling that the family inside had lost someone in the war. Names like Rommel and Montgomery and Patton filled the news as the tank war in the deserts of North Africa intensified. Hollywood went to war, with actors ranging from Eddie Albert, James Garner, and Clark Gable to Robert Taylor, James Stewart, and Eli Wallach joining up. War movies dominated theaters: *Bomber's Moon*, *Assignment in Brittany*, and *Wake Island*, like so many others, centered on the war in the air, on the ground, and at sea, while movies like *Casablanca* and *Mrs. Miniver* explored the lives of civilians caught by the war's snares.

My sister and I saw *Mrs. Miniver* at the Hart, a new theater in Baton Rouge with a sleek and very modern decor that contrasted with the ornate design of the Paramount, a former stage theater, as so many movie theaters were. I own a copy of that movie, and it is still as wrenching for me now as it was the first time I saw it. But what I remember most about that first viewing is what I saw as we made our way up the aisle when the movie ended.

A large man in a soldier's uniform with master sergeant stripes on the sleeves sat in the very back row, sobbing as though he would never stop. I had never seen a grown man cry, and to see this soldier, medal ribbons forming a colorful row on his jacket, crying with such deep felt grief remains one of those moments in my life when I had a glimpse into real emotion and knew that underneath lay experiences this man would never be able to forget.

Ten months before Pearl Harbor, 1,200 men plus WPA workers had been employed to build the runways at Harding Field, an airport to the northeast of the Esso Refinery. Workers were divided into three round-the-clock, seven-days-a-week shifts, a stepped-up pace that finished, in record time, the base that would train fighter pilots flying the newest planes. Quartermaster units, as well as fighter and bomber squadrons, trained at Harding Field and departed for overseas assignments from its runways. A new way to support our military opened for the people of Baton Rouge, one my parents embraced, as did many of their friends.

Every Sunday and holiday, off-duty airmen would congregate at a spot just off the base to wait for Baton Rougeans to pick them up and take them home for dinner. The number of airmen a family could feed depended, of course, on available food, but never did a Sunday or holiday go by in our family without at least one airman, and more usually two, at our table. These boys came from all over the United States. Most of them had never been in the Deep South, and I remember one young man asking my mother, one Christmas Day, if he could cut one of her roses and send it to his mom to prove that roses bloomed in December in the South. Our guests were all polite, mostly reserved, though we would occasionally get a city boy with more sophistication and experience, and he would flirt mildly with my sister, but pay the most compliments to his hostess, who deserved every one of them.

My brother André got a Lionel electric train the Christmas of 1941, one of the last manufactured until well after the war. We had three airmen as guests that day, and though my brother had hardly had time to play with his new toy, between Mass and the time the boys arrived, he made his own contribution to military morale and watched while they lay on the floor and put the train through its paces. That Christmas, we also continued our caroling with our usual walk around the neighborhood.

Many years later, during the Vietnam War, when the children of Ned and Laura Clark, Dick and Vicki Hearin, Bobby and Stratton Leonard, and our girls sang carols in that very same neighborhood, a wonderful connection occurred. When we arrived at one house, the man came to the door and told us that at that very moment he and his wife were talking to their son in Vietnam. "Would you come in and sing a carol for him?" he asked. "I know it would mean so much." His mother asked her son what he'd like to hear, and, not surprisingly, he chose "Silent Night." We found ourselves holding hands as we sang. The women cried openly, the men developed sniffles, which we tactfully ignored. It is a moment I cherish. Despite all the reasons I may have to become cynical about human behavior, I have seen so many examples of kindness and compassion lying beneath the hardest exteriors that I still believe cynicism is often a defense used by people who might have gentler emotions, but are afraid to show them because they might be teased by those who present bold fronts, criticizing people, food, homes, cars, and whatever else they can diminish. I've known many people who put up with such attitudes, but I am not among them.

After caroling in our neighborhood, we climbed onto the city bus Mr. Leonard had engaged to take us to the two hospitals, Our Lady of the Lake near Huey Long's state capitol, and the Baton Rouge General on Government Street, to serenade not only the patients but the overworked doctors and nurses who rarely left those walls.

Baton Rouge's doctors had gone to war. The only two that I know of who remained were Dr. Tyler, whose son Louis would later be my children's pediatrician, and Dr. Wallace, who took over the practice when his partner Dr. Browne left for the army. In those days of house calls, Dr. Wallace literally worked around the clock. Concerned for his health, whenever he made a house call to us—and because I was susceptible to tonsillitis, that occurred fairly often—Mother would insist he sit and have a sandwich and coffee before he went on with his rounds.

I remember once he looked so exhausted Mother said he had to take a nap. He refused, saying if his nurse called, he wouldn't allow Mother to lie and say he wasn't there. "Then sleep in your car. If she calls, I won't look out the window, so I won't be lying when I say you're not here." That was the first, but not the last, time neighbors could see a weary doctor, eyes closed and head back, sleeping in his car on our street.

The constant tonsillitis attacks resulted in surgery in the summer of 1942. Mary Leonard's face, behind a huge bouquet of flowers from her extensive gardens, was the first thing I saw when I woke. The flowers were welcome, but the gift of a pint of the richest cream from a friend who kept cows ranked first. With that, Mother could make ice cream to soothe my aching throat, using a bit of the sugar she had been allowed to have for preserving food, most of which came from the Victory garden my father planted in our backyard.

Never a gardener before nor after that, Daddy tended his garden in the long evenings of daylight savings time, as did anyone else with ground enough to plant a few rows of carrots, tomatoes, beans, and even corn. The Hearins' gardener, helped by Dick, took care of their garden, a very large one that produced a very large yield. Dick arranged the vegetables in artistic circles on one of his mother's big, flat gardening baskets, put on a white linen jacket over white linen shorts, and made the rounds of neighbors either too elderly or too disinterested to have gardens of their own, buying Victory stamps with the money he earned.

Not long after we became friends with the neighborhood children, our father and Mr. Hearin made a gate in the wooden fence that separated our yard from theirs, a device that enabled us to get from one house to the other without having to venture onto Claycut Road, then and now a very busy street with blind curves dangerous for cycling children. When we moved away, Dick insisted the gate be boarded up. "I'm not going to want to know anyone who moves in," he told us. To ease the parting, he gave us one of his beagle's pups. That dog lasted until hunting season in Lafayette, when it disappeared to become someone's coon dog.

The diversions of childhood, though limited by gas rationing and other shortages, continued to occupy us. We explored the wooded areas bordering our neighborhood and built a fort on a large piece of property that angled away from the Clarks' house, a plot we called Clark's Field, which was later used by Ned and Laura's children and their neighborhood friends, including my five girls, as a site for adventures and games, just as we did then.

Again to keep their children off busy roads, the fathers in the neighborhood collaborated to build a swinging foot- and bicycle bridge over the stretch of Ward's Creek that separated one end of Moore Street, where the Clarks lived, from the other. Someone, either Dick or Ned, still has a photo of a parade of bicycles decorated with ribbons and flags crossing the bridge the day it opened, while parents looked on and clapped.

During fifth grade, in what turned out to be my last year in Baton Rouge, new experiences let me peek into the strange and scary world of approaching adolescence. The first of these came in the form of a dancing class, organized by Sally Clark with the help of the other neighborhood mothers. They engaged an instructor from LSU's Department of Physical Education and Dance, and every Friday afternoon we gathered in the Clarks' living room,

where Mrs. Clark accompanied on the piano our stumbling attempts to follow the instructor's agile feet.

When Laura gave Ned a surprise fortieth birthday party thirty years
later, she asked the guests to dress as someone from his past. I had a boldly
flowered, tight-fitting silk dress very much the same style as those our dance
teacher wore. That, with high-heeled platform sandals, earrings dropping almost to my bare shoulders, and more makeup than I would normally use up
in a week, completed my outfit—one that made Ned's jaw drop before he
burst out laughing.

The class ranged in age from sixteen-year-old Nick Stein to ten-year-old
Dick and me. Nick had good looks, more charm than anyone needed, and
what older women called sex appeal and young ones called scary. Of course,
he smoked, drove like a madman, and drank, though no one in the class ever
saw him do it. As a matter of course, each boy in the class had to dance with
each girl. My head came about midway up Nick's chest, and since he always
held his partners close, regardless of their age, my memories of dancing with
him are being pressed against either a cotton shirt or wool sweater scented
with a mixture of shaving lotion and cigarette smoke.

At the dance held at the end of the year, he put his name down for two
dances with me, when one would have fulfilled his obligation. I wore a long,
pale pink organdy dress with a demure sweetheart neckline, short puffed
sleeves, and a long, deeper pink taffeta sash with rosebuds edging the ends.
I had grown a little taller, so my head came just under his chin. And when
I felt that chin resting on it, I felt something that I wouldn't feel again for a
few years—the thrill, or tremble, or shiver, that certain human touches create,
sometimes for good, sometimes not, but always exciting.

My first date also occurred in that fifth-grade year. A classmate, Jimmy
Pierson, decided that instead of having the usual whole-class-invited birthday
party, he would have a movie date. He and his good friend Jimmy Lilly would
take two girls—me and a newcomer from Texas, Patsy Branch—to a movie,
followed by hamburgers at the Toddle House downtown. His older brother,
Roy, would be both chauffeur and chaperone. On an autumn Saturday, we
went to a western at the Paramount, then had hamburgers, french fries,
and Cokes at the Toddle House, followed by cake and ice cream back at the
Piersons' home.

To Patsy and me, this had been a pleasant but not extraordinary occasion.
But when we got to school on Monday, we were surrounded by a group of girls,
led by two future femme fatales, Arabella White and Anne Wilkinson. As the
questioning got more specific, with people wanting to know if we held hands

or even kissed, Patsy turned to me and in her slow Texas drawl summed up our feelings: "If I'd known there'd be all this commotion, I would've said no."

I forgot about Arabella and Anne's interest. Both Jimmy Pierson and Jimmy Lilly were friends, as were Ned, Carl Harvey, Lyle Edwards, George Heath, and many other boys in the class. But then, in late January, one of my friends told me that Arabella and Anne had started a campaign to make sure I received as few valentines as possible—none, if they could manage it.

Our school, like so many, had mailboxes into which students put valentines for their friends. I can remember being asked by teachers on several occasions to give a valentine to a shy or lonely child who might not receive many or any. The boy and girl who received the most valentines were crowned the King and Queen of Hearts, an honor I had had the previous year.

I couldn't understand why two girls who had never been either friends or enemies wanted to do such a mean thing. As far as I knew, I'd done nothing to earn their enmity, and as the days went by, and February 14th approached, I became more and more upset. Normally, I would have taken my concern to my father, but at the time, a union had gone on strike at the Gulf States plant, and my father, along with other management personnel, had to be on-site, not only to run the plant, but maintain order.

Valentine's Day dawned. I dismissed the idea of pleading sick as cowardly and walked into the classroom with the box of valentines for my friends, slipping the envelopes into the mailbox slot, and then waiting with growing sadness for the fateful hour to come—only to hear my name called over and over again, until valentines spilled over my desk and onto the floor. Every boy in the class had sent me at least one valentine, some two. But the core of my friends had sent more than that—one boy sent thirteen. Those, added to the ones from the girls with whom I always exchanged them, added up to a sum so much more than the next highest that even the teacher showed her surprise.

Arabella and Anne never looked at me. Nor did I look at them. I had too much to think about to want to spend any time on them. On the way home, I knew why I felt sad. Up until that day, I had considered the boys I knew as friends, comrades, people to do homework with, go to dance class with, play with. But Arabella and Anne had brought a new element into the arena, and its name was jealousy. I thought of those thirteen valentines and of how much they'd cost. That money could have bought Victory stamps or a treat for the sender. Instead, he and the other boys, like the knights in the stories we read, had come to the defense of a maiden in distress, rescuing her honor from the wicked witches. And that was a sad realization, indeed.

The strike ended that week, and my father was once more available. I didn't tell him the exact story but put my problem in a more general way. "There are people at school—well, girls—who seem to be getting jealous about things like grades, and how many boys like you, and if your curls are longer than theirs."

My father looked me in the eyes. "Sweetheart, there will always be girls smarter than you are, prettier than you are, with more talent, more money, and more boyfriends. There will also always be girls not as smart, not as pretty, with less talent, less money, and fewer boyfriends. Do we ever have to have this conversation again?"

No, we never did, because he had made it clear that depending on whom you compare yourself to, you may feel like the Queen of the May or the ditchdigger's daughter, but you, for better or worse, will be the same you.

I realize that many girls would take such a problem to their mothers. But from the day my father told me about Buttons, we had a bond made up of two things. First, I knew he wouldn't duck telling me hard things, and two, I knew he would never lie. And as I grew older, I realized that my mother's view of the world was, understandably, constrained by her mother's, while my father's view of the world came from his observations of the human condition and his compassionate interpretation of it. That first meeting with jealousy marked the end of innocence, because I had learned, to my great sorrow, that the purity of friendships and caring for other people can be spoiled by girls collecting scalps just because they can.

Losing spiritual innocence is, to me, a much more significant loss than losing one's virginity, because it affects one's trust in the people one meets and how one negotiates the often dark and rocky paths of life. Until this moment, as I'm writing those words, I hadn't realized the full impact of those girls' jealous designs. But now I understand that my trust in men, and my willingness to turn to them for help, stems not only from my relationship with my father, but also from the gallantry of those fifth-grade boys, determined to keep that green-eyed monster from doing me harm.

My second kiss came from Dick when we parted at the gate in the fence the night before my family left for Lafayette. He took my hands and said, "You are so beautiful," and kissed my lips, a sweet, tender kiss that marked not the end of childhood, but a hint of what lay ahead. Years later, at a small dinner party, Dick and his second wife—his first wife, one of my closest friends, had died a few years before—were present. I could have told her I had my first date with her first husband, and my first kiss from her second. That did not seem wise.

Recipes from Wartime

Since eggs were not rationed, dishes using eggs became popular meat substitutes.

PERFECT SCRAMBLED EGGS

1 egg per person, extra for larger appetites
Butter/margarine, 1 tablespoon per two eggs
Salt and pepper to taste

Beat the eggs with a fork until well mixed. Heat the butter/margarine over a low heat in a thick-bottomed skillet until melted. Pour the eggs in. Do not stir until the eggs are almost cooked. If the heat is low enough, the eggs will cook slowly and evenly. When they are done, serve immediately on warm plates with crisp toast.

Optional: Chopped parsley or chives, bits of bacon or ham may be beaten in with the eggs.

HAM CAKES AND EGGS

A good way to use leftover ham. Some wartime housewives would have used Spam.

1 cup cooked ground ham
1 egg
1 tablespoon water
⅛ teaspoon paprika or black pepper
4 eggs
Toast rounds

Mix the first four ingredients and press into 4 greased muffin tins. Leave a large hollow in each one.

Drop an egg into each ham hollow.

Bake in a preheated 325° oven until the eggs are firm. Serve immediately on toast rounds.

SUGARLESS CAKE

3 cups sifted cake flour
4 teaspoons baking powder
½ teaspoon salt
½ cup shortening
1½ cups light corn syrup
3 egg yolks
2 teaspoons grated orange rind
1 cup milk
3 egg whites

Sift together flour, baking powder, and salt. Cream shortening, add 1 cup of the corn syrup gradually, and cream until fluffy. Add egg yolks, one at a time, and beat well. Add sifted dry ingredients alternately with milk, stirring well after each addition. Add grated orange rind. Then, beat egg whites until stiff and add to them the remaining ½ cup corn syrup gradually, beating until mixture stands in stiff peaks. Fold into batter until well-blended. Bake in two greased 9-inch layer cake pans in a preheated moderate oven (375°) for 25–30 minutes. Cool and frost as desired.

White Cake: Use 5 egg whites and no egg yolks. Beat the egg whites until stiff, then gradually beat in the ½ cup corn syrup.

Chocolate Chip Cake: Add ⅔ cup semi-sweet chocolate, broken into small pieces, to the cake batter just before folding in the beaten egg whites.

SUGARLESS FROSTING

¼ cup corn syrup
3 egg whites
2 teaspoons flavoring (vanilla or other flavoring)
1 teaspoon baking powder

Boil corn syrup in a saucepan over direct heat until it spins a thread when dropped from a spoon. Beat egg whites until foamy, add baking powder and beat until stiff. Add corn syrup slowly, beating vigorously while adding. Add flavoring and continue beating until frosting is stiff and stands in peaks.

Yield: Frosting for two 9-inch layers, one medium loaf cake, or 16 large cupcakes.

APPLE CORN MUFFINS

¾ cup sifted flour
⅓ cup cornmeal
3 teaspoons baking powder
½ teaspoon salt
¼ cup sliced raw apple
1 egg, well-beaten
⅓ cup milk
¼ cup honey
3 tablespoons melted shortening

Sift together flour, cornmeal, baking powder and salt. Wash, pare, and cut apple into eighths. Remove core and cut crosswise in very thin slices. Combine egg, milk, and honey. Add to dry ingredients, stirring only enough to dampen well. Stir in melted shortening. Fold in apple. Fill well-greased muffin tins ⅔ full and bake in a moderately hot oven (400°) for 25 minutes.
Yield: 12 medium-sized muffins.

QUICK LOAF BREAD

¾ cup sifted flour
3 ½ teaspoons baking powder
¾ teaspoon salt
1½ cups whole wheat flour
1 cup corn syrup
⅔ cup milk
¾ cup chopped nut meats (optional)

Sift together flour, baking powder, and salt. Mix with whole wheat flour. Blend corn syrup and milk, add to dry ingredients, and mix well. Stir in nut meats, if used. Bake in a well-greased loaf pan (8 x 4 inches) in a moderate oven (350°) Check for doneness after 45 minutes; continue baking until top is a golden brown. Cool before cutting.

WHITE BEAN SOUP

1 lb. pkg. Great Northern beans
1½ cups diced ham
1 cup chopped white onion
¾ cup chopped celery with tops
5 teaspoons chopped parsley
¼ teaspoon garlic salt
¼ teaspoon black pepper
10 cups water
⅔ cup mashed beans for thickening
2 teaspoons salt
3 tablespoons cooking oil
1 clove garlic, chopped

Rinse and sort beans. Place in large, heavy soup kettle. Cover with water, put on the stove, and bring to a hard boil. Cut the heat to simmer. Sauté ham, onion, and garlic in oil; add to beans and cook about two hours. If necessary, add water while cooking. Then, add all other ingredients except the mashed beans, and cook 10 minutes more. Stir in the mashed beans; if soup is not thick enough, remove some of the beans, mash them, and stir in. May freeze.
Yield: 8 to 10 servings.

CODFISH CAKES

1 can codfish (canned salmon can be used instead)
6 medium boiled potatoes
2 eggs
2 tablespoons cream
1 teaspoon grated onion

Drain and flake the cod. Put the potatoes through a ricer or mash well. Combine with cod. Beat the eggs well, add to mixture. Beat the cream with the onions until fluffy. Add to mixture. Form it into 2-inch cakes, dip them in flour, and sauté in butter until brown. Serve at once.
May also make the mixture into patties and bake in a preheated 375° oven for 30 minutes. Dot with butter and serve.
Yield: Serves 4.

Lagniappe

BREAD AND CHEESE PUFF

8 slices white bread, buttered and cubed
2 cups shredded sharp cheddar cheese
6 tablespoons grated Parmesan cheese, divided
2 cups whole milk
5 eggs
½ teaspoon dry mustard
½ teaspoon salt
Dash of white pepper

Place half of bread cubes in a greased 2½ quart soufflé dish; put half of the cheddar cheese over it and 2 teaspoons of the Parmesan. Repeat layers.

Beat eggs with an eggbeater or whisk until fluffy. Blend in milk; add seasonings. Pour over layers of bread and cheese; sprinkle last 2 teaspoons of Parmesan on top. Press ingredients down with a spatula if necessary to make them fit into dish. Cover tightly with foil or plastic wrap—wartime cooks, not having access to these products, would use a tight-fitting lid or waxed paper secured by a large rubber band. Refrigerate for at least 2 hours or overnight.

When ready to bake, remove covering, put soufflé in a preheated 350° oven. Bake 45–50 minutes, or until a knife inserted in the middle comes out clean. Serve immediately.

Yield: 6 to 8 servings.

Note: This is of course not as light as a cheese soufflé, but it is similar in taste and consistency and much easier to make. Excellent for breakfast and also for lunch, accompanied by a green salad in summer or an apple and walnut salad in winter.

CHAPTER SIX

Gulf States Utilities transferred my father to Lafayette in October of 1943, but in order not to take us out of school again, and because Lafayette also had a housing shortage due to the influx of contractors and workers coming to join the war effort, Mother, my sister, my brother, and I remained in Baton Rouge until the end of the school year. During those months, my father stayed in Lafayette during the week, coming home on weekends bearing bourbon, cigarettes, chocolate, and beef, items rarely available in Baton Rouge.

"Don't they have rationing over there?" my mother asked, leery of using items that might have been sold on the black market.

"They do. When someone gives me cigarettes, or bourbon, or chocolate, they always say an old aunt who didn't want it passed it on. Which we both know can't always be true, but they have their own ways of doing things, Kateen." (This was his pet name for her.)

One of these ways explained gifts of beef. A farmer whom my father had met in the course of negotiating for rights-of-way would appear with a roast and a few steaks. When asked the source, he would answer something like this: "Well, Mr. Dubus, I tell you. One of my cows, it broke its leg and I had to shoot it. Now, the rest of my beef I'm raising to feed our soldiers, but how could you ship a dead cow? So, I think, I can't let it go to waste, not in wartime. So, my brother and me butchered it." Cajun logic has always cut through what is seen as unnecessary red tape, and faced with a fait accompli, my father accepted the meat.

I knew nothing about Lafayette except for glimpses when we drove through on our way to visit relatives in New Iberia. So, when my father gave me a book titled *Bayou Suzette* by Lois Lenski, I read it with great interest, hoping to learn more about my future home. What I learned disheartened me, to say the least. A true child of the bayou, Suzette roamed the swamps in a pirogue, a sort of canoe made from a single cypress log. Suzette and a young Native American girl named Marteel pick blackberries, chase off snakes and alligators, and gather moss to be cured for mattresses—all of this barefoot with unkempt hair and dresses made of flour sacks.

We arrived in Lafayette in early June, and though the D-Day invasion on June 6 seized adults' attention, all children my age knew was that we needed to pray even harder for men fighting their way inch by deadly inch from the Normandy beaches into German-held territory. With no television and no satellite communication systems, my parents and their friends depended on radio commentators like Edward R. Murrow, H. V. Kaltenborn, Eric Sevaried, William L. Shirer, and Gabriel Heatter to bring them news, and though I rarely processed the words, those voices—steady, assured—formed a backdrop for the small scenes of my life.

We had been in Lafayette only a few days when I met Louise Cornay, who had been born in Lake Charles, as I had, and where her father, Howard, and her mother, also named Louise, met my parents. By a stroke of good fortune, the Cornays' home was within walking distance of the house we rented on Taft Street, not far from Southwestern Louisiana Institute, the local college my grandfather Walter James Burke had been instrumental in founding.

Louise was the perfect playmate, loving movie star paper dolls as much as I did and owning as many. Every morning we took turns walking to each other's house, carrying a large dress box filled with our collections. Hedy Lamar and Lana Turner had the most glamorous outfits, with Gene Tierney in a class by herself. Her wardrobe had the kind of sophistication that has to come from within, and the slightly "foreign" cast of her features made even the simplest outfit unique. Veronica Lake was another movie star of that era who, like Gene Tierney, brought something mysterious and secretive to every scene she played.

Paired with my favorite, Alan Ladd—I would have paid good money to watch him recite the alphabet, just as I would Paul Newman, Sean Connery, and Clint Eastwood later on—in early films noir like *The Blue Dahlia*, *This Gun for Hire*, and *The Glass Key*, Lake could create a mood with one quick move, veiling half her face with her signature long, blond hair. Like many other girls, I tried vainly to master this trick, just as when we began to smoke, my crowd and I practiced smoking with Patricia Neal's panache or Katharine Hepburn's patrician insouciance.

From a contemporary viewpoint, it seems strange that at that young age I saw these "adult" films. But since the Hayes Office forbade even married couples sleeping in the same bed, when low-cut necklines stopped before showing cleavage, and when swear words relied on color rather than crudeness, my friends and I saw many movies like the ones cited above and were none the worse for it.

Now that we lived only twenty miles away from New Iberia, we spent at least one day a week visiting family there. Those drives through the cane fields lining both sides of the road introduced me to another facet of wartime: prisoners of war. After the tank war in North Africa, with the British General Bernard Montgomery and the American General George Patton victorious over General Erwin Rommel and his troops, thousands of POWs were transported to camps in the United States. Such a camp had been established near St. Martinville. The men worked in the cane fields, guarded by soldiers with not only side guns, but also rifles. The number of guards, spread out a fair distance from each other, didn't seem sufficient to guard all those prisoners, but my father pointed out that because of the hostile nature of both the climate and the terrain, particularly to people who had never endured either, the probability that any of the prisoners would succeed in an escape was small.

"First of all, they're stuck out in the boondocks," Daddy said. "In a city like New Orleans, they might be able to hide until they could sneak onto an outbound ship. But here? Where could they go? And even if they did try, think of the swamps. Mosquitoes, snakes, alligators, no drinkable water, and oppressive heat. It would take a madman to try it."

The people of St. Martinville's behavior toward the POWs was, I think, typical of the unique humanity of the Acadian people. The town got up a band, and on Sunday afternoons, the townspeople would bring food out to the camp and give concerts, the performers on one side of the barbed wire fence, the audience on the other. Town doctors and nurses offered their services, housewives put baskets of food together, a lending library provided books for those who could read English. Nor was this sort of kindness unusual. I learned that the people in many small towns with a POW camp nearby reacted in the same way, and I imagine that in their hearts they prayed that American prisoners would also find friends.

I know of two instances for certain in which they did. My lawyer's father was captured and held in a prison camp near a small German town. Those townspeople, on rations far more meager than those of St. Martinville's citizens, brought food, visited the prisoners, and, when the war ended, sent the Americans home with wishes for happier lives. This same thing happened to the father of a close friend. Joe was shot down over Italy, marched over the Alps, and ended up in a German POW camp until the end of the war. He, too, reported the "kindness of strangers." Both men, accompanied by their families, returned to the villages where people had befriended them and had the kind of reunions possible only to those who have endured horror and pain and fear together.

World War II expanded the horizons of not only those in military service, many away from home for the first time, but also those who stayed at home. Even children my age saw foreign places and people and events via newsreels and heard adults discussing the latest news.

Because reading had always been important in my family, I knew many of the places in the news through books, particularly those by a writer/illustrator named Lucy Fitch Perkins. She had two series, the Geographical Series, with books geared to readers from Grade I to Grade VII; and the Historical Series, with books geared to readers from Grade III to Grade VII. Each book in both series starred a pair of fraternal twins, a boy and a girl, and described the environment in which they lived, their activities, their food, their holidays, and other interesting information.

The first book in the Geographical Series was titled *The Dutch Twins*, followed by stories of Eskimo, Chinese, Japanese, Swiss, Norwegian, Filipino, Irish, Italian, Mexican, Scottish, Spanish, Belgian, and French twins. The Historical Series began with *The Indian Twins*, followed by Cave, Spartan, and Pioneer twins, as well as *The Colonial Twins of Virginia*; *The American Twins of 1812*; and my all-time favorite, which I still own, *The American Twins of the Revolution*. These books opened a wider world to me.

Mother's lessons in etiquette taught Kathryn and me how to act in the small world we lived in. She taught us everything from how to speak with adults to how to pay proper visits to the elderly and ill who were not so ill that they couldn't be visited in their parlors. Mother also taught us to visit the very ill, the dying, and the bereaved.

"The visit is not about you. Many people excuse themselves from making these difficult visits because of their feelings. Only the feelings of the person visited matter. You must make them feel cared for and loved. If you can manage to make an ill or dying person laugh, fine. But it must not be a 'joke.' It must be a little anecdote about someone the person knows. A child's humorous or clever comment is always appropriate."

When Kathryn and I accompanied our grandmother and mother to visit elderly ladies, we learned that their conversations often centered on the ailments of their relatives and friends, solemnly discussing the chance of recovery or conceding that would not happen. A favorite story about growing up in Lafayette is proof of this.

One of my friends, Marie Ellen Voorhies, nicknamed Monie, had a grandmother who reigned unquestionably as the dominant Grande Dame. Autocratic, sharp-witted, strong-minded, and with a fluid tongue, she ruled her family and friends with the *je ne sais quoi* of the aristocrats from whom she descended. In her late eighties, her health was better than that of many women half her age, but one winter she succumbed to pneumonia, well-named "the old person's friend," as it took so many of them off each winter. With no antibiotics or miracle drugs, few measures other than the body's own forces could conquer it, and Marie Ellen reported that her parents didn't expect her grandmother to live many more days.

Until a member of her rosary group sneaked by the nurses' station and entered a room clearly marked NO VISITORS ALLOWED, where Mrs. Voorhies lay under an oxygen tent, to all appearances already dead. But one eye opened as the woman greeted her, and, encouraged, the lady bent over the bed. "*Mais*, Voorhies, *chère*—you look terrible, yes. We've been praying the rosary for you to get well, but now I guess we'll pray for a good death." And then, the final blow. "But, Voorhies, it's good you can tell me what flowers you want, that way we won't get the wrong kind." The adrenaline that had begun flowing with her visitor's first words coursed through Mrs. Voorhies. She sat up, rang for the nurse, and after ordering her visitor out, proceeded to get well.

Probably because Roman Catholics were 95 percent of Acadiana's population in the 1940s, and for quite a while after that, religion formed a much greater part of daily life than it ever had in Baton Rouge. Of course, we went to Mass on Sunday, didn't eat meat on Fridays, and I assume Mother fasted in Lent. But we found a different level of religious practice waited for us in Lafayette.

We went to Mass at St. John's Cathedral, where Cajun families from the outlying rural area arrived in horse-drawn buggies, not to save gasoline but because that had long been their mode of transportation. I continued to see those buggies well into the early fifties, and even after that, occasionally one could be seen on a farm-to-market road.

The cathedral had very high ceilings and windows that opened to let in whatever breeze might sail by, augmented with tall circulating fans that did little more than stir the summer-hot air. Children got off lightly in terms of clothing. The boys could wear short pants and short-sleeved shirts, the girls light cotton dresses that, even with a cotton slip, were still cooler than what the grown-ups wore.

At the eleven o'clock Mass, men wore suits, starched dress shirts, and ties. Ladies wore layers of clothing, beginning with brassieres, panties, girdles, and stockings held up by garters, proceeding to a slip, and then finally a dress, either cotton or linen, worn, of course, with de rigueur gloves and a hat. Even constant fanning with hand fans brought from home, or the ones the town's two funeral homes placed in the pews, couldn't combat the late morning heat.

The prescribed fast from midnight before taking Communion didn't help. Take extraordinary heat and humidity, throw in an empty stomach, and it's astonishing that so few ladies had to be revived at the back of the church, the ushers holding the smelling salts they all carried under the ladies' noses, while a family member fanned them back to consciousness.

Kathryn, André, and I did not go to the eleven o'clock Mass where such drama occurred. We went to the eight o'clock children's Mass, where the sermon had been prepared to address the ears of children, leaving heavier topics and blacker sins for the later Mass.

My father joined the Episcopal Church during college, and he went to that church in Lafayette, a small chapel with perhaps a hundred or so worshipers all told.

All of these different times might have caused logistics problems had Mother's new friends not assured her that it was perfectly safe for her children to ride their bicycles to Mass, and that if we cut through the college campus and the residential neighborhood on the other side, we would ride not only in shade, but within sight of a friend's house.

There were Masses in French in Acadiana's small towns. At least one radio station broadcast in French, and though the concerted effort to restore and preserve the French language had not yet begun, and in many places children who spoke French at school were punished, still the language of their forebears remained in hearts and heads, and thank goodness for that because the loss of the Acadian culture, one of the most unique in the many that form this melting pot of a nation, would be a tragic one and not only to Louisiana's people.

The summer of 1944 wore slowly on, and the first day at school approached. Though my parents had made many new friends, either through family connections or my father's business, none of them except the Cornays had a child my age. As few families in Catholic Acadiana had babies in 1933 as in Protestant Lake Charles, and since I doubt this was an accident, I imagine even then French Catholics made up their own minds as to what was the Pope's business and what most definitely was not.

Three of Louise's brothers would go to St. Paul's in Covington, across Lake Pontchartrain from New Orleans, a Lasallian school run by the Christian Brothers, with only the youngest remaining at home. Louise, too, would go to boarding school at the Academy of the Sacred Heart in Grand Coteau, some twenty miles away.

Thus, I faced my first day at a new school with neither sibling nor friend by my side. André began third grade at the Cathedral School, a boys' school also run by Christian Brothers, and though Kathryn would also be going to

Mt. Carmel Convent, the Catholic girls' school recommended by my mother's friends, she would be in ninth grade and therefore on a different floor from me, a distance much further than one flight of stairs would imply.

With visions of Cajun children's bare feet and soup bowl haircuts, I followed my mother to the principal's office, where Mother Dolores welcomed us. Mother stayed only long enough to kiss me goodbye and then left to take André to Cathedral, Mother Dolores's assurances that I would be well taken care of following her out the door.

"I've asked Mary Alice Blanchet to come meet you and take you to your classroom," Mother Dolores told me. At that time, and in fact at no time while I was at Mt. Carmel, did we wear uniforms. I was in a new cotton dress of the kind I'd worn to public school in Baton Rouge: a simple plaid in shades of pale yellow and rust with a white piqué collar. When Mary Alice entered, I thought that for the first time in my life I was wrongly dressed, and would have rushed after my mother if there had been anything in my closet approaching what Mary Alice wore: a white batiste dress over a lace trimmed slip, with a bodice finely tucked and edged with delicate lace. With that, she wore white stockings and black patent leather Mary Jane's. She was an exquisitely beautiful child, with dark eyes and long, dark curls tied back with a white silk bow. When she spoke, I was still so bemused by her appearance that it took me a moment to realize that not one twinge of an accent marred the purity of her speech. Clearly, *Bayou Suzette* was not the only game in town.

I have little memory of those first days at Mt. Carmel. I felt acutely lonely at recess, but never admitted that at home. Overseas, our men were not only homesick but risking their lives for our freedom. Surely, I could stand a little loneliness. All very Pollyanna, I suppose, but being born in the worst year of the Great Depression and then spending half your childhood with the whole world at war does give you a certain perspective, and the strongest voice is the one that says there are always people on the planet much worse off than you, and you'd better pull up your socks and get on with it.

And then, on the day the class elected officers, I got one of the biggest surprises of my life. Not only did someone nominate me for president, but I won. As if that were not enough, the two girls who had been the top contenders, Adele Sonnier and Lois Trahan, seemed okay with this. Too shocked to say anything, I resolved I would do my best to live up to the trust my classmates had put in me. I didn't dare ask why they'd done this until many years later when I asked Gail Dugal, one of the straightest arrows I have ever known. "Well, Dubus," Gail said (she called me this her whole life; I never asked why, and she never said), "we knew you were going to be either really great or really terrible, so we decided to give you a little power and find out."

"What if I'd messed up?"

A long stare. Then, "You didn't."

I am still impressed by that wisdom. To think that eleven-year-old girls had gotten together, discussed this newcomer, and instead of forming an immediate judgment, gave me an opportunity to either become one of the gang or to outlaw myself, amazes me. But that's typical of that culture. One does not prejudge, nor make decisions without sufficient observation and facts.

After that, I slipped into life in Lafayette as easily as though I had always lived there. And a delightful life it was. No German submarines threatened Acadiana, and since its war industry lay in the fields and farms that made up the bulk of land in these rural parishes, we had none of the sense of urgency that permeated Baton Rouge. One could almost forget the war, particularly because, though rationing continued, it didn't seem as limiting in Lafayette. Part of this came from the proximity of farms to towns. The wives of farmers with only a few cows had always made butter and cheese, including cottage cheese, for their families, and had always given the extra away. Now, they sold these to "city dwellers" with no cows of their own, sending them in on vegetable wagons that made daily rounds from spring until fall.

And, in an agricultural area, housewives had much more produce available for canning, and so received larger allotments of sugar, a bit of which was saved to make treats for the family table. Thus, on Friday nights when our crowd of girls gathered at one house or another, each of us brought one or two tablespoons of sugar, which made enough for a respectable batch of fudge.

In that fall semester of sixth grade, we had a substitute PE and Civics teacher for a few months. Not only was she not a nun, she was a young married woman who looked like a cross between Maria Montez and Dorothy Lamour, and of course became the idol of every girl in the class.

Mrs. Dupuis did not believe in athletic exercise. She decided we would forgo the usual routines of a PE class and concentrate instead on poise and beauty. First, we learned to walk properly, mincing around the classroom with books balanced on our heads. I still remember the advice she gave us to help us remember to stand tall: "Pretend a string is attached to the top of your head and is pulling you up." Then, we learned to sit without turning to make sure the chair was behind us, to rise without hauling ourselves up. She must have studied acting or modeling, or maybe she just avidly read women's magazines, but at any rate, if there were any useful trick to attain poise and beauty she didn't know, it must not have been worth knowing.

She also gave us advice about using makeup, though it would be a few years before any of us did. "The point is not to give yourself a different face," she said, "but to carefully enhance the one God gave you." She had numerous diagrams from magazines that showed how to make eyes look larger, noses smaller, cheeks thinner, and lips fuller. Since she had one of those perfect oval faces, huge blue eyes, and fair skin with just a hint of olive, we doubted that she ever availed herself of any of these pointers. But we appreciated her passing them on to us.

What Mother Dolores thought of all this I've no idea, but the more I got to know that remarkable woman, the more I realized how completely autonomous she was, and that if she had not approved of Mrs. Dupuis's version of PE, it would have ended.

Mrs. Dupuis and her husband lived not far from the street on which a number of our crowd lived. One night as the fudge bubbled on the stove, someone suggested we take some to Mrs. Dupuis, a suggestion that found immediate approval. When we consulted our hostess's mother, she said she thought it a good idea, cautioning us that even if Mrs. Dupuis invited us in, we were not to accept.

The fudge cooled, we cut it into squares, put some into a small box lined with waxed paper, and then ventured forth. I doubt that there are many eleven-year-olds left who would approach a teacher's home with the mixture of anticipation and trepidation we all felt. The boundaries between a teacher's life at school and at home were strict, and the right to personal privacy paramount. Though I never asked, I suspect that Mrs. Dupuis received a call warning her of our approach. While we would never have thought that the Dupuis might be engaged in a private activity, any wise adult would.

At any rate, we were greeted with proper surprise and delight, and when we refused the invitation to come in, Mr. Dupuis came to the door to meet us. Tall and handsome, he was precisely the man we would have chosen for our glamorous teacher. We knew that he was on leave before going overseas, and that made the meeting especially poignant.

When he shipped out, Mrs. Dupuis left Lafayette to return to her family to wait until her husband came home. I've no idea whether he did or not, as I never heard from either of them again. Like so many people one knows briefly, Mrs. Dupuis remains in my mind as she was then: a beautiful, young woman who gave us a glimpse into the adult world of glamour and some of the tools we would need to enter it.

Along with Gail, Lois Trahan, Carolyn Littell, and Pat Jardell, I joined the Girl Scouts, a troop that drew its members not only from Mt. Carmel, but from a public school as well. Two girls who later became good friends, Gay Meyers and Pat O'Brien, were members, and when I think about their lives just a few years ahead, the memory of them in Girl Scout uniforms working on badges makes me laugh.

Gail put the same energy and determination into scouting as she did everything else. I remember sitting on the swing on her front porch, turning the pages of the *Girl Scout Handbook*, reading the list of activities to be accomplished before earning a particular badge. The troop worked on some badges in concert. But our leader, Miss Shirley Kurzweg, encouraged individual effort, so long, of course, as a reputable and responsible adult certified that we had indeed performed every activity required. Such an adult could be a parent—even Miss Kurzweg would not dare question their honor—but an adult with some competence in the activity was considered a much better judge.

Fortunately, Gail's father taught in the School of Agriculture at SLI, and through his contacts, we had access to experts in any field we chose. Mr. Dugal was a quiet man, at least when at home. He had two avocations: hunting and grafting camellias. Gail and I earned one badge helping him do the latter. It's a simple enough process, needing patience and care more than expertise, and it is one skill that, though I have never put it into practice, I keep thinking one day I will.

Gail had an aunt who owned a fabric shop on Jefferson Street, and many a summer morning Gail and I would ride our bikes and spend an hour or so looking at patterns and fabric. We planned to earn the Girl Scout sewing badge over the summer, with Mrs. Dugal as our teacher. Mrs. Dugal started Gail and me on aprons with bibs, the only ones useful to any serious cook. She had sufficient scraps to make these, but when she decided we were ready to make a dress, we went to buy new fabric from Gail's aunt's shop. "Don't choose a stripe, a check, or a plaid," Mrs. Dugal advised, "because it's not always easy to match the pattern and I want you to concentrate on basic techniques." Solids or prints remained: both Gail and I found the prints more interesting. I chose a cotton fabric with a cream background with small roses scattered all over it in a random pattern, and Gail chose a bolder print with fruits in bright colors against a hunter green background.

We both used the same sewing pattern, a full-skirted dress with a simple bodice augmented by puffed sleeves and a sweetheart neckline that Mrs. Dugal changed to round, as that would be easier for us to bind. With her guidance, we completed our dresses in three mornings of steady work. As I remember, only putting in the zipper needed constant redoing; like my grandmother, Mrs. Dugal didn't consider "almost perfect" good enough. "A zipper is meant to be used, not seen," she said, and finally, both zippers lay neatly behind the bound edges of the bodice, and all we had left was to put in the hems.

Many years later, when I sewed for five daughters, one year making sixty-five garments between the beginning of March and the end of May—leading my mother to ask if I were opening a branch of New York's garment district—I thought of those sewing lessons and thanked both my grandmother and Mrs. Dugal for their patience and perseverance, without which I know I would have given up.

The sewing badge behind us, Gail and I turned to the cooking badge, again with Mrs. Dugal's help. We worked our way through the requirements, measuring, sifting, stirring, blending, learning the difference between a rolling boil and a slow boil, learning how to test when milk had just reached the scalding stage and when candy had reached the stage known as "soft ball."

We celebrated completion of that badge with an afternoon gathering for our friends. We decided to make a pièce de résistance that Keller's, a local bakery founded in 1938 and still in business, was famous for: éclairs. The pastry turned out perfectly, the custard was just right. But before we filled the éclairs, Gail suggested putting a little color in this special treat. We considered yellow or pink, but then Gail decided we should blend blue and green food coloring and make the custard a nice shade of aqua. Which we did. And learned that food presentation may be adventurous, it may be unique, but it must never be such that it discourages diners from eating something because, as one of our guests said, "They look like they have mold."

My experience with scouting ended when Miss Kurzweg expelled our entire troop. Our nickname for our leader was "One Match Kurzweg," because she allowed us only one match with which to light the fires we built. After several experiences with that one match going out and having to eat uncooked hot dogs or nothing, we took prepared food along on hikes. This food was hidden in the woods, and though we tried to cover the disappearance of several scouts with excuses, Miss Kurzweg finally caught on and expelled the whole troop.

I thought this a rather harsh punishment. Most of the scouts had achieved the highest rank and taking sustenance on a daylong hike was our only rebellion. As usual, I discussed this with my father.

"Well, Beth, Miss Kurzweg is a very smart and competent lady. But unlike most of the women her age, she doesn't have a husband and children. Which leaves a lot of energy to be put someplace else."

Mrs. Dugal, a Red Cross volunteer, introduced Gail and me to the Junior Red Cross. We did practical service, such as rolling bandages and knitting wool squares, which the women would connect to make helmet liners for the troops. We also had pen pals, children our ages who lived in England, Scotland, or Ireland, the only European countries where civilian mail could be delivered.

My pen pal's name was Maureen, and she lived in London. She was eleven, and in one letter told me she would probably fail her eleven-plus tests, and in that case, would go to a secondary modern school until she was old enough to train to be a beautician. I had no idea what a secondary modern school was at the time. Later, I looked it up and learned that children who were in the top 25 percent of those who passed their eleven-plus tests went on to grammar schools, where an academic curriculum prepared them for university educations. Those who failed the eleven-plus tests but had the ability to master technology could attend technical schools, while those like Maureen, almost entirely working-class, went to secondary moderns, which prepared them for very little.

Reading this letter, I no longer asked Maureen about the books she liked, but asked questions about life in wartime London and told her about my life in Lafayette. Maureen's courage impressed me. Her only reference to bomb raids came from a statement that she and her family had spent half the previous night in a bomb shelter or a comment that she took a different route to school because buildings destroyed in a bomb raid blocked the old one. I'm sure she lost friends and relatives, but she never wrote about it.

The Christmas of 1944, I made Maureen a wool scarf with a long fringe on either end, then added a batch of fudge, each piece wrapped separately and put in a tin box that could withstand the trip across the ocean. I mailed this package weeks before Christmas, and I remember coming out of the Lafayette post office, surveying a calm and peaceful street, and wondering what Maureen's street would look like when the package arrived.

As in any rural community, life in Lafayette changed with the seasons, and during my first fall there, I learned that hunting season is one of the most important, for a number of reasons. First, a good hunter can fill a freezer with enough game to feed a family through the winter. Second, hunting provides men with an opportunity to acquire and perfect a manly skill. Third, and perhaps the most compelling reason of all, hunting gives men an opportunity to get away from civilization and all its pressures, and for the length of a few hours—or a few days, if they hunt from a camp—return to a simpler life when men were men and women were absent.

I had not yet learned from my father this primitive need men have to put their everyday world behind them and pit themselves against the wild. But when he explained it to me, everything I had observed about hunters and hunting growing up in Lafayette fell into place. I don't remember how the subject came up. My father had a way of using a comment or anecdote as a stepping off place for an exploration of yet another aspect of the human condition he found instructive.

"Some ladies never seem to understand why their husbands want to go off with a bunch of men and live like savages," he said. "But it's bred in the bone, and the veneer of manners and social rules that a few thousand years have imposed can't overcome a history that goes much farther back than that." He went on to explain that from the first human beings, when a man's property and life, as well as the lives of his family, depended on being able to trust others, knowing who you could count on and who you couldn't, was paramount to survival.

"It's why most men are suspicious of meeting men they haven't met in the course of their daily lives," he said. (I incorporated this wisdom into a creative entertaining course I gave in Baton Rouge, explaining to my students why their husbands were reluctant to meet the husbands of their friends for the first time in their own homes.)

His final words: "When you marry, let your husband have his time with his friends. So long as he doesn't drink too much or gamble too much, kiss him goodbye and welcome him home with a smile."

Like all hunters I knew, Mr. Dugal valued his hounds right up there with his family. He trained them himself, and when they weren't out in the field, he kept them in a kennel behind what had been a maid's quarters and which Gail and I had turned into a clubhouse. Also like many hunters in Acadiana, Mr. Dugal cooked for his hounds, a favorite being cornbread, though, as I learned the hard way, one not nearly as tasty as that made for humans.

Gail and I walked to her house after school one cold fall day and found a pan of cornbread still warm from the oven sitting on the kitchen counter. We cut generous slabs and slathered them with jam. I bit into mine and then grabbed a paper towel and spit into it. Even the sweetness of the jam couldn't disguise the sour taste of the cornbread, and to my relief, Gail spit out hers, too—cuing Mr. Dugal's entrance. He took one look at the cornbread, another at our faces, and said, "Serves you right, eating my hounds' supper."

Mr. Dugal also made cracklings in the fall after a *boucherie* (a pig butchering), cutting the pork rind with a layer of fat still attached into small squares and deep frying them until crisp. I never developed a taste for cracklings but ate them at the Dugal's as an act of politeness.

With the advent of hunting season came something I had never seen before—flocks of ducks in V-shaped formations flying overhead, filling the Mississippi flyway from Minnesota to the Louisiana coast. Although the Wildlife and Fisheries Service regulated the number of ducks hunters could kill and the seasons in which they could shoot them, Cajuns had been accustomed to feeding their families with wild duck and geese, as well as wild turkeys and deer, since they arrived in Louisiana. This separated them, in their minds, from hunters who belonged to ritzy hunting camps, one so splendid the hunters had bearers to carry their guns. Cajuns held such clubs in great contempt. Why pay good money to belong to a club when you could take your Lab, your pirogue, and your gun and shoot all the ducks you wanted by yourself? Which they did, and were sometimes caught shooting out of season, a crime punishable by law.

Lafayette's sheriff at the time owned a restaurant on Jefferson Street called Autin's, his last name. He served wild duck gumbo year-round, adding oysters to it when they were in season. Wild duck and oyster gumbo is one of the world's best dishes, and his restaurant was constantly filled. The diners knew they ate ducks shot by poachers, but in true French style, agreed with the sheriff's logic that since you couldn't put the ducks back in the sky, you might as well eat them.

This went on until some aspirant to the sheriff's office, knowing he could never win by fair means, chose foul. (Literally, as it turned out.) He reported Autin to Wildlife and Fisheries, which resulted in a hearing to investigate the charges. Sheriff Autin freely admitted using the ducks in his restaurant, asking his judges what else they thought he should do?

"Destroy them," came the answer, along with a warning that he would be let off this time, but that if he ever again accepted poached ducks, he would be fined and perhaps have to serve time in jail. Hearing this, the sheriff removed his badge and threw it on the table before him. "*Mais*, it's a lot of trouble to be a sheriff," he said, "and now you take all the fun out of it. I quit."

And so ended the year-round source of wild duck gumbo, the only justice, in local minds, being that the informer did not win the race.

My father's hunting days ended when he left Abbeville, but enough of his friends hunted to supply us with ducks, only in season. Of all wild duck, teal are not only the most delicate in flavor, but the smallest and fastest, making them difficult to hit. A friend had given us half a dozen teal, one for each of the children and Mother, two for the man of the house. Mother cooked them and as we sat down for our noon meal, my father said grace and then announced that since it was an Ember Day, none of the Roman Catholics present could eat meat. "Such a shame, when we have teal." Ember Days are no longer observed, but at that time, they occurred seasonally and required fasting for those over eighteen and abstinence from meat for anyone more than seven years old. My father had an astonishing amount of knowledge about the Roman Catholic Church, usually welcome additions to family discussions, but today, most definitely unwelcome, as he well knew.

Mother rose from the table and headed for the telephone. We could hear her conversation with someone who was obviously a priest. "Yes, Father. Thank you, Father." She returned to the table, a victorious glint in her green eyes. "Well, André, Father Boudreaux said to tell you that since teal eat nothing on land, but feed only in water, I can bless them and call them fish. He also said to tell my Anglican husband that greed is a capital sin."

Many years later, the same friend who teased Wesley Brummett about giving me measles shot enough teal for me to serve at a dinner party, letting mallards and wood ducks fly by as he waited for his chosen targets. This took some time, and he reported that when the last teal fell to the water, and the Lab went out to retrieve it, the guide poling the pirogue said, "She must be one hell of a woman."

To which my hunter replied, "She is."

Some women get expensive jewelry, some women get ducks, and one Lafayette woman got both. Her husband, Roy Hawkins, was one of the most avid hunters in town. Mabel Hawkins was one of the most beautiful and feminine women. Made even more prosperous when oil was found on his property, Mr. Hawkins resolved to surprise his wife with a custom brooch from Cartier, made from his own design. I'm sure you've guessed what Mabel found when she opened her gift on Christmas morning: a mallard duck, its colors executed in emeralds; black, gray and white pearls; and smoky brown topaz, set in twenty-four karat gold.

In a display of devotion and appreciation that the thought is what counts, Mabel wore the brooch in the daytime, as its subject hardly qualified to be pinned on a cocktail or evening dress. "But," she confided to friends, "I do hope people realize I know it's not proper to wear precious stones before six, but in this case, what can I do?"

I still occasionally wonder if that mallard duck ranks as one of Cartier's most challenging orders, because, as Roy told his friends, he had sent one of his prized mallard decoys up there to make sure they got the coloration right. For a true huntsman, realism trumps art where ducks are concerned.

A major event in the fall of 1944 came in the form of Dudley LeBlanc's Hadacol Caravan. He had founded the Happy Day Company in the 1930s, producing Happy Day Headache Powders, a preparation that was seized by the FDA. Undaunted, LeBlanc developed a tonic that he marketed as a vitamin supplement. Taking the first two letters of Happy Day Company, and adding L from his last name, he came up with Hadacol, a name that was soon known all over the South.

Early on, despite the tonic's 12 percent alcohol content, he began directing sales promotions to elementary school children. One of the most successful promotions centered on a comic book named *Captain Hadacol*, a wonder man who rescued children from misfortune and peril, always after a big swallow of the potent tonic. LeBlanc distributed these comic books free and gained a large following among children as a result. He also organized a Hadacol Caravan, modeled after the medicine shows commonplace on the American scene until the late forties. Many of these featured vaudeville acts and comics. LeBlanc hired Hollywood stars like Lucille Ball, George Burns and Gracie Allen, Judy Garland, Chico Marx, Cesar Romero, Carmen Miranda, Dorothy Lamour, Mickey Rooney, Bob Hope, and James Cagney to draw crowds. Adult admission cost two Hadacol box tops; children's one. An eight-ounce bottle cost $1.25; a thirty-four-ounce bottle $3.50. Adjusted for inflation, $1.00 in the 1940s would be $15.00 today—of course, customers got the tonic in the bottle as well as the pleasures of the show.

In the fall of 1944, Bob Hope headlined a show meant not only to sell Hadacol, but also war bonds. Other Hollywood stars of varying magnitude appeared in that show as well, but my memory is dimmed by a personal high point, one that came about because our Girl Scout troop, along with others, was given the job of taking pledges from audience members seated in McNaspy Stadium, where SLI's football team played. The crowd packed the concrete part of the stadium, which also contained athletic dorms, and the overflow found seats on the wooden bleachers across the field. My parents sat with friends, and because almost none of them had girls my age, I soon had a stack of pledges in my hands.

A friend of my father's, who had been watching me, beckoned me over. He pointed toward a seat several rows up from ours. "See that man wearing the Stetson hat? I want you to go up and ask him for a pledge." It was one thing to ask my parents' friends for pledges, since I barely had to open my mouth. To approach a total stranger, and such an imposing one, seemed impossible. "I promise you he'll make a pledge. Just go up and smile at him and ask him nicely."

And so, I went, a small figure against that big crowd, my sash with rows of badges across my shoulder, my troop patch sewed to my uniform sleeve.

My target sat on the end of the row, which made it easier for me to talk with him. I introduced myself, mentally forming the words I would speak next.

"You're André Dubus's daughter," he said. I couldn't tell whether he thought this a good or bad thing. "Well, I tell you what. I've been sitting here waiting for someone to ask me to make a pledge—that's why you're here, right?"

I nodded, not believing I had achieved my goal so easily.

"Then, take this down," he said. He dictated his name and paused. "Aren't you going to ask me how much?"

"Yes."

"Ten thousand dollars." I looked at him, expecting to be told the true amount. "Write it down." Then, he smiled. "You may as well know, your father's friend and I set this up. He told me what a nice little girl you are, and what a fine man your father is, and I thought—well, since I'm buying a bond anyway, why not buy it from her?"

A memorable night indeed, one which reinforced a long-held belief that there are people in the world who know how to do things with style, and though the tangible outcome may not change, the intangible ones do.

Recipes for Game

JOE'S SPECIAL DOVES

25 doves
Salt and black pepper to taste
½ cup vinegar or red wine
1 cup roux, made with equal amounts of oil and flour
2 cups chopped white onion
2 jalapeño peppers, finely chopped (optional)
3 cloves garlic, finely chopped
½ cup cooking oil
½ cup chopped parsley
½ cup chopped chives
½ cup dry red wine
1 cup chicken stock or bouillon

Twelve hours before cooking, wash birds, sprinkle with salt and pepper, sprinkle with vinegar or wine, and cover tightly. Refrigerate for 12 hours, turning once. Remove birds from marinade and pat dry. Brown in oil in large iron pot. Remove birds from pot, put the chopped vegetable in, and simmer until wilted. Add red wine and stock. Combine this with roux and thin with 2 to 3 cups water. Return birds to pot. Cover and simmer about 3 hours or until meat begins to fall off wings. Correct seasonings. Sprinkle with parsley and chives before serving.

WILD DUCKS WITH TURNIPS

2 wild ducks
6 turnips, young, sweet ones (boiled for 20 minutes)
2 tablespoons shortening
Flour
1 large white onion
Salt and red pepper to taste
Parsley and green onion tops, finely chopped

Cut up ducks as for frying and in a heavy iron pot brown in hot shortening but do not burn. Remove from pot. In same pot, add flour and make a roux. (The amount should be sufficient to make not a paste, but a mixture about the consistency of thin custard.) Add onion and cook until limp. Add ducks and boiled turnips; cover with water heated on the stove, *not* from the tap. Season with salt and red pepper. Cook slowly until ducks are tender. If water gets low, add enough to make gravy. Add chopped onion tops and parsley 10 minutes before removing pot from the fire.

Note: Turnips are an excellent accompaniment for wild duck. I frequently put cut turnips and apples in the duck cavity when baking them. I would use half red wine, half water, for the liquid in this recipe or make your own vegetable stock with turnip and green onion tops.

AUTIN'S WILD DUCK AND OYSTER GUMBO

2 mallards or 4 teal
1 teaspoon Tabasco sauce
1 teaspoon salt
2 tablespoons vegetable oil
2 tablespoons butter
3 tablespoons all-purpose flour
1 cup chopped yellow onions
1 cup seeded and chopped green bell pepper
½ cup chopped celery
2 garlic cloves, chopped
3 cups chicken broth (made from necks and wings)
2 dozen shucked oysters
¼ cup chopped green onions, tops and bottoms
¼ cup chopped fresh parsley leaves

Rub the salt over the ducks. Heat the oil in a cast iron pot or Dutch oven over medium-high heat. Brown the ducks on all sides; remove and set aside. Pour off the fat. Lower the heat, then melt the butter in the same pot. Add in the flour and stir constantly, making a roux. Add the vegetables and cook, stirring frequently, until they are soft. Pour in the chicken broth slowly so that the roux doesn't curdle, and then add the Tabasco. Cook until the mixture is slightly thickened. Now add the ducks, bring to a boil, cover, reduce the heat to medium-low and simmer about an hour, or until ducks are tender. Add the drained oysters, the green onions, and parsley. Cook until the oysters curl. Before serving, adjust the seasonings. Serve hot over rice.

Yield: Serves 4.

VENISON ROAST

Marinade for Venison #1:
1 quart vinegar
1 quart water
1 tablespoon red pepper
1 tablespoon black pepper
1 tablespoon salt
3 cloves garlic, chopped
3 bay leaves
1 teaspoon ground cloves
1 teaspoon ground allspice
1 teaspoon mustard seed
1 teaspoon thyme

Mix marinade ingredients and pour over meat in a bowl that can be covered. Place in refrigerator and turn several times during a 12-hour, or longer, period.

Marinade for Venison #2:
1½ cups vegetable or olive oil
¾ cup soy sauce
½ cup Worcestershire sauce
2 tablespoons dry mustard
⅓ cup vinegar
1 tablespoon black pepper
1¼ teaspoons salt
1 teaspoon parsley
⅓ cup lemon juice
1 teaspoon garlic powder

Put ingredients as listed in large bowl. Stir well, pour over venison. Marinate for 24 hours in refrigerator. If roasting the venison, cook the venison in the marinade. If venison is cooked on a grill, baste it as it cooks.

Preparation:
10 lb. venison roast
½ lb. salt meat cut into strips
1 medium onion, cut into strips
12 strips of celery
½ cup sour cream
½ cup currant jelly
1 tablespoon brandy

Before roasting, punch at least 10 holes in the roast with a sharp knife. Insert the salt meat, onion, and celery strips. Insert a meat thermometer. Roast at 325–350° as for a beef roast. Baste frequently with the remaining marinade and meat drippings. When roast is done, add sour cream, jelly, and brandy to skimmed meat drippings for a truly delicious gravy.
Yield: 12 to 16 servings.

WILD RICE AND OYSTER DRESSING
(Perfect for Game)

2 cups cooked wild rice
2 cups cooked white rice
4 strips bacon
1 medium white onion, chopped
½ teaspoon thyme
1 bay leaf
2 tablespoons finely minced parsley
2 dozen oysters, cut in half, drained, with liquid reserved
Salt and pepper to taste
Oyster liquid

Cook rice according to package directions. Cook bacon until crisp; remove and crumble. Sauté onion in bacon drippings until soft and yellow. Add remaining ingredients, using enough oyster liquid for a moist dressing. Season to taste with salt and pepper. Bake at 325° for 30 minutes.
Yield: Serves 8.
Note: You may prepare the dressing except for the oysters ahead of time and freeze. In this case, use chicken broth to moisten the dressing. When ready to use, thaw the dressing, stir in the drained, halved oysters, and bake as above.

BAKED WILD GOOSE

Wild goose
Green bell pepper
Garlic
White onion
Salt, red and black pepper to taste
Bacon strips
Red wine, if desired
Fresh mushrooms, if desired

Note: The amounts of vegetables are not given. After you see the size of the goose, you will have an idea of how much of each you need.

Wash goose and pat dry. Slit under breasts and fill with peppers and salt, a piece of garlic, white onion, and bell pepper. Now season inside and out with salt and black pepper. Place a piece of bell pepper and half an onion inside. Melt bacon in large skillet and brown goose, then put in roasting pot, breast side down. Add a little flour, about one tablespoon, to drippings in skillet, stir until brown. Add a little water or wine until smooth. Pour gravy over goose. (Note: Do not season gravy until after it has cooked with the goose for a while and then add if needed.) Place roaster, top on, vent closed, in 325–350° oven and cook until tender, which depends on the size of the goose, usually from 2–5 hours. Add ½ cup wine and the caps from a pound of fresh mushrooms during the last half hour of cooking. Sprinkle with chopped parsley.

Serve with rice.

Yield: 2 to 4, depending on size of goose.

ZIPPY GLAZED CARROTS

2 tablespoons butter
¼ cup brown sugar
2 tablespoons prepared yellow mustard
¼ teaspoon salt
3 cups sliced carrots, cooked and drained
1 tablespoon chopped parsley

Melt butter in saucepan. Stir in brown sugar, mustard, and salt. Add cooked carrots, stirring constantly, until glazed—about 5 minutes. Sprinkle with parsley.
Yield: Serves 4.
Note: You may use canned carrots, but be sure to rinse them well. This is a great dish for wild game dinners. It has just the piquant sweetness that sets off the flavor of the game.

YAM PIE

¾ cup brown sugar
½ teaspoon salt
1 teaspoon ginger
1 teaspoon cinnamon
½ teaspoon nutmeg
2 eggs, beaten
1 tablespoon dark cane syrup
1½ cups mashed sweet potatoes (3 medium if you bake them yourself)
1 cup light cream
½ cup dry sherry
1 unbaked 9- or 10-inch pie shell

Mix salt and spices with brown sugar. Add eggs, syrup, and yams, mix well. Gradually add cream and sherry. Bake in pie shell in a preheated 425° oven for about 40 minutes or until set.
Note: This is a good dessert for a wild game meal, as the flavors blend well with game.

Lagniappe

ALLIGATOR PROVENÇALE

1 medium white onion, chopped
1 small green bell pepper, chopped
2 ribs celery, chopped
½ stick butter
1 tablespoon flour
3 cups canned tomatoes
1 cup plain (mild) barbecue sauce
2 lb. alligator fillets, cut into 1-inch cubes

Sauté the first three ingredients in butter in a large skillet until they are soft. Add flour and cook to a thick paste. Add the next two ingredients gradually, stirring to blend them in. Cover and simmer 30 minutes. Add the alligator and continue cooking until meat is tender, about an hour. Serve over rice.

Yield: Serves 6 to 8.

Note: When asked how alligator meat tastes, the response is usually the same as when people are asked how rabbit or frog legs taste: "Like chicken." Cooked properly, alligator meat is tender and tasty. Cooked improperly, it can be like eating a piece of rubber.

CHAPTER SEVEN

With children in school, the ladies of Lafayette returned to the social and club calendar that ran from September to May. Les Vingt Quatre, a group of twenty-four civic-minded women, had been formed in Lafayette in the 1930s and began their civic efforts by establishing Lafayette's first public library in a narrow, brick building across from the parish courthouse. My mother was invited to join this group not long after we moved to Lafayette, and that group of ladies formed the core of her friendships.

Besides civic projects, Les Vingt Quatre members undertook a serious subject for study each club year. At the monthly meeting, a member would read her paper, which explored one aspect of the chosen topic. These papers ranked, in terms of research and depth, with any master's thesis. I remember the year my mother prepared a paper on the Russian novelists of the nineteenth century. I was in college at the time, and I read it with awe and admiration. I knew my mother was highly intelligent, but until then I hadn't known she was also a scholar of the first rank.

The library Les Vingt Quatre started has long been replaced, but the Alexandre Mouton House Museum they founded in 1954 is still operating. The Mouton home was in disrepair, and funds were raised for its restoration. I remember going through it when it opened and seeing a date and a pair of names scratched into one of the original windows with, the story goes, the engagement diamond of a young lady who had just accepted a proposal. Both a historical and decorative arts museum, it is well worth a visit.

My parents both loved to play bridge, as do I. Mother had several foursomes that met in the afternoons, and when she hosted a table, I had the opportunity to watch the play and get some sense of how the game was played. I soon learned that the personalities of the bridge players helps make the game one of constant variety.

One lady, Maggie Richard, had the kind of optimism that can lead to bids on hands that have little chance of making it. Her battle cry to her partner, "But, *chère*, you have thirteen cards!" signaled a wild leap that more often than not succeeded. One memorable day, Maggie opened her hand to find thirteen spades. Wanting to make the highest bid she could think of, when her turn came, she said, "Seven no-trump," which meant that the few tricks she took came from those thirteen cards in her partner's hand.

Bridge would later replace canasta as the game of choice for my crowd on summer days when we had to remain out of the sun between 10 a.m. and 4 p.m. Since the color I turned was not one anyone would choose to be, I stayed out of the sun as much as possible, and now, into my ninth decade, I have very few wrinkles, due also to inheriting my mother's skin.

On October 20, 1944, General Douglas MacArthur made his promised return to the Philippines, landing at Red Beach, Palo, Leyte. By New Year's Eve, the entire Philippines archipelago would be in Allied hands. In Europe, Allied forces freed country after country, encouraging progress that would grind to a halt in December when the Battle of the Bulge, as that last-ditch struggle for the Ardennes was called, began.

As Thanksgiving approached, people began talking about "when the war is over," in voices that held not just hope, but also a surety that this would soon happen. Still, in families like ours who had members serving overseas, until they came safely home, there would always be an undercurrent of tension and fear beneath the most ordinary day.

All my relatives did come home, thank heaven. I don't remember where the four men in Aunt Roberta and Uncle Francis's family served, but I know that my Uncle Donald Robert's son, Cousin Dracus Burke, served in the Judge Advocate Department and, I suspect, also Military Intelligence. Cousin Walter Binnings commanded a PT boat in the Pacific, and Uncle Julian, my Aunt Bertha's husband, went as a medic because, as he told the draft board, he couldn't kill someone who wasn't trying to kill him. They asked him if he could kill someone trying to kill a wounded soldier or him, and he said yes. He carried a sidearm, but I never knew whether he had to use it. I would think so, as he was part of some of the worst fighting in Europe, including the battle for the Remagen Bridge.

Uncle Julian had always been a gentle, kind man, who trained hunting dogs as an avocation. He had instant rapport with dogs and was rarely seen without one at his heels. But when he came home, something had changed. For one thing, he slept on the floor the first year, saying he had slept on the ground so long he didn't feel comfortable in a bed. The most significant change happened inside. His eyes, still gentle, still kind, had a look that I didn't understand until my father, after seeing me watching Uncle Julian one day, explained it. "Your uncle is one of those people who should never have seen the terrible things human beings can do to others. He saw things over there that he will never be able to forget, and that's what you see in his eyes."

Later, a close friend and I named the kind of pain my uncle suffered—and we both suffered for entirely different reasons—"dirty pain," because it has absolutely nothing good about it. It's not productive pain, like childbirth, or healing pain, as when an injured arm or leg slowly recovers. It settles into your soul and stays there, sometimes sleeping but always ready to spring to life at the slightest provocation.

Cousin Walter had terrible headaches for years after his service on that PT boat. He told me once they lived on vitamin tablets when in action, as they couldn't keep anything else down in a high-speed boat pounded by waves. A few years ago, I learned that PT boats were not much more than manned torpedoes, and I realized how fortunate we were that Cousin Walter came home.

We spent what would be the last wartime Thanksgiving at Aunt Roberta and Uncle Francis's house in New Iberia. When they married, they bought the house in which they'd met in kindergarten and named it Halcyon House, a house particularly well-named because they were two of the most contented people I knew. The phrase "bon vivant" could have been coined just for my Uncle Francis Voorhies. He loved life, and that joie de vivre inhabited everything he did, particularly the life he shared with my aunt. Given to spontaneous plans, Uncle Francis would call Aunt Roberta from the bank—he helped found two banks in New Iberia—and tell her to get ready, they were going to drive to New Orleans and take a plane to New York or Miami or San Francisco the next morning. This was all very well, except that Aunt Roberta, while she too loved life, had a more orderly way of living it. And so, she found a way to appear as spontaneous as her husband while still maintaining the preparation she required.

Her solution lay in the various "kits" waiting in a closet for one of Uncle Francis's sudden announcements. She showed them to Kathryn and me one day. The New York kit had a tailored suit, several blouses, stockings, appropriate shoes, bags, gloves, and accessories, as well as a costume suitable for dining out in the evening. The San Francisco kit had the addition of a stylish raincoat, while the Miami kit contained resort clothes and bathing suits.

"Girls, if you are fortunate enough to marry a bon vivant, never do anything to squelch him," she said. "And though sometimes it is necessary to engage in a little subterfuge to keep him happy, it is all done in the name of a good marriage."

Like any meal when a large family with a wide range of ages gathers, that Thanksgiving dinner at Aunt Roberta and Uncle Francis's house had both the sublime—a solemn toast proposed by Uncle Francis after grace for the safe return of all our boys—and the ridiculous, when the young boy cousins, relegated to the children's table, amused themselves by using knife blades to propel green peas at targets all over the room. Aunt Roberta, whose strong suit was "rising above" such incidents, signaled the boys' mothers to leave them alone, waiting until bits of roll became part of the arsenal, at which point she told the combatants they could be excused.

Due to careful conservation of ingredients, and a contribution to the meal from each household present, the Thanksgiving feast had all the traditional dishes: turkey with rice and oyster dressing and cranberry sauce, yam casserole, creamed spinach, a molded cherry and Coca-Cola salad, homemade rolls, and pecan, mincemeat, pumpkin, apple, and lemon meringue pies.

The only problem with eating Thanksgiving dinner away from home is that there are no leftovers to make turkey and cranberry sauce sandwiches, and no pies for late-night snacks. A good friend and I solve this problem on occasions when we don't have Thanksgiving dinner at home by buying whole turkey breasts, making cranberry sauce, and at least a pumpkin and pecan pie so that when people who stuffed themselves to the gills just a few hours ago open the refrigerator, they'll find "leftovers" inside.

Right after Thanksgiving, preparations for Christmas began. Many women had made their fruit cakes in early September and had been "curing" them with bourbon every week since. Though we always had fruit cake, Mother didn't make it. Her specialty was a date nut cake that I make every year. That, with the ambrosia my father made every Christmas Eve, had the star roles among the desserts served on Christmas day. Two favorite candies, pralines and Divinity fudge, can only be made on days of low humidity, which, even in December, can be few and far between. On the first cold, crisp day, women all over Lafayette would cancel whatever plans they had to make these candies, knowing that they must literally "seize the day" or have their families do without them.

Like gumbo and potato salad, praline recipes vary. There are four recipes in *Talk About Good*, my favorite Lafayette cookbook; three in *Cotton Country*, a Monroe, Louisiana, cookbook; and one, in which the pecans are toasted before being added to the candy, in a cookbook from Avery Island. I use a friend's praline recipe. It's simple and good. Not foolproof, but then, no cooked candy is. Before candy thermometers could be found even in hardware stores, one had to be able to determine the precise moment when candy was ready to take off the heat, either by testing the "soft ball" in a cup of ice water or by dripping syrup slowly from a spoon to see if two strands met and made one.

Advent, though not as solemn as Lent, is also a time of fast, as well as preparation for the birth of Christ. Advent wreaths, for a long time now a tradition in both Catholic and Protestant churches and homes, weren't in use then, but every home had a crèche, with the empty manger waiting for the Christ Child to be born. Churches had elaborate crèches, as they do now, usually taking over one of the side altars. The Ladies' Altar Society, with the help of husbands and sons who went out into the woods to gather greenery, made a background for the stable. Some churches had backdrops with starry skies, one brilliant star pointing to the manger. And occasionally a church would sponsor a living Nativity scene, with caroling on the evening it began.

We put our crèche under the Christmas tree, where it held ground against an increasing pile of presents. Though by Christmas 1944, my siblings and I no longer believed in Santa Claus, I think my brother and I believed past the age most children did because of our father. Every Christmas morning, as long as we believed, we would first go to our parents' room while they had their morning coffee.

Every day of his life until the last, my father got up first, dripped coffee, and brought two demi-tasse cups to their bedroom, letting my mother start her day with coffee in bed. On Christmas morning, those two tiny cups seemed to hold coffee enough to last until noon, but then we would hear a horn blow from the living room, and my parents would take their last sip, finally rising and leading the way to see what Santa brought. An empty glass where milk had been, cookie crumbs, carrot tops left by the reindeer, and the horn Santa had just blown. What other proof did we need?

When we were too young to make our own lists, Mother would write down the gift and the name of the giver so that we could thank the right person for a particular gift. Writing thank-you notes occupied hours in the days between Christmas and New Year's. We usually got a box of notepaper in our stockings, and though my handwriting left a lot to be desired, and still does, with effort I could write legibly enough for my notes to be read.

These notes were a foundation for our social training. No mere "Thank you for the gift," as so many notes I have received these past years read. "You must write something that will let your aunt know why you enjoy the book," Mother would say. "Quote a particular scene or make a comment about something you found especially interesting." Handkerchiefs, jewelry, games, and toys—each had to be examined for the qualities that made it a welcome and much appreciated gift, and this had to be expressed in words not overly fulsome, but with a recognition of the care the giver had taken in choosing it.

What with writing notes, reading new books, and playing new games, as well as exchanging visits with friends to see their gifts, the Christmas holidays sped by, climaxing in New Year's Day, which followed a set routine: Mass in the morning, and then we usually went to a buffet hosted by friends of our parents, a gathering that gave the men a group of football fans to listen to the bowl games with, and the women fellow bridge players with whom to spend the afternoon. We children, left to ourselves, played outside if the weather permitted, inside if not.

Though other menu items could be left to the hostess's choice, no New Year's Day table would be complete without the traditional greens for money and black-eyed peas for luck. Some people served mustard or turnip greens, cooked down with salted pork and accompanied by a bottle of pepper vinegar, a seasoning guests could apply to their own taste. Some served cabbage, simmered down with white onions and bits of ham or creamed and baked with cheese on top. Ham, cornbread muffins or sticks, cauliflower au gratin, and a yam casserole usually appeared on the menu, not only because they were universal favorites, but because they could be kept warm for hours, accommodating the comings and goings of guests.

Desserts would be equally manageable. A New Year's Day buffet provided the perfect opportunity to finish off Christmas goodies, and so a sideboard would be covered with plates holding date nut and pound cake, along with an array of pralines, Divinity fudge, and one or more versions of chocolate fudge, as well as whiskey balls, which, since they were not cooked, were forbidden to children. And, of course, the ubiquitous French drip coffee, sometimes with a brandy bottle nearby for those who wanted it.

Five football bowl games—the Rose (the oldest), the Sugar, the Cotton, the Sun, and the Orange—were played on January 1, as they had been since their inception, and fans could follow the games on radio. Conveniently enough, only two bowls, the Sugar and the Cotton, were in the same time zone, Central Standard. The Orange Bowl was in Eastern Standard Time, the Sun Bowl in Mountain Time, and the Rose Bowl in Pacific Time. A very long afternoon and evening of football, but, with good food and good drink available, the men around the radios managed to stay the course.

With January comes what we call the "monsoon" season in Louisiana. There are weeks when the skies are never any shade but gray, and rain pours and pours and pours until even the most stoic allow themselves to complain. Still, bad weather outside makes being inside even nicer, and the ladies of Lafayette brightened the calendar with a succession of afternoon teas, beginning in early January, usually right after Twelfth Night, which comes on

January 6, and lasting until Ash Wednesday, which is always forty-six days before Easter and the beginning of Lent.

Twelfth Night, which marks the three kings' arrival in Bethlehem, is the first event of Mardi Gras. On the morning of Twelfth Night, flags of former royalty waved from flagstaffs, with distinctive symbols indicating over which ball they reigned. That evening, Twelfth Night parties officially open the Mardi Gras season, with a ball in New Orleans as well as events ranging from formal dinners to informal neighborhood gatherings everywhere Mardi Gras is celebrated.

The traditional king cake, an oval-shaped pastry more like a bread than a cake, is always served at these events. These confections are now enjoyed anywhere a UPS or mail truck can get, carrying at least one Mardi Gras custom to those who have never witnessed the event themselves. The cake is decorated with purple, gold, and green sugars. King Rex, whose parade is on Mardi Gras day in New Orleans, chose these colors in 1872, and in 1892, the theme of the Rex parade, Symbolism of Colors, gave them the meaning they still have. Purple is for justice, green for faith, and gold for power. The tiny baby hidden in the cake is said to bestow luck on the person who finds it and also the responsibility of hosting the Twelfth Night party the following year. King cakes sold by bakeries now either leave the baby out altogether or give it to the buyer to insert (or not).

Many of the teas held in Lafayette during Mardi Gras season honored the maids who would be in the Krewe of Gabriel court, Lafayette's oldest carnival organization, founded in 1939. This krewe, like those in New Orleans, holds a parade on Mardi Gras day, with the queen and her court on a reviewing stand. As in New Orleans, the king's float stops in front of the court and a champagne toast is made. The ball that evening presents the queen and court as they make their debut into formal society. In earlier times, a debut meant that a young lady could now be courted. By the time I made my debut, the message had changed. The debut marked the end of a young woman's social training and meant that she could now be invited anywhere without a mother or aunt to guide her and be counted on to be a good guest.

Although the queen's identity is not known until the day invitations to the queen's luncheon arrive, the members of the court are announced early enough for a season of luncheons and teas leading to the main event. Those winter teas form some of my loveliest memories of growing up in Lafayette. They provided my friends and me opportunities to observe how ladies conduct themselves as both hostesses and guests and to learn valuable lessons that could apply to any meetings of friends.

Afternoon teas, at which my friends and I served as tea girls, were the perfect places to learn these lessons. We wore our prettiest dresses, usually made of taffeta or velveteen, and carried silver trays laden with tiny sandwiches and cakes through rooms crowded with women wearing afternoon costumes complete with small-brimmed hats. (Large brims are not appropriate in crowded rooms, although at every tea at least one woman showed her independence by wearing a broad-brimmed "picture" hat, so called because the brim framed the face.)

We spoke only when spoken to. These exchanges would begin with a guest greeting us, our low-voiced, "Good afternoon," in reply. If we knew the lady, we would address her by her surname, though I doubt I was the only one who, fearing her memory would betray her, used names only when I was absolutely positive I had the right one.

Someone might compliment our dress, in which case, only "Thank you," was required. I have no idea when girls and women began responding to a compliment on an outfit by saying, "This old thing. I've had it for years," continuing with a history of the costume. When anyone says this, I suggest we start from the top, adding that when one's outfit is complimented a simple "Thank you," is all that is necessary.

We also had the responsibility of letting the kitchen staff know when trays on the table needed refilling, or when the punch bowl, teapot, or sherry decanter ran low. As well, the hostess asked us to look out for tea napkins discarded around the reception rooms and to discreetly pick them up and take them to the kitchen. Very much the size of ladies' handkerchiefs, some inadvertently found their way into guests' purses, and so, having us retrieve as many as possible saved the expense and trouble of replacing those lost.

Lafayette had no caterers then. It did have a marvelous bakery, called Keller's, established by a family from Alsace who arrived in Louisiana in the 1760s and in Abbeville in 1895, where they opened a bakery, moving the operation to Lafayette in 1929. Still in operation, Keller's recipes are the same ones used more than ninety years ago, and if I want to have instant memories of my childhood, all I have to do is visit Keller's and buy their butter flake or cinnamon rolls, an éclair, a petit four, or any of the other breads, cakes, pastries, and cookies that have made them deservedly famous.

Hostesses would order petit fours from Keller's, and perhaps sand tarts as well, though these are simple to make. Most of the refreshments, however, came from their own kitchens and those of friends. The stacks of tins with cheese straws, roasted pecans, lemon squares, and other goodies tempted the male members of the household to sample them. Only the knowledge that while hell hath no fury like that of a woman scorned, earth hath no fury like that of a hostess who finds her stores decimated held them back.

When I think of those teas, I am assailed by sensual memories, beginning with the aroma produced by pecan logs burning, French perfumes, the scent of hot wax, and, as I drew closer to the table, the smell of crabmeat from a chafing dish. Not of flowers, because camellias grown in hostesses' own yards provided more than enough to fill epergnes, to tuck into the open-work gilt frames of mirrors, to float in cut-crystal dishes, or, when ancient bushes produced blooms on long stems, to put in silver vases.

I remember, too, the way highly polished silver looks with firelight playing off it, the delicate designs on porcelain teacups, the intricate surface of cut-glass punch cups, and the shifting colors as ladies moved in and out of my sight, leaving images of deep burgundy or hunter green silk crepe dresses or a swirling skirt of silk brocade in taupe or gray or teal. And jewelry, gold or silver set with semi-precious stones, usually brooches and bracelets and earrings because necklines then carried much of a dress's style and necklaces weren't needed. Tiny purses large enough only for a compact, lipstick, handkerchief, and comb. Car keys were left in coat pockets along with gloves and scarves. Some of the guests would linger, to be joined by husbands coming for a drink accompanied by the remaining sandwiches, cheese straws, and roasted pecans.

Mardi Gras parades were canceled during World War II, but the balls went on. As I was far too young to attend a ball, Mardi Gras, for me, came and went without much more importance than an ordinary day.

This was not true of Ash Wednesday. My first Lent in Lafayette, as Ash Wednesday approached, I heard classmates talking about what they would give up. Although I went to Saturday catechism classes in Baton Rouge, until I moved to Lafayette I had never been immersed in the daily practice of my faith as these girls were. I soon learned that Lent offered opportunities for two kinds of penance: giving up favorite foods and pastimes and performing works of mercy.

Since, at our age, our sins were hardly severe enough to require penance other than the usual one Our Father and three Hail Mary's prescribed by a priest after hearing our bland confessions, the nuns suggested that we offer up whatever grace we earned from giving up Cokes and chocolate and visiting the shut-in and elderly, for the poor souls in Purgatory. This gave impetus to our Lenten observances and helped us persevere until noon on Holy Saturday, when, at least in Acadiana, Lent came to an end.

The nuns helpfully reviewed the Corporal and Spiritual Works of Mercy, recommending we place a bookmark on the pages detailing them so we could refresh our memories if needed. I read them over, trying to decide which I might be able to perform.

Of the Corporal Works of Mercy, feeding the hungry, giving drink to the thirsty, and visiting the sick seemed the most likely; I couldn't imagine circumstances in which I could clothe the naked, shelter the homeless—unless stray animals counted— ransom captives, or bury the dead. The nuns stressed that the first three spiritual works of mercy—to instruct the ignorant, counsel the doubtful, and admonish sinners—did not apply to those lacking the proper tact, knowledge, and training to do so. However, anyone could bear wrongs patiently, forgive offenses willingly, comfort the afflicted, and pray for the living and the dead. Naturally, girls our age had many occasions to bear wrongs patiently and forgive offenses willingly, though these were usually pointed out to us by parents or well-meaning older siblings.

I had already decided, like most of my friends, to give up movies and all sweets for Lent, including Keller's cinnamon rolls. As for works of mercy, I felt that normal kindnesses, like fixing a sandwich for my brother or getting my father a glass of water, hardly constituted an act of grace, and so I relied on praying for the living and the dead.

Then, at a Friday night gathering, Gail suggested we all announce a wrong we had been bearing patiently, allowing us to forgive willingly the person who caused it. That we remained friends after this exercise was, Gail said, a sign that we had indeed been given grace.

As it happened, one of the charitable endeavors we had been engaged in all year lent itself to both kinds of penance. This was ransoming pagan babies through monetary donations, which would be larger now that we no longer spent money on the movies and treats we'd given up. Our teacher pointed this out to us on Ash Wednesday, after each of us had announced what we planned to do for Lent. "You will be performing both a corporal and spiritual work of mercy," Sister Dorothy said. "Because the missionaries feed and clothe the babies as well as saving their souls."

Impressed by the effect my self-imposed denial would have, I talked about the project at dinner that day. I waited for a natural opening for my topic to appear. When none did, I took advantage of a small break in the conversation to announce, "My class is ransoming pagan babies."

"How do you ransom a pagan baby?" André asked. His eyes lit up, and I knew he was thinking of the stories about pirates we read and then acted out on summer afternoons.

"We put money in a box and when there's five dollars in it, we get to choose a baby and give it a name."

My mother, schooled at Sacred Heart Convent in New Orleans, took nuns in her stride. The nuns in the Mt. Carmel Order were well educated and were fine teachers, but they didn't come from families of the same social status as did those of Sacred Heart. My mother, therefore, did not hold them to behavioral standards that might judge ransoming pagan babies as not quite the thing. "Well, I imagine the babies are symbolic, don't you?"

"We have pictures of the ones we ransomed already."

"Really?"

"Three girl babies who live in the Belgian Congo, and we named all of them Dorothy."

"I wonder how their parents feel about that. Unless they're baptized, too? But no—if they were, their babies wouldn't need to be saved." She shook her head in a way that reminded me of her response to things beyond the code of living she understood. "Well, I suppose they don't really use the name." I could see her relegate these distant babies to an unused corner of her mind.

"Poor little bastards," my father said. He caught mother's quick glance. "Sorry." He looked at me. "But seriously, isn't it rather sad? Little babies depending on schoolgirls' nickels to give them a better life, when all the time their people are exploited and robbed." I could read the look on my father's face, too. He wore the same look when he listened to the war news or read accounts of refugees fleeing their homes. He could not generalize horror. He could not depersonalize war. He carried the fate of individual victims in his heart.

The glow had gone out of ransoming pagan babies, not because of my parents' reaction, but because when I dropped my donation, augmented as expected by the smaller drain on my allowance, into the box, I felt not charitable but resentful that I wasn't free to choose other charities like the poor box in the church vestibule or the Red Cross containers in drug and grocery stores.

Even more than that, I suspected that Sister Dorothy had a motive other than saving pagan souls. Though there was no formal prize, still, at the end of the year in the final assembly, the class ransoming the most babies would be announced and congratulated. And, of course, the teacher who led the effort would bask in reflected praise. If this were true, Sister Dorothy was not the last person I would meet whose charitable efforts had a personal element as well. And though I have always been much happier working with a group who honestly believe in the cause they support, still, over the years I learned not to look a gift horse in the mouth, especially when it comes in the form of a large, tax-deductible check.

Another nun, Sister Veronica, the oldest in the convent, gave Adele and me an opportunity to do a unique work of mercy, one that combined comforting the afflicted with discovering a saint. Sister Veronica taught fourth grade, but in such a small school, she could easily find students with the talents she needed. One afternoon, Adele and I were summoned to her classroom and given a most unusual task. She wanted us to visit the LeBlancs, a family whose fifth-grade daughter, Annette, had recently died of pneumonia, and write up her life for submission to *Young Catholic Messenger*, which published a feature on deceased children who were saints in each issue. Not in the canonical sense, she hurried to explain, but in the sense that their lives had been so good, and so pure, that, having no need to live longer to earn their crown, they had been called home to heaven.

Annette's older sister would join our class the next year, held back to repeat seventh grade. We knew her—a tall, lanky blond with freckles and athletic ability that probably accounted for her poor grades, because she would much rather be on the basketball court or softball field than inside studying.

I don't know if Adele told her mother the whole story. I did not. I merely said that Adele and I had been asked to write an article about a schoolmate and that we would ride our bikes to the LeBlancs' to keep a Saturday morning appointment.

With the other girls in my class, I had been to the funeral home to say a rosary for Annette the afternoon before the Requiem Mass. I may have seen a dead person, I don't remember, but certainly I had never seen a dead child. Annette looked as pale as the white satin pillow behind her head. She wore an elaborately embroidered batiste dress and held a rosary in her hands, and I wondered if it would be buried with her. Then, I said a quick prayer and turned away before I got sick.

That image had been at the back of my mind ever since Sister Veronica made her request. When Mrs. LeBlanc opened the door and invited us in, I saw a dark hall stretching behind her, and if Adele hadn't been with me, I'm sure I would have cut and run.

We followed Mrs. LeBlanc into the living room and accepted her offer of Cokes. "We gave them up," I reminded Adele when Mrs. LeBlanc left the room.

"I know," Adele said. "But we have to be polite." Manners over morals—I had neither the time nor desire to think that one through, so accepted my Coke, sipping it slowly while Mrs. LeBlanc waited for us to begin.

Sister Veronica had made a list of questions for us. Adele and I'd agreed to take alternate ones, and having lost a toss of the coin, I began. "Did Annette show early signs of being a spiritual child?" I tried to think of an example, but nothing came to mind.

"Maybe a devotion to a special saint?" Adele prompted.

"Well, there's a statue of the Blessed Virgin in the rose garden," Mrs. LeBlanc said. "She used to play out there a lot."

"What about books? Stories about the lives of the saints? Like—oh, Joan of Arc," I suggested.

"Annette never was much of a reader."

We went through the list of questions, not daring to look at each other as it became more and more apparent that whatever Annette might have been, she was no saint. She wasn't bad, only a perfectly normal child who considered going to Mass, Novenas, and other services interruptions to be put up with, and daily prayers part of adult expectations like washing your hands and brushing your teeth.

Not that Mrs. LeBlanc put it this way. We got our information from what she didn't say, and the only thing that saved us from feeling absolutely awful about being there was that we could see Mrs. LeBlanc had no real interest in the interview or its purpose, if she even knew what it was. She had allowed us to talk with her only because a nun had asked it. Like so many French Catholics at the time, she considered nuns, brothers, and priests to be true emissaries of God, and it would never have occurred to her to refuse a request.

When we left, she pressed quarters into our hands. "Stop at Walgreens and get an ice cream soda. Chocolate was always Annette's favorite." Then, and only then, did we see the tears she had held back.

"I don't know about you," Adele said as we walked down the steps. "But I'm not only *not* going to put this quarter in the pagan babies' box, I'm going to Walgreens for a chocolate ice cream soda."

In that moment, I think we had a very dim intimation of what war correspondents feel coming off a tough story. We gave the article our mutual best, trying to convey a hidden spirituality in our subject's life without telling outright lies. The result seemed thin and unsatisfactory, but Sister Veronica thought otherwise and sent it off. A few weeks later she told us *Young Catholic Messenger* had written her that although Annette LeBlanc seemed to be a child of innocence and purity, and surely gazed down on her loving family from heaven, still, her story did not quite measure up, and they, with regret, would not be using it.

"Well," said Adele after we heard this news, "at least she's up in heaven, which is more than that stupid editor can say."

My first rejection, drawing a line in the sand on one side of which stand editors who don't recognize brilliant writing when they see it, and on the other, writers who, like doting parents, can rarely admit that their child, no matter how loved, has flaws.

Recipes for Debutante Teas and Lent

LAFAYETTE TEA PUNCH

2 quarts strong, hot tea
3 lb. sugar
1 dozen oranges, juiced
4 dozen lemons, juiced
2 (no. 2) cans pineapple juice
12 quarts ginger ale

Dissolve sugar in hot tea, add juices. Chill. Add chilled ginger ale to this base just before serving.

Yield: 75 punch cup servings.

Note: You may use a ring mold to make an ice ring with maraschino cherries and small chunks of pineapple frozen into it. Do this by layers so that the fruit won't all sink to the bottom. Many people make the ring mold with the punch base rather than water, so when it melts, it doesn't dilute the punch.

CHAMPAGNE PUNCH

2 quarts pineapple juice
4 quarts lemon juice
3 quarts orange juice
5 lb. sugar
14 fifths champagne
1½ quarts of sparkling water to every gallon of mix

Yield: 100 punch cup servings.

Note: Sauterne may be substituted for champagne.

HOT CRABMEAT DIP

1 large pkg. Philadelphia cream cheese
1 stick butter
1 lb. white crabmeat, picked over for shells
1 small finely chopped onion
Dash Tabasco sauce
Dash garlic

Melt cream cheese and butter in a double boiler; add crabmeat and seasonings. Serve in a chafing dish with small patty shells. (Fills a quart-size chafing dish.)

CUCUMBER SPREAD FOR SANDWICHES

2 medium size cucumbers
1 large pkg. cream cheese
3–4 drops Tabasco sauce
¼ teaspoon salt

Chop cucumbers into fine pieces—do not use blender. Cream into cheese with remaining ingredients. Use on thin wheat bread or on rye bread rounds.
Yield: 2 cups, enough for 24 open-face sandwiches, each on half a slice of crustless bread.

SHRIMP SANDWICHES

2 4½ ounce cans shrimp, rinsed and drained
1 rib celery, chopped fine
1 teaspoon minced green onion flakes
1 teaspoon lemon juice
¾ cup mayonnaise

Chop the shrimp very finely. Add celery, onion flakes, and lemon juice. Mix in well and blend in mayonnaise. Spread evenly on crustless slices of thin white bread. Cut into fours.
Yield: 60 sandwiches.
Note: You may use fresh or frozen shrimp, but canned shrimp, so long as it is well rinsed, serves equally well. I wouldn't use it in any other recipe, but here, it works.

SAND TARTS

1 cup soft butter
5 tablespoons sugar
1 tablespoon vanilla
2 ¾ cups flour, sifted
½ cup chopped nuts
Pinch of salt

Cream butter and sugar together. Add vanilla, flour, nuts, and salt. This will be rather dry, but you just work it with your fingers until blended. Roll into small crescents or balls and bake in a preheated 350° oven for 15–20 minutes, but check to make sure they are not getting too brown. Roll in powdered sugar and cool.
Yield: 3 to 4 dozen, depending on size.

LEMON BARS

Bottom layer:
1 cup flour
½ cup butter
2 tablespoons sugar

Top layer:
1 cup sugar
5 tablespoons flour
½ teaspoon baking powder
1 eggs
3 tablespoons lemon juice

Frosting:
1½ cups sifted powdered sugar
½ stick butter
2–3 teaspoons lemon juice

Mix bottom layer ingredients and press into a 9 x 9 pan, then bake in a preheated 350° oven for 15 minutes.
For the top layer, sift sugar, flour, and baking powder. Beat eggs with lemon juice. Mix with dry ingredients and pour over crust. Bake 25 minutes.
Mix frosting ingredients, using lemon juice sufficient to make a spreading consistency. Let the frosting set, then cut into 1-inch squares or larger if desired.
Yield: 81 squares.

Lenten Fare

BAKED MACARONI AND CHEESE

1 package (8 ounces) elbow macaroni
3 tablespoons butter or margarine
2 tablespoons flour
1 teaspoon salt
Few grains black pepper
2 cups milk
½ lb. sharp Cheddar cheese, grated
1 tablespoon grated onion
1½ teaspoons dry mustard
1 teaspoon Worcestershire sauce
½ cup buttered crumbs

Cook macaroni in boiling, salted water until tender; drain; rinse with hot water. Melt butter/margarine, blend in flour, salt, and pepper. Add milk slowly, stirring over low heat until smooth and thickened. Add cheese, onion, mustard, and Worcestershire sauce, stir over low heat until cheese melts. Add macaroni and stir well. Pour into a greased casserole, top with buttered crumbs. Bake in a preheated 375° oven about 25 minutes or until browned.
Yield: 6 to 8 servings.

TRUE SPANISH OMELET

2 medium-sized raw potatoes, peeled and diced
⅓ cup olive oil
4 eggs, beaten
Salt and pepper to taste

Cook potatoes in oil, turning often until tender but not brown. Remove from the oil and drain on absorbent paper; cool to room temperature. Drain any surplus oil from skillet, leaving just a film. Reheat skillet. Combine beaten eggs, salt, pepper, and potatoes. Pour into the hot skillet, lifting the edges frequently until the omelet is browned on the bottom. Turn and brown the other side.
Yield: 4 servings.

SCALLOPED OYSTERS

2 dozen oysters
Milk
½ teaspoon Worcestershire sauce
¼ teaspoon salt
⅛ teaspoon black pepper
½ cup melted butter or margarine
2 ½ cups coarse soda-type of cracker crumbs
1 tablespoon butter or margarine

Drain and measure liquid from oysters; add enough milk to measure 1 cup liquid; reserve. Stir Worcestershire sauce, salt, and pepper into melted butter/margarine. Arrange alternate layers of half the cracker crumbs, oysters, and seasoned melted butter/margarine in shallow baking dish. Repeat, ending with crumbs. Pour oyster/milk mixture over all just before baking. Dot with remaining butter or margarine. Bake in a preheated 350° oven for 30 minutes or until top is golden brown.

Yield: 4 servings.

Note: If you have never eaten scalloped oysters, I recommend them for an easy and delicious supper or lunch, accompanied by a green salad and Muscadet wine, often called "oyster wine" because it is one of the few that truly complements oysters' delicate taste.

Spinach is a good vegetable to serve with oysters, but avoid acidic ones.

Lagniappe

OYSTER STEW

1 quart oysters
¼ cup butter or margarine
1 teaspoon paprika
1 teaspoon Worcestershire sauce
1½ teaspoons salt
Few grains white pepper
1½ quarts milk

Pick over oysters, removing bits of shell; strain oyster liquid. Melt butter or margarine in deep, heavy saucepan. Add paprika, Worcestershire sauce, salt, and white pepper; stir until smooth. Add oysters and oyster liquor. Cook over low heat a few moments until edges of oysters curl. Add milk. Heat slowly over low heat just to scalding point. *Do not boil.* Serve at once with crisp French bread to get up the last delicious drop.

Yield: 6 servings.

Note: Because the Lenten months all have an "R" in them, oysters are in season and so appear often on Lenten tables.

CHAPTER EIGHT

Easter Sunday fell on April 1 in 1945, and Gail invited me to attend the Dugal family barbecue in Girard Park. After attending Mass and hunting for dyed eggs with Kathryn and André, I went with Gail's family to the park.

I've no idea how many people were there, but it must have been close to fifty. Some of the men had dug pits on Holy Saturday and built fires in them. The wood turned into coals that burned all night, roasting the kid, lamb, pig, and calf turning on metal spits, and all night, the men basted the meat with the Dugals' special sauce. There were several shifts doing the basting so that no one would have to stay up all night.

Squab, chicken halves, pork chops, and T-bone chops cooked on grills set over bricks while the ladies of the clan filled several long tables with their offerings: potato salad, cabbage slaw, dirty rice, marinated cucumbers, rolls of various kinds, pies in every imaginable flavor, as well as layer cakes, sheet cakes, and pound cakes. Ice-filled tubs held beer for the grown-ups and soft drinks for the children.

The ladies urged me to sample every dish, but Gail said we didn't want to take more food than we could eat and would come back for seconds. The men were easier to please. They asked what we wanted and served it to us. I remember choosing a T-bone chop because meat was still rationed at that time, though given the amount being roasted, you wouldn't think so.

The boys in the ten to thirteen age range had brought their dyed eggs with them so they could engage in an old custom in Acadiana, egg-knocking. Two players knock their hard-boiled eggs together, and the egg that cracks first goes to the winner.

One of Gail's cousins, a Dugal from the Erath branch, had a winning streak that made one of his uncles suspicious. "Let me see that egg, James," he said. Reluctantly, James handed it over. "Just as I thought. It's a duck egg. No wonder you're winning." Whereupon James not only had to return his ill-gotten eggs, but also go help the ladies clean up.

Charles Dixon "Dick" Baldridge Jr.

The next day, the news reported the beginning of the battle for Okinawa, launched on April 1. The casualty toll ranked as one of the worst in the war. More than 12,500 American soldiers and more than 110,000 Japanese soldiers died. Almost one-fourth of the civilian population died, many by suicide.

Though we eventually won that battle, the horrific number of casualties resulted in a change of military strategy. It was clear that to defeat the Japanese, our military would have to go island to island, searching out pockets of resistance. Later, when it was learned that Japanese soldiers in isolated Pacific Islands continued fighting into the 1970s, this was proved true.

Thus, the decision was made to use a new and terrifying weapon, the atomic bomb. In April, US civilians knew nothing about that, only that the Nazi forces lost strength daily and that since February, B-29s, long-range bombers with the fuel capacity to fly 5,830 miles from the Marianas to the Japanese mainland and back again, conducted an air campaign intended to force a Japanese surrender.

My second husband served as a bombardier in XXI Bomber Command, based in Guam. Nine years older than I, in 1945 he was twenty-one years old—the pilot, at age twenty-five, was the "old man" of the group. In 1994, Dick and I went to a reunion of his squadron at the US Air Force Academy in Colorado Springs. A monument with the names of deceased squadron members would be dedicated in one of those military ceremonies that manage to be moving, solemn, and celebratory all at once.

Four out of ten crew members, accompanied by their wives, came to the reunion. Dick and I had a suite, and one evening we ordered sandwiches and chips and set up a bar so the men could reminisce. As is usual with war veterans, we heard only stories with a laugh at the end, like the one about the time a five-hundred-pound bomb got stuck in the bomb bay. The pilot brought the B-29 down to a lower altitude, and then crew members held the radio man by his legs over the open bomb bay while he pushed the bomb loose to fall into the ocean below.

"We picked him because he was the smallest," Dick said.

"You picked me because I was the only non-officer on board," Sam retorted.

Dick's crew set a record for the longest bombing run, twenty-eight hours, which was surpassed only when the Black Hawks flew to Kosovo. He flew twenty-eight missions in all, and though he said planes bombing Japan had an easier time of it than those bombing Germany—because the German planes and pilots were superior to those of the Japanese—a large number of B-29s did get shot down by antiaircraft guns and Japanese fighters. On May 25, 1945, twenty-six B-29s were lost, totaling 5.5 percent of the 464 dispatched.

Our own fighters could escort them only so far, lacking the fuel capacity to go the whole way. The B-29s relied on their own armament, twelve .50 mm machine guns and one .20 mm. cannon. The bombardier sat in a bubble under the plane, an easy target for a Japanese Zero. As the plane approached the target, the bombardier took over the navigation, making sure they were in bombing range of the target before they dropped the bombs.

I never asked Dick about his war experiences unless he brought them up. Causing death and destruction you can't see might seem to be impersonal, but knowing Dick, I know that to him it wasn't. One evening, when we were watching a movie about World War II, he took my hand. "We knew we were killing civilians, too." I still feel honored that he told me that.

I was putting clean socks in his sock drawer one day when I saw a box with four medals in it. One of them was the Distinguished Flying Cross, the highest medal except the Medal of Honor a military person can earn. I had it and the other three framed, and Emile, who had worked for me since 1988 and now worked for us, asked Dick where he'd like to hang them.

Dick said, "It's only four medals."

To this, Emile answered, "That's four more than most people I know have."

On the afternoon of April 12, 1945, Aunt Roberta hosted an informal tea, meaning afternoon instead of tea dresses and a guest list comprised of family and intimate friends. The news that President Franklin Delano Roosevelt had died at Warm Springs, Georgia, came not as a shock, since he had been in increasingly poor health for a very long time, but as more proof that the war took its toll on many beyond those on the front lines.

Never in robust health, Roosevelt's responsibilities would have fatigued a much younger man. Fortunately for the country, Harry S. Truman had much better health and stamina that had not been tested by the endless crises and crucial decisions that ended at the president's desk—though at sixty-one, he was only two years younger than his predecessor. His folksy and pragmatic style could hardly have contrasted more with Roosevelt's patrician persona, and his wife, Bess—quiet, desiring privacy, and performing only those social duties her husband's office required—was distinctly different from Eleanor Roosevelt, whose interest in the plight of those reduced to poverty in the Depression had led to activism that continued throughout her life.

Newsreels showed the train carrying Roosevelt from Warm Springs to Washington and the horse-drawn casket being driven through the streets, as well as the last train journey home to Hyde Park. Joseph Stalin allowed Russian newspapers to carry the story of Roosevelt's death on the front page, which was usually reserved only for national news. Winston Churchill broke down as he gave the news to the British House of Commons, and a young soldier cried out, "But the war's nearly over!"

The war in Europe was, indeed, nearly over. On April 30th, 1945, Adolf Hitler, besieged by Russian troops flooding into Berlin, first married his longtime mistress, Eva Braun, and then, after making farewells to the staff in the bunker with them, retired to his study, where they committed suicide, Eva by taking cyanide, Hitler by shooting himself. He caused millions of Jews and other people to die in concentration camps and sent armies of young men to their deaths, though I doubt that when he pointed a pistol at his head, he thought of any of them. Rather, his last thoughts were probably about how close he had come to ruling Europe and the British Isles.

I have always believed we owe thanks for this failure to the courageous British citizens and military who held on until the United States finally came in. The first time I visited London, I thanked everyone I met who seemed to be of age to have been alive during the war for Britain's tenacity, because without it, Hitler would have prevailed.

Honoring the president's death, flags flew at half-staff until May 12. On May 8, German troops on the Channel Islands surrendered, following the surrender on Europe's mainland a few days earlier. I heard the news from Gail, who bicycled across the SLI campus to ask me to go with her to Our Lady of Wisdom Chapel, which served the Catholic students, and thank God for prayers answered.

Church bells rang all over Lafayette, and, I'm sure, all over the country, just as they had in late August 1944, when General Charles de Gaulle led the march into Paris, followed by the US Second Armored Division and the Fourth Infantry Division. A woman who later moved to Lake Charles, where she and my mother became close friends, had fought in the French Underground throughout the war, and she told us what Paris was like on that glorious morning.

"The first sign that the longed-for day had arrived came from church bells," Denise said. "For the first time since Paris fell, they rang all over the city, bringing people out on balconies, flooding the streets—and all over the city, hidden radios were taken out and turned up full volume, so that no matter where you went, you could hear the 'Marseillaise.'" I knew that anthem perhaps better than most of my classmates because Hazel Hearin used to ask my father to sing it at the annual Christmas party after caroling. He always obliged, standing next to the piano while Sally accompanied him, singing the rousing words in French to the delight of all present.

Looking back, I'm grateful we didn't have television and instant internet streaming. We may have heard news, but we never saw images of the events described. Our parents read *Life* and *Time*, but we didn't, and so, as dramatic and often tragic events dominated the last spring and summer of the war, for children my age, life went on in its usual seasonal path.

One of the first signs of spring in Lafayette came from the rumbling of wagon wheels and the high, melodic call of, "Strawberries—fresh strawberries. Bush Beans—cauliflower—spinach and sweet corn." Housewives along the street left whatever they were doing to go outside and watch the slow progress of the vegetable man from house to house, welcoming the return of spring vegetables to the table.

The vegetable man must have had another name, but I never knew it. Unlike his cohorts in New Orleans, who obtained their produce from the stalls at the French Market, our vegetable man grew his own, rotating his crops throughout the year, making use of every inch of his patch of earth. Later, he would hawk blackberries and dewberries and figs, as well as tomatoes and cucumbers, okra and squash. But no later appearance could compete with the first one. Menus went under instant revision, with bush beans seasoned with onions and ham or bacon accompanying sweet corn immersed in boiling water just long enough to make each kernel tender.

Now, when I can buy almost any fruit or vegetable all year-round, I feel that, despite the convenience, something essential has been lost. Living with the seasons in a natural rhythm cannot be replicated in climate-controlled buildings and hothouse farming. I pick up a microwave-ready packet of organic string beans or carrots or green peas, and though usually I'm perfectly happy to trade convenience for connection, still there are many times when I buy fresh vegetables so I can snap or string the beans myself, pare and slice the carrots, and pop the peas from their spring green cases. When cutting open a package of frozen chopped seasonings, I smile when I think of the horror with which a Cajun lady would greet such an abomination.

When asked for a recipe, the phrase, "*Mais, chère*, it all depends," occurs frequently.

"How much chopped onion?"

"*Mais, chère*, it all depends how fresh the onion is."

The fresher the onion, the more juice, and chopping it yourself was the only way you could know that.

"How much flour should I use in the roux?"

"*Mais, chère*, it all depends on the flour. Flour may look alike, but it all depends on how much rain the wheat got. So, you need to make a test, *chère*. You need to put a tablespoon of flour in a cup and then add water until it makes a paste. Then, you know." Many times when making pastry, I've been grateful for this lesson. Instead of using the amount of ice water the recipe calls for, I test the flour ahead of time, adding or subtracting liquid depending on the results.

Although the vegetables the vegetable man brought to our door from early spring well into autumn were much fresher than any purchased in a grocery store, still, people who had their own gardens could serve corn just picked from the stalk, tomatoes still warm from the sun, snap beans so tender they hardly needed to be cooked.

That summer my good friend Diane Lee and I taught catechism to children in Cade, a tiny community between Lafayette and New Iberia. I had just finished sixth grade, Diane fifth. Sister Veronica, perhaps thinking we would be more successful instructing the ignorant than Adele and I had been trying to create a saint, had chosen us for this spiritual duty—a duty that, although it involved our mothers taking turns driving us to and fro each day for a week, neither of us thought of refusing.

When we asked Sister Veronica if we should bring our lunches, she said no, we would dine with the priest in the rectory. This added an entirely new dimension to the venture. In high school, priests would teach us religion. But in elementary school, we only saw priests on the altar at Mass or in the pulpit, delivering sermons designed for young ears.

I did know Father McGlynn, a great friend of my parents. He was a White Father, which is a missionary order. He served as pastor at a Catholic church in an African American neighborhood, an assignment given him because, as he aged, the order felt he should have the comforts and conveniences not available in their missions in the third world. Single-malt Scotch and Havana cigars were among Father McGlynn's favorite comforts. He used to arrive at our home for dinner about once a month, bearing a fifth of Scotch and a fresh box of cigars, as well as his pinochle cards. After dinner, we would leave the men to their evening, an evening that usually stretched into the wee hours, ending only when the bottle was empty and most of the cigars smoked.

Father McGlynn was also a golfer. He had a marble hearth in his rectory study chipped from countless use as a putting green. My father and other friends called it the "Golfer's Altar," and I imagine Scotch and cigars found their way into the celebrations there. My father became a golfer under Father McGlynn's tutelage, and later, when he became an avid devotee of the game, my mother told Father McGlynn that it seemed ironic that the same priest who married them was now breaking up their union.

Armed with this knowledge, that priests were human beings just like anyone else, I told Diane that having dinner with the priest was nothing to worry about. If he were anywhere near as nice as Father McGlynn, we might even enjoy ourselves.

From the first words that came from the Cade priest's mouth, we knew we were in trouble. Father McGlynn spoke English with a thick Irish brogue, which only made everything he said more charming. Father Picou spoke English with a thick Cajun accent, which may be charming under some circumstances, but not if you are a schoolgirl trying to understand what he wants you to do. Fortunately, though Sister Veronica venerated priests as channels of sacramental grace, she had no illusions about their competence in everything else. Thus, she had gone over every lesson in the catechism books we would use, teaching us how to teach so that our students would understand.

"Simplicity is key," she said. When we met our class, we understood why she said that so often.

These children had never been away from Cade. If that seems astonishing, let me remind you that even if the war hadn't rationed gasoline, Cajun families living that far off the beaten path rarely went anywhere. After the Great Depression, they didn't trust banks, and even when the oil boom hit Acadiana in the mid-1950s, Cajuns who were well paid for mineral leases on their land would stuff thousands of dollars under their mattresses rather than put it in a bank.

The children went to school only when they weren't needed to help their fathers during trapping season or with planting and harvesting crops. Most of the houses had no electricity or indoor plumbing. Once we turned off Highway 90 onto the gravel road to Cade, we could have been in Oz.

When I got to know the essence of the Cajun people, I understood that our students' amiable response to what we asked of them came from the innate good manners abundant in that culture. Everyone is welcome until they do something that changes that; everyone's peculiarities are accepted unless they cause harm. To sit inside with electric fans creating a small breeze, to be given a midmorning treat of lemonade and vanilla wafers, were new and welcome experiences, and the children knew our presence was responsible.

With the first morning behind us, Diane and I walked over to the rectory and knocked at the screen door. Father Picou bade us come in and pointed out the direction to the bathroom. When we emerged, hair smoothed and faces and hands washed, he beckoned us to come to the table, set with three places, its center occupied by bowl after bowl of food. Then we heard a door bang and saw the housekeeper enter the kitchen from the back porch, bearing half a dozen stalks of corn, which she quickly shucked and dropped into a large pot from which steam rose.

Father Picou bent his head and said grace, and at the moment we echoed his "Amen," the housekeeper came in from the kitchen, six ears of corn on a platter. Every day that week, we feasted on vegetables that had been picked that morning, and every day that week we ate fresh corn, knowing that rarely in our lives would we again know what "fresh-picked" corn really tastes like.

Although our vegetable man provided us with seasonal vegetables from spring into fall, as well as fruits such as strawberries brought in from Hammond and Ponchatoula, still Louisiana's strawberry capitals, and peaches shipped down from Ruston, we picked some of the favorites ourselves, not always because we wanted to, but because of necessity.

Figs headed the list of summer fruits. When I was growing up in Lafayette, almost every yard had a fig tree, and many had two or even three. Figs become ripe in July, at just the time a Louisiana summer is settling in for a long spell of hot and highly humid days. Also, fig leaves and stems contain a milky substance that many people are allergic to. Add to that the mockingbirds who claim the figs for their own, and you will understand that a picker must like figs a great deal to attempt to gather any, which I did.

Armed with nothing but insect spray, a bucket or basket hanging from my arm, I went out as early in the morning as possible, hoping to escape the worst heat and perhaps steal a march on the omnipresent mockingbirds. The dog of the moment would try valiantly to bark the birds away, but they had long discovered his limitations, flying just above his back and diving down to peck his head. My reward for this persistence came at breakfast, when peeled figs topped homemade cream cheese, a summer breakfast I rank near the top of the list, right under leftover blackberry cobbler with cream. Until I peeled figs for five little daughters, I didn't realize that although my mother didn't fight mockingbirds or heat, peeling such small fruit in such quantity was proof that in the South, food is indeed love.

Fig picking was usually a solitary occupation, unless a family member was on hand to help. But blackberry and dewberry picking were communal activities, as they involved driving to a levee or pasture where wild berries grew. Adults always initiated these outings, either a parent whose family owned land on which wild berries grew or an older brother who had spotted berry bushes on a levee or pasture and offered to drive a group out to pick them.

The adventure began with the girls of the party putting together a picnic: sandwiches, cookies, and lemonade in big thermoses, carried in grocery bags that would serve to bring home the trash. Stout shoes and thick socks were de rigueur. The possibility of snakes was real, and since cottonmouths, copperheads, rattlesnakes, and even coral snakes sought out the same terrain where berries grew, the boys carried heavy sticks and sharp knives. Years after these adventures, I read that contrary to common belief, it was not necessary to cut a blood vessel above the snake bite and suck out the poison. But at the time, had one of us been bitten, one of the boys would have done precisely that and been called a hero.

Even if we saw no snakes and avoided pastures dominated by the Brahman bulls brought in from India to crossbreed with Angus, producing a strain of cattle more resistant to both insects and heat, the thorns on the wild berries wrought their own havoc, particularly on girls' hands not accustomed to such work. Undaunted, we went from bush to bush, adding berries until our buckets were filled to the brim. Then, the best part of the outing: the picnic on quilts spread under a tree, lemonade cold and sweet on our parched throats, sandwiches devoured with the healthy appetites of young people whose only concern at the moment was whether to ask for blackberry dumplings or blackberry cobbler first.

One of the benefits of living in Lafayette was that, in the summers, Kathryn and I visited our cousins Anna and Pascal (nicknamed Pack) Sartwelle in their home in Lake Charles. Anna was a cousin on Mother's side. She was a Cannon, connected to the Burkes through marriage, and, as she was one of the most interesting, talented, and entertaining of that vast army of relatives, was embraced by everyone, regardless of age. Her husband, Cousin Pack, was a founding member of the Southwest Cattlemen's Association. He, along with his brothers, owned a ranch near Palacios, Texas, but he and Anna had moved to Lake Charles and lived there for many years until, after Cousin Pack's death, Cousin Anna returned to Palacios.

They lived in what is still one of my favorite houses, on a street running off Shell Beach Drive, which borders the lake that gave the town its name, one story, raised on four-foot piers, with a porch that wrapped around three sides of the house. That, plus high ceilings, windows set so as to provide cross-ventilation, and the cool air from under the house, kept the rooms cool except during the hottest part of the day, and even then, the attic fan pulled in a strong breeze that formed an oasis.

Attic fans also pulled in dust, which is why women used muslin slip-covers, called "summer dress," over their upholstered furniture, took down draperies, hanging instead filmy lightweight curtains, and rolled wool rugs up in butcher paper with moth balls, storing them in the attic until cool weather returned. I have muslin slipcovers for my upholstered furniture, because though I welcome central air-conditioning as a vital element in surviving a hot, humid Louisiana summer, I like to open my windows whenever possible. Besides, "summer dress" creates an ambience in which, no matter what the thermometer says, the room looks cooler.

In summers when Kathryn and I visited Cousin Anna and Cousin Pack, the noon meal began in the garden, where Lad, a man who lived on the place, surveyed its offerings, picked the vegetables he thought ready, and brought them into the kitchen, where, after checking the basket's contents, Cousin Anna created the menu for the day.

My cousins also kept chickens, and though now I'm astonished that a sensitive child like me could watch such a spectacle, I remember Lad selecting a hen and then choosing its method of execution. Sometimes he used a hatchet, holding the chicken's head against a tree stump and whacking it off with one swift blow. Sometimes he grabbed it by the neck, whirling it around until the neck snapped. And yes, I did see headless chickens run around the yard, blood spurting, and why I didn't have nightmares I still don't know.

One explanation might be that I considered Cousin Anna and Cousin Pack to be magical. The curio cabinet in the wide hall held things I'd never seen before. Tiny ivory chess sets that even a small doll might find hard to use; a tiny pair of binoculars with real lenses, through which minute objects became one degree larger; a mother-of-pearl desk set with gold tips on the pens; and a Japanese tea set for dolls. Their bookshelves had books from their own childhoods, as well as games Kathryn and I had never played, with wooden toys from the late nineteenth century on a shelf all their own.

Cousin Anna, an accomplished pianist, had a concert grand piano in her front parlor, and on summer afternoons, Kathryn and I would lie on the cool, bare floor under the piano and listen to her play. A lot of Chopin and Liszt, as well as Schumann and Schubert, but she also played old favorites like "Annie Laurie" and "Beautiful Dreamer," and I can think of no pleasanter way for children to be introduced to the joy and beauty music provides than listening to a beloved relative play.

As if all these pleasures weren't enough, Cousin Pack added to them when he told us Lad's story. Lad had been born on a ranch in the Texas panhandle and had begun working with the horses as soon as he was old enough to stay on one. His primary job was to look for broken spots in the rail fences and to notify the foreman so they could be repaired. One day, Lad didn't return from the pasture, and when the foreman went to look for him, he found the horses and the boy gone, taken, he felt sure, by the notorious James brothers, whose headquarters were to the north not that many miles away.

As it turned out, that is exactly what had happened. The James gang, either not wanting to leave a witness or just not bothering to take him off his horse, had swept the boy—ten years old at the time—along with the horses, riding north to safety. When the James brothers came to their violent end, and the federal marshals rode out to the ranch to mop up the remnants of the gang, they found Lad, in his twenties by then, with no notion of what his real name was or where he came from. Wisely deciding that Lad never knew what Mr. Jesse and Mr. Frank did, they gave him a horse and some money, and he rode south, eventually ending up at the ranch from which he'd been kidnapped.

Cousin Pack found out about him from a fellow member of the Cattlemen's Association and brought Lad, then in his fifties, to Lake Charles, establishing him in a small cottage at the back of their lot and looking after him the rest of his days.

Once I heard this story, I tried to get up enough nerve to ask Lad how he'd felt when he found himself galloping along with stolen horses, led by a gang of strange men. Cousin Pack must have intuited this, for he told me that he and Cousin Anna never asked Lad anything. "Someone who lost his whole family at that young age needs to be left with the memories he still has. He's an old man. Leave him in peace."

I did, using my imagination to create a life for someone who couldn't remember his own. Perhaps that experience stirred something in me that later impelled me to imagine other lives, not only those of real people but also those who lived only when I put their stories on a page.

Some years after Cousin Pack died, Cousin Anna, having no children of her own, decided to give most of her jewelry as well as some of her china to her nieces and cousins. I received several pins, among them a gold one with a flower made of blue enamel and tiny diamonds, and another set with turquoises and pearls. She also gave me a Belleek lemonade set, which French nuns had hand-painted in gilt for Cousin Anna's great-grandparents to commemorate their fiftieth wedding anniversary. The set has a pitcher with six tumblers. Each piece has an elaborate design of gilt scrolls around the top, with the initial "M" under it. Their name was Mistrot, my first married name was Michel, and so she chose me to be the next owner. I have never used it for lemonade, but I have used it for hot eggnog, because the tumblers are the perfect size for a serving of eggnog with enough room left over for brandy or whiskey to be added.

When Cousin Anna asked me if there were any mementos in particular I'd like to have, I asked for the turquoise glass knife rest Cousin Pack used for his carving set. Now it stands with the lemonade set and the rest of my Belleek collection on the top of a glass-fronted cabinet that used to be in my Grandfather Burke's law office and currently holds my collection of tea and coffee cups. When I look at that knife rest, I remember looking past it up into Cousin Pack's face, a genial face with laugh lines at both eyes and mouth, a face that beamed down on me and taught me what it means when one says, "His smile warms my heart."

Over the years, I have had many children in my various homes, coming for cookie bakes at Halloween, Christmas, and Valentine's Day, and for egg-dying and hunting at Easter. Invariably, one of the children, and so far, always a boy, sees that knife rest and is drawn to it as though the memories it holds attract him, too. They always want to hold it, and despite the mother's objection, I always tell them of course they may. I watch them while they handle it carefully, holding it to their eye to look through it, and then finally giving it back to me, though I know very well they'd like to put it in a pocket to take home.

There is, in my mind, a distinct difference in material goods that come to stand for home and family and material goods acquired for status only. That Belleek lemonade set probably would fetch a good price at an antique shop, because it is painted on "blank" Belleek, which predates the pieces with a design. Its value for me and my daughters rests in the fact that family members used it and that one of these gave it to me to take care of until I give it to a member of the next generation. When my first marriage ended and my girls went through such a long, dark passage, I gave each of them things that had belonged to my mother and also things they had grown up with, as reminders that our family had lasted a very long time, through good times and bad, and that they would do the same.

In a time when extended families are spread out, when marriages end even when children are small, it seems to me to be more essential than ever that home is more than just a place to eat and sleep, but instead is a place that helps the people who live there feel connected, not just to each other, but to all those who went before them. All too many children, not having that, seek connections with their peers, and that, as we know, does not always have positive results.

Looking back, I see how fortunate I was that my peers came from stable families and were being reared with the same rules as I was. Temptations, if they arose at all, were of such trivial nature that even if one gave in to them, nothing of consequence resulted. I was also fortunate to have Gail as a best friend, because had it not been for her, I think my life would have been much less fun than it was. She had an older brother, Donnie, and had learned through him and his friends to put up with boys and their teasing and jokes and roughhousing, and though she never said so, I believe she decided she should take me under her wing.

And a great wing it was. I had never been to a watermelon party before, and when we were invited to a party to be held in Girard Park, hosted by a boy our age, Gail prepared me. "The main point for the girls is to eat watermelon. The main point for the boys is to take the rinds and chase us with them. When they catch us, they rub the rinds all over our arms and legs and hair, though usually they leave our faces alone."

My face told her what I thought of this. "Now, here's what you do. While we're eating, try to figure out who the shyest boy is. I'd tell you, but you need to learn these things for yourself in case I'm not around sometime. Then, eat your melon slow enough that the chase starts while you're still eating. A shy boy will be hanging back, too, so when you finish your watermelon, you sort of walk past him, and he's almost sure to pick up a watermelon rind and start after you, because you don't look scary the way some of the girls do. He'll start running, only not all that fast, so you run, too. You can look back every once in a while, if you want to. You need to run far enough so he'll think you're really trying to get away. Even shy boys have their pride. Then, you start huffing and puffing and slowing down, and then he catches you. Only since he's shy, he won't get you too messed up. Then, you say you need to rest, and you both sit on the grass until the game's over."

I remember my astonishment as I listened to Gail talk, my respect for her rising with every word. Clearly, she had spent a great deal of time figuring all this out, and I could see that the plan she gave me had every possibility of working.

"Any questions?"

"What makes a girl scary?"

"She's getting breasts."

"And the boys know that?"

"They always know stuff like that."

My initiation into watermelon chases proved, thanks to Gail, not at all bad, and as the summer went on I gained more confidence. I also learned to wear white shorts and a white blouse, as watermelon stains could be bleached out.

When Gail found out I didn't know how to swim and heard about the two disastrous events that had led me not only to fear the water, but also to distrust anyone trying to get me into it, she neither sympathized nor judged me. She just encouraged me to take Red Cross-sponsored lessons, saying she would take the Advanced class while I took the Beginners. The instructor, Elsie Cancienne, taught PE at SLI. A no-nonsense woman, she frightened me more than the water, and so I passed, not only Beginners swimming but, the next summer, Advanced as well as the life-saving program.

The municipal pool had two diving boards, a lower one that most people used and a very high one that only proficient divers attempted. That diving board became part of a rite of passage devised by the boys who would be part of our crowd as we entered our teens. Already they left what had been their end of the pool, meaning the deepest and most dangerous, to come into our area, swimming underwater and grabbing us, rising up suddenly and ducking us, and letting us know they had finally noticed us in the usual adolescent boy way.

A favorite game was to circle a girl and dare her to break out. This, of course, allowed for a lot of careless touching, but since few of us had anything much to touch, it seemed innocent enough and preferable to the final test— jumping off the high diving board.

Certainly, we could have said no. But the early skirmishes in the battle between the sexes already have a hint of the power later ones do, and none of the girls in the crowd would have refused to jump off that board. Finally, my turn came. Gail insisted on going up with me, standing at the top of the ladder, daring any boy to come up and harass me, while I walked out to the end and stood looking down at water, which seemed farther away every instant.

Then came Gail's voice. "Go on, Dubus. It's only water and I'm right behind you."

Summertime with friends (I am on the far left).

I jumped, arms by my side, legs straight, plunging deep and then immediately swimming to the surface, shaking hair out of my face and turning to see Gail beside me.

"That wasn't so bad."

I agreed it wasn't. And felt a small jolt of surprise. I'd done something I never thought I'd do and found in myself a seed of courage I didn't know I had.

Gail wanted me to join her, Patsy Quoyser, and Lois Trahan to go to Camp Windywood for a two-week session beginning the final week of July and lasting until the end of the first week of August. "There won't be any boys. That's a reason to go in itself."

That summer, boys our age had begun to follow us on our bike hikes to Girard Park, circling the tables where we set out our picnics, but never coming any closer than that. Still, their presence changed the nature of those outings, creating small tensions that I wouldn't understand for a year or so yet.

Windywood was near a north Louisiana village called Fishville, not far from Alexandria, set in the pine wood forests that cover that part of the state. The cabins, made of dark stained wood with screened upper halves and deep eaves to provide both shade and protection from the rain, held eight campers and two counselors, one junior, one senior.

We had bunk beds. Gail took the upper and I took the lower, with our footlockers neatly arranged against the wall. That first evening, as we walked into the dining hall and saw the tables of "old girls" already filled, I felt all my shyness rising up, and then Gail's hand came out and took mine. "It's going to be fun, Dubus. You'll see."

And it was. We learned to ride, we played endless games of tetherball, we learned crafts and new songs, and swam twice a day in the coldest water I have ever been in, including the Atlantic off Hollywood Beach, Florida, in February. An underground spring fed what had been a small swimming hole that had been enlarged to make an area about three-fourths the size of the Lafayette municipal pool. It had docks with ladders at the deeper end and a roped-off area for beginners, who could wade out from the muddy bank. There was no diving board, but a rope swinging off a tree that provided the quickest, and in the long run, the easiest way of making yourself get into that arctic water. Grab the rope from the bank, hold on, take a running jump— and leap. And then swim as though your life depends on it, as it well might if you lounged around and let hypothermia set in.

Despite it being late July, when south Louisiana is blanketed in hot humidity day and night, as soon as the sun set behind the dark shapes of pine trees, cool air chased away the heat, and we actually slept under wool blankets at night. The evening campfires made a welcome spot, with campers seated on logs placed in circles, roasting marshmallows and singing songs I remember still. We sang "Yellow Rose of Texas," "Cotton-Eyed Joe," "My Bonnie," "Do Your Ears Hang Low," "Clementine," "Polly Wolly Doodle," and other fast-paced, peppy songs at every meal, as well as spontaneous serenades in between. But we sang "Tell Me Why" only at campfires, its pensive mood quieting us for sleep. When the last thin line of light blacked out, and we could see stars thick overhead, we sang "Taps," thinking of the many soldiers who had been laid to rest to the notes of that song and praying that there were not going to be many more.

On Saturday, August 11, when my parents and André came to pick me up to go home, André hurtled toward me shouting something I couldn't understand until he reached me and finally slowed down. "We bombed two Japanese cities with atomic bombs. They're the biggest bombs ever made and everyone's sure now they'll surrender."

He turned nine that day, and I know that if my almost twelve-year-old mind couldn't process the idea of one bomb being big enough to destroy an entire city, his certainly couldn't. Nor, I imagine, did adults understand the vastness of the devastation until pictures began to appear in magazines and newsreels. But that day, with relief that finally a long and bloody war would soon end, I think probably only those with a deeper knowledge and more profound understanding of what had been leashed upon the world did not rejoice.

Recipes for Summer's Bounty

MAQUE CHOUX (STEWED CORN AND TOMATOES)

1 dozen ears fresh corn (the fresher the better; as corn dries, it loses its "milk")
2 tablespoons vegetable oil
1 medium size white onion, thinly sliced
2 tablespoons fresh tomatoes, chopped
½ medium-size green bell pepper, chopped
⅓ teaspoon sugar
Salt, black pepper, red pepper, to taste

Using a very sharp knife, cut corn off cob lengthwise, cutting as close to the cob as possible. Use a cutting board with a rim or else a shallow glass pan, so as to retain the "milk" from the corn. Mix all ingredients except salt/peppers and place in a heavy-bottomed skillet in which the oil has been heated. Cook over medium to low heat, stirring constantly, until corn is tender, and onion, bell pepper, and tomatoes are cooked. If the mixture becomes too dry while cooking, add a little corn milk. After corn is cooked, add 1 level teaspoon butter and salt and black pepper to taste.

Yield: Serves 8 generously.

SUMMER DAY SQUASH

1 stick butter
1 large thinly sliced lemon
12 thinly sliced yellow crookneck squash
1 medium onion, chopped
2 tablespoons fresh parsley, chopped
Salt and black pepper to taste

Melt butter in a large heavy-bottomed skillet over medium heat. Add remaining ingredients. Mix well. Cover skillet and sauté over medium heat for 7–10 minutes, or until squash is tender. Remove lemon. Serve immediately.

Yield: Serves 6 to 8.

Note: Depending on how hot the medium setting on the burner gets the skillet, you may need to adjust the heat so that the liquid doesn't evaporate.

SPINACH CREOLE

1 large bunch of fresh spinach, washed and drained but not blotted dry
1 small onion, chopped
1 tablespoon butter
Four pieces bread, toasted and buttered

Garnish:
Grated hard-boiled egg or a slice of crisp bacon

Melt the butter in a heavy-bottomed saucepan over medium heat; add chopped onion and cook until it is wilted. Then, add the spinach; the water adhering to the leaves should be sufficient. If necessary, add water in very small amounts at a time, so as not to leach vitamins into the liquid. When spinach is cooked, season to taste, then chop fine and put on the buttered toast. Garnish as desired.

Yield: Serves 4.

Note: Frozen chopped spinach may be used. In this case, thaw and let drain in a colander until most of the liquid is gone.

BAKED TOMATOES

6 Creole tomatoes (any truly flavorful, field-grown, thin-peel tomato may be used)
Breadcrumbs as needed (may be mixed with grated Parmesan cheese, if desired)
Fresh parsley, chopped
Herb vinaigrette dressing (recipe follows)

Peel the tomatoes by holding each one over steam (use a meat fork) until the skin starts to peel. It will then easily come off without further steaming. Cut the tomatoes into chunks and place in a lightly oiled, flat casserole dish. Spoon herb vinaigrette dressing over the tomatoes, lightly covering each piece. Spoon breadcrumbs into spaces between tomatoes, not tightly. Sprinkle chopped parsley over the tomatoes and breadcrumbs.

Put top on dish or cover with aluminum foil. You may now either bake the dish in a preheated 350° oven or refrigerate until ready to use. Do not refrigerate longer than overnight.

Yield: Serves 6.

HERB VINAIGRETTE DRESSING

4 tablespoons lemon juice or vinegar (cider or wine)
½ cup olive oil
¼ teaspoon dry mustard
6 fresh basil leaves, bruised
6 sprigs fresh thyme, bruised
Salt and pepper to taste

Shake all ingredients well; let herbs marinate in dressing at room temperature for at least an hour before removing. Double the recipe if necessary.

SMOTHERED OKRA

2 quarts freshly cut okra
¼ cup vegetable oil
3 medium tomatoes, chopped
2 medium white onions, chopped
Salt and pepper to taste

Sauté all ingredients in a heavy skillet over medium heat approximately 30 minutes, or until okra doesn't "string" any more. Season to taste.

Yield: Serves 8.

Note: Smothered okra is a favorite summer dish. It is served over rice and very often accompanies chicken fricassee, as the flavors complement each other.

SUCCOTASH

1 lb. fresh butter beans, shelled
¼ lb. salt meat
1 medium onion, chopped
1 clove garlic, minced
4 ears of fresh corn
½ stick butter
Half-and-half

Cook the butter beans, salt meat, onion, and garlic in water to cover until beans are done. Drain the bean and reserve the liquor. Cut the corn off the cob into a heavy skillet containing melted butter. Add the beans. Pour cream and enough of the bean liquor into the skillet to barely cover the succotash. (Pour very slowly simultaneously, so as to get equal proportions of each.) Season with salt and black pepper to taste. Simmer slowly for 15–20 minutes, until corn is tender.

Yield: Serves 4.

GREEN PEAS TARRAGON

1 lb. fresh green peas, shelled
1 beef bouillon cube
2 tablespoons butter, melted
¾ teaspoon sugar
½ teaspoon salt
⅛ teaspoon fresh tarragon leaves, finely crushed
⅛ teaspoon fresh chervil, finely crushed
Black pepper to taste

Put peas in water just to cover; add bouillon cube. Cook peas until just tender; drain. Add the rest of the ingredients, heat, toss to coat peas.

Yield: Serves 4.

BLACKBERRY DUMPLINGS

1 lb. fresh blackberries, rinsed and picked over
1 cup sugar
1 cup all-purpose flour
1 cup yellow cake mix
1 teaspoon baking powder
1 large egg beaten with ½ cup water

Combine berries and sugar in a heavy saucepan over medium heat. Cook for 15 minutes, stir occasionally. Reduce heat to medium-low. Combine the dry ingredients in a bowl and mix well. Make a well and pour in the egg/water mixture. Stir with a wooden spoon to make a smooth dough. Using a teaspoon, drop heaping spoons of dough into the hot fruit, half a dozen at a time. Poach for about 2 minutes, then gently flip over with a fork. Cook 1 to 2 minutes longer, or until the dumplings are puffy. Transfer them to a shallow bowl and cook the remaining batter. Serve in 8 dessert bowls; spoon fruit mixture from pot, dividing it equally among the bowls. Top with dumplings.

Yield: Serves 8.

Note: These may also be made with blueberries. The dumplings may be topped with ice cream or heavy cream. Leftover dumplings, if there are any, make a great breakfast treat.

BLACKBERRY COBBLER

1 stick butter
1 cup sugar
1 cup flour
1 teaspoon baking powder
1 cup milk
1 quart blackberries, picked over and rinsed
Sugar to taste

Melt butter and add dry ingredients, mix well. Stir in milk. Flour a baking board or waxed paper. Put dough on the board, pat to shape to fit over an oven-proof baking dish. Put blackberries in the dish. Dot with butter and sprinkle with sugar to taste. Cover with the dough. Bake in a preheated 350° oven until brown.

Yield: Serves 6.

Note: Blueberries or peaches may also be used in this recipe. Top with vanilla ice cream or heavy cream, or just serve plain. Again, nothing like leftover cobbler for breakfast!

Lagniappe

MARINATED CUCUMBER RINGS

2 large cucumbers, thinly sliced
4 4-ounce cans pimientos, drained and sliced
⅔ cup vegetable oil
¼ cup white wine vinegar
½ teaspoon salt
2 cups sour cream

Put thinly sliced cucumbers in salted ice water for at least 30 minutes; drain and rinse. Now mix together cucumber and pimiento strips. Shake oil, vinegar, and salt together in a jar. Pour over cucumber mixture and chill 1 hour. Drain well. Just before serving, blend with sour cream. Chopped green onion tops may be added while cucumbers are marinating, if desired.

Yield: Serves 12.

CHAPTER NINE

On August 14, Japan surrendered, and though it would not be official until September 2, still, as far as most Americans were concerned, the war with Japan was over. As predicted, there were many pockets of Japanese resistance in the Pacific Islands, but at least our military, particularly the Marines and the Army Infantry, wouldn't have to continue the high-cost struggles to take one island after the other.

When it became known that American and British POWs had been executed after the surrender, and when the Allies took over the POW camps and heard the stories of how the prisoners had been treated, the decision to end the war, even with such horrifying weapons, seemed more understandable.

When I studied literary criticism in college, the professor told us that we must judge the work in the context in which it was written or in which it was set. "Hindsight is useful only when we can use it to see our mistakes and learn from them," he said. "In fiction, it just doesn't work to apply contemporary judgment to books written a century, even decades, ago." It's one thing to examine something like the use of the atomic bomb to learn from them and develop policies and procedures to keep them from happening again. It's quite another, in my view, to judge the choices made in another time and another place by people who, in many instances, were in situations where panic and desperation had greater influence than standards of fairness.

It would be a while before our family members in the military returned home, but we knew they would, and that was all we needed to know. The aftermath of victory over Japan, as had been the aftermath of victory in Europe, was bittersweet. For every family who would welcome a son or brother or husband or father home, there were hundreds who wouldn't, and when later pictures of the cemetery holding the dead from the Normandy invasion appeared in newspapers and magazines and newsreels, they created a lasting image of the ultimate and most lasting cost of war, not only to the Allies but to everyone caught up in that maelstrom.

The human feelings of anxiety, fear, and deep grief are not restricted to one group of people, but are universal to all humans, excepting the psychopaths

163

who design and execute death camps and the terrible tortures practiced in prisons all over the world. When the prisoners in the death camps were liberated and the stories of what had happened there told, we knew that not only had western civilization been saved, but a darkness that came from hell itself had been conquered. This knowledge cast a shadow over the victories. It was impossible not to think of the terror, the agony, the people in these prisons had suffered. For the survivors, their lives would forever be affected by the insane cruelty of people they didn't even know.

I had the great privilege of meeting Dr. Bruno Bettelheim when he came to Louisiana to give the Flora Levy Lecture at the University of Southwestern Louisiana, as SLI had become. I was teaching in the English department as an adjunct, driving over from Baton Rouge every day. The chairman of the English department asked me if I could pick Dr. Bettelheim up at the New Orleans airport, take him to his hotel, and drive him to Lafayette the next day. I agreed, arranged to spend the night with my Burke cousins Walter and Lettice Stuart, and, after Lettice and I met him at the airport, we drove him to his hotel. Dr. Bettelheim was somewhat frail, and so, on the way to Lafayette, I made an excuse to stop at the duplex I lived in so he could have a pit stop and I could get him some orange juice.

By that time, he had asked me many questions, which turned personal when we resumed our journey. He had noticed antique rugs and furnishings, and other signs that my life had at one time been lived on a more elaborate scale, and gradually, the story of my divorce came out. The story was one of a destructive campaign by my ex-husband to destroy me and our daughters, and it included a sanity hearing along with many other horrors that still cause me nightmares.

At the end of this, Dr. Bettelheim turned to me. "That is the most brutal story I have ever heard."

"But Dr. Bettelheim, how can you say that? The Holocaust—"

"Was not personal. This is."

I don't agree with Dr. Bettelheim that the Holocaust was impersonal. It was personal in a barbaric and demonic way. Victims couldn't look at their lives and try to see signs that might have led to a choice whose path would have taken them somewhere else. Nor were they random victims, cases of being in the wrong place at the wrong time. They were being exterminated because a madman had convinced himself, as well as other human beings, that they were degenerates, traitors, or unfit to live. I think the unfairness—what a weak word to convey such a large concept!—of this must have been one of the hardest things to bear.

Anyone who has suffered rejections has learned that they are hated not because of who they are but how they are perceived. This is why I have told my daughters and friends that when I die, I do not want God to tell me that for a huge number of people, an act or word of mine was *the last straw*. Since I have no idea what burdens the strangers or acquaintances I meet in the course of day may be carrying, I try very hard not to do or say anything that is rude, unthinking, or unkind. My parents, as well as the nuns, reinforced this attitude by word and example. Thus, I found myself unable to understand what some acquaintances of my parents did.

The incident, one of the most bizarre of my childhood, began one day in September of sixth grade. As we ate our noon meal, a knock came at the door. Mother asked André to answer it, and he returned to the dining room to report that "a man in uniform" wanted to see our father. Daddy rose and went to the door, and when Mother heard the word "eviction," she went to find out what in the world was going on.

It turned out that this was the final step in a long campaign by a family who were close friends with our landlords, the Mancils, and who had long been trying to find a way to legally get us out of the house so they could have it. Wartime housing regulations, seeking to keep landlords from accepting "bids" for their rental properties, had strict rules about how and under what circumstances renters could be evicted. The Spencers (name changed to protect the innocent) had been living with Mr. Spencer's father. Wanting a place of their own, they filed a request that we be evicted on the grounds that their presence in old Mr. Spencer's home had such a bad effect on his deteriorating health that his doctor predicted a heart attack if he did not get his home back to himself. No one who knew the Spencers doubted that the boisterous presence of his relatives robbed the old gentleman of needed peace, but few people believed him in imminent danger of a heart attack.

My sister, brother, and I had fallen silent when Mother left the table, and now we barely breathed in our effort to hear what was being said at the front door. "No member of my family has ever been served a subpoena or warrant of any kind," Mother said, using a tone of voice we had never heard her use before. "We are not going to start now."

"But, Mrs. Dubus," the deputy said, "I have to give this to you. It's my job."

"Then leave it on a chair on the porch."

"I have to put it in your hand. . ." The voice trailed off. We looked up to see our parents returning to the table, and past them, a khaki-covered back going out the screen door.

"Kateen," my father said. "Don't worry about this. I'll take care of it."

And he did, so quickly that we had the great satisfaction of telling the Mancils we would be out of the house by the end of the week. This meant that my parents didn't have to go to court, but also meant we had to pack quickly, find a place to live, and, in the event we couldn't find a house right away, a place to store furnishings until we did.

There were, very simply, no houses for rent in Lafayette. Two of my parents' closest friends, Harry and Dorothy Steiro—whom they met when Harry, a Madison, Wisconsin, contractor, came down to Louisiana with a military contract—lived in a trailer, a circumstance that gave my mother pause when Daddy came home from the golf course and told her about this nice couple he'd met.

"Now, Kateen, I know you're thinking of the kinds of trailers people used to live in during the Depression. But I assure you, theirs is nothing like that." Nor was it. Brand new, it was compact and comfortable, and André and I would have moved in with the Steiros in a New York second.

With no place to go, but determined to save his wife from having to appear in court, my father called a good friend, Tom Parkerson, who owned Lafayette's only respectable motor inn. I say respectable, because there were others, owned by a family known for dealing in prostitutes, gambling, and drugs, that were never mentioned in polite society, though everyone knew where they were.

(In eighth grade, a daughter of the family came to Mt. Carmel. For the rest of her time there, she was delivered to school and picked up in the afternoon by a man driving a long, black limousine, with another sitting beside her on the back seat. She was not allowed to date or attend our inno-cent parties. Her father arranged her engagement to a nice young man who owned part of a lumber yard and whose reputation in town was impeccable, and they married the day after she graduated from high school. We saw her once after that, when she attended an early summer class party, and when the grown-ups were out of the room, told us about her wedding night. I still remember some of the details—and, particularly, her gratitude to her father that out of all the suitors he could have picked, he'd chosen one who knew his way around a bedroom.)

Fortunately, Mr. Parkerson had rooms enough for all of us, and so, af-ter packing clothes and personal items, we moved to his motor inn, located catty-corner from the Cathedral School, and only a few blocks from Mt. Carmel. Daddy had men bring trucks from Gulf States Utilities to move our furniture to storage space out there, and for the next six weeks, we lived like we were on vacation, a sort of life that my friends envied, partly because the housekeeping staff took care of our rooms and partly because Mr. Parkerson gave us tokens to use in the soft drink vending machine.

I don't remember what we did about meals, but obviously we ate them. I do remember that instead of eating at a café called Camos' on Thursdays only, I ate there more often, walking with Kathryn the one block from Mt. Carmel and meeting the rest of the family. Lois, Jane Matthews, and I ate at Camos' on Thursdays because our fathers were in Rotary, which met that day, and our mothers took a day off from fixing a noon meal. The café was across the street from the courthouse, so its usual clientele were lawyers, staff, clerks, and, of course, litigants in the various suits being heard. The menu offered an array of items, but the majority of customers ordered the daily plate lunch, which, at 35 cents, served a meat, a starch, two vegetables, rolls, a beverage, and a dessert. Like any café, Camos' had its star dishes, white beans being one of them, and round steak in gravy being another. Bread pudding appeared on the dessert menu year-round, with fruit cobblers in the summer, and pumpkin, yam, pecan, and apple pies taking over the main roles in the fall.

The first time I entered this mostly-male enclave with Lois and Jane I felt shy until a few of the men spoke to us and said they knew our fathers. Their positive comments made me feel right at home.

Another café, Jack's, had the best chili hot dogs I have ever eaten in my life. Like most Lafayette restaurateurs at the time, Jack expected his customers to know quality meat when they tasted it, even in hot dogs, so he used top-grade weenies and top-grade ground beef in his chili sauce to make a succulent concoction that, with an ice-cold Coke poured over a glass of ice, made a lunch that even now I have to make myself once in a while, if it does mean another ten minutes on the treadmill.

When we did find a house, it was the only house in Lafayette that had a basement, dug by the man who built the house, and a mule, much to the gratification of the neighborhood small boys, who had never seen anything like that in their lives. Neither had we. My Burke grandparents' house had a basement, because it was built into the side of what in south Louisiana is called a "hill" and anywhere else "a small mound." The basement, built out from the foundation of the house, was ground-level at the back, and the washing machine, garden tools, and other such things had storage space there.

(Here, too, the gardener killed and plucked the Thanksgiving turkey. One Thanksgiving, my grandmother heard terrible cries coming from the basement and hurried down the back steps to find the gardener plucking the bird live. When told to stop immediately and kill the poor thing first, he replied that it was so much easier to pluck alive, and what did it matter to the bird? My grandmother told him it mattered to her and that was all he need know. But the next day, so family lore says, she ate no turkey, nor did she eat any of the turkey gumbo made from the carcass and leftover meat.)

The basement in our new home had a pump for the rainwater that cascaded down the slanted driveway. Since it is not at all unusual to get four inches during a hard downpour, that pump had to work overtime to keep water from rising above the running board of the car. André and I thought that basement the greatest feature we'd ever had in a house. Besides the driveway, which was a great place to coast down on skates or a bicycle, it had a flight of steps opening into the backyard, providing a stage for all sorts of adventures from Ali Baba and the Forty Thieves to the Three Musketeers to Robin Hood.

We liked the neighborhood, too. Lionel Abshire, André's age and soon best friend, lived on one side, and the Richards, with a daughter Pat, Kathryn's age, and a son, Laurie, two years older than I, lived behind us. Diane Lee's family lived next door to the Richards, and further down St. Mary Boulevard, the Conners, whose son Pierre, in Laurie's class at Cathedral, would be my first beau.

The area had only begun to be developed when the war started, and civilian construction was put aside. Diane and I both loved to walk, and on fall afternoons and mild winter ones, we would take an apple and walk to the woods at the end of St. Mary Boulevard, finding a tree to sit under where we munched our apples and compared notes on books we'd read.

I still have many of the books I had in childhood. My godfather, Tommy Keiller, and his wife, Kitty, had no children, but he certainly knew how to furnish a library for a child. Tommy was an electrical engineer, and he and my father met when they were on the same project. Tommy joined the Navy and rose to the rank of lieutenant commander before he retired. He worked on the Manhattan Project at Oak Ridge, Tennessee, during the war years, helping to produce the enriched uranium that made nuclear fission possible.

But to me, he was Uncle Tommy, who had stocked my library with such books as *The World's Hundred Most Famous Paintings*, *The Parade of the Animal Kingdom*, *Dogs As I See Them*, books of poetry and folklore, and anything he thought would challenge both my intelligence and my imagination. Many times in my life, I have entered a gallery in a museum and seen for the first time, "up close and personal," one of those pictures I pored over, lying on the floor, turning the pages of that heavy book, drinking in the beauty of portraits and landscapes, seascapes and still lifes. *The Polish Rider* in the Frick, *The Laughing Cavalier* in London's National Gallery, the *Mona Lisa* in the

Louvre, Monet's *Waterlilies* at MOMA—all of these I met first between the pages of a book, and I owe a great deal of my love of the visual and plastic arts to my godfather.

Following in his footsteps, years later in my own home, in summers I used to string clotheslines across the room we called "THE BIG LIVING ROOM," using clothespins to attach prints of masterworks, introducing them to my children as my mother introduced music to my siblings and me. She would put on a record, and at the end give its name as though speaking to herself. A few days later she'd play it again, only this time she would pretend she couldn't remember the name. It might take more than twice before a little voice piped up with the name, but it always happened. The first two I remember recognizing were "The Evening Star" from Richard Wagner's *Tannhäuser* and "Meditation" from Jules Massenet's *Thaïs*. I did this with my children, too, and the happy outcome for all of us is that we have interests we share and can combine visits to museums and concerts with family gatherings we will never forget.

Among childhood books on my library shelves, the Little Colonel series are favorites. They follow the life of a girl living at a place called The Locusts, not far from Louisville, Kentucky, from age six until she marries. While telling engrossing stories of Lloyd and her friends, the author, Annie Fellows Johnston, reinforces the values that my family imbued in me: honor, courtesy, generosity, kindness, tolerance, forgiveness, patience, and loyalty. When I drive by a billboard giving the element of character being stressed in public schools that month, while I applaud the sensibility, I'm sorry that some parents no longer seem to think character important and leave the tremendous responsibility of instilling it in their children to people who see them for such a relatively short period in their lives.

The Nancy Drew mysteries fill almost two shelves, while the Mary Poppins books, the Five Little Peppers, and Louisa May Alcott's fill two more. There are also anthologies of poetry, and a series Aunt Bertha and Aunt Pamela gave us one Christmas titled The Junior Classics. It has ten volumes, each one devoted to a special subject, such as myths of Greece and Rome, stories of heroes and heroines, stories that never grow old, and the tenth volume devoted to poetry. These books covered the classics' waterfront, as well as giving sources for every selection and suggestions for further reading. I can thank my godfather and those two aunts for furnishing the foundation for a personal library that remains one of the most treasured elements in my life.

During the divorce, my ex-husband allowed me into our family home only with a court order, and after three years, when I finally got one allowing me to remove my personal books, I entered the house with my lawyer and his with a terrible fear that I would find most of them gone. His lawyer, a woman I had been in a religious study group and bridge foursome with for years, insisted that I make a list of every book I took. My lawyer, an honorable, kind man whose appearance belies his tenacity in a courtroom, told her if she wanted a list, she could make it herself. After the first few entries, she stopped. I rarely ran into her, but when I did, I think she didn't understand why my attitude toward her cooled, not only because she represented my husband—one of a chain of eight—but had started dating him within two weeks after I moved out of our house. When she complained to a mutual friend that people wouldn't speak to her and my husband, my very dear friend Helen said, "Most people wait until a body is dead to bury it."

My lawyer helped carry the books to my car and his and also helped carry them inside the house where my two youngest daughters and I lived. I spent the evening arranging them on shelves and called him the next morning to tell him I had slept better than I had in years, because my friends were back under my roof.

My good friend Walker Percy said the only way to learn to write is to read, and when I began writing, I think that years of reading well-written literature, graduating from children's books to the great nineteenth-century novelists of England, France, and Russia, had provided an inner structure on which I could build my work.

Mother, mindful that he or she who samples the best rarely settles for lesser quality, began giving me—and I suppose Kathryn—reading lists the summer before seventh grade. Some of the girls I knew passed Gwen Bristow's *Jubilee Summer* around. It had the reputation of being quite risqué, but now I imagine it could be found in the children's section. At any rate, I had begun reading Charles Dickens's *The Old Curiosity Shop*, and when Mother asked me if I were in line to borrow *Jubilee Summer*, I admitted I was. "Well," she said, "you might remember that your intellect is part of your soul, and your soul will last forever. If you really want to take Miss Bristow along with you, by all means, do."

After reading a few pages, I decided that while Miss Bristow might know a good story, she didn't seem to have the craft to tell it.

A fondness for the same books is, to me, one of the happiest bonds between friends. Reading an excellent book is one kind of pleasure, discussing it with someone else is another, and both are, I think, essential to experiencing the richness being an avid reader can bring to our lives.

My fourth daughter, her husband, and her son lost every book they owned when Hurricane Katrina flooded their home in New Orleans, among them Aimée's cherished children's books. They happened to be in the Northeast when Katrina hit, and being unable to return to New Orleans, they stayed in a summer home belonging to a friend of her sister DeLauné. Aimée had taught in Tulane's Theater Department and was the Artistic Director of the Shakespeare Festival at Tulane, but, displaced by the hurricane, ended up living in Massachusetts. I was visiting them on the third anniversary of Katrina, and we decided we would drive to a restaurant in another town we enjoyed rather than be sad. She and her son, Sebastian, and I happened to drive past Berkshire Books, a noted bookstore we had long wanted to see, on the way back. We went in, passing the adult sections and heading straight for the children's, where the three of us began perusing the shelves. My daughter kept exclaiming, and when I asked her what she was finding, she said, "You won't believe it, but they have almost every book I lost in that flood."

The stack of books grew higher, and her excitement with it. Finally, she stopped, and began looking through them, trying to decide which to buy. I knew what losing those books had meant to her: not just the books themselves, but the memories of a childhood shared with four sisters and all the happy times we'd had.

"We're getting all of them," I said.

"Momma—that's too much," she protested.

"It is not too much. Besides, it's all Monopoly money."

When I say that, the girls know they have to give in. They understand when I started saying that and why. It means that if you have shelter, food, clothing—the basic necessities of life—then when something comes along like the truly miraculous discovery of those books, you must, like the French, put flowers before bread. And when you think of it as Monopoly money, that's very easy to do.

CHAPTER TEN

A lthough public schools had elementary, junior, and high schools, all of Mt. Carmel's classes were in the same building. Still, as seventh graders, our classroom was upstairs, and that, along with the fact that some of the girls had already entered puberty, made us feel we were no longer children. Since most of us were twelve, at least until after the first of the year, we weren't teenagers, either. However, we were close enough to that mysterious state to want to find out a little about it, which meant adopting the activities of real teenagers, beginning with going to record stores on Saturday mornings and listening to the newest songs.

Since the booths in which we could play records held at the most three people, and since no store had more than four or five, lines formed. But, as we soon realized, those lines offered opportunities for casual meetings, which, since they took place in a record store, could begin with a conversation about music and move on to the more personal if that were mutually desired.

Gail, ever mindful of my shyness, would decide whether to respond to an overture from a boy we'd never met, and, if she did, would take the lead until she could bring me into the conversation. I never saw Gail at a loss for words, I never saw her flustered by male attention, and though for years I attributed this to great poise, I later realized that Gail, self-sufficient and independent, didn't really give a damn if boys liked her or not.

Like most people of my generation, I have a shelf with songs from the forties and fifties, and when I play them, memories flood back, which is why I have them. Thanks to dancing classes, and with the help of Kathryn, Marilyn Trahan (Lois's older sister), and other girls in their crowd, Lois and Gail and I brushed up on our dance steps and learned some new ones, particularly the classic jitterbug, which had taken hold during the war.

Our crowd didn't have planned mixed gatherings, but it wasn't unusual for a few boys to turn up at a girl's house, and what had begun as a sleepover for three or four friends ended up with Cokes, popcorn, and rugs rolled back so we could dance to the newest records. Fast tunes like Johnny Mercer's "Atchison, Topeka and the Santa Fe" and Stan Kenton's "Tampico" suited the girls better, because the space between bodies never closed. The boys preferred slow tunes—Doris Day singing "Sentimental Journey," Henry James and Kitty Kallen with "It's Been a Long, Long Time," and Woody Herman with "Laura"—not because they would hold us close, but because it's easier to fake slow steps than fast ones.

Freed from the restrictions of dancing class, I found that I really loved to dance, and since my first husband was one of the South's best dancers, we spent many happy hours on the dance floor. The month after that marriage ended, the Alvin Ailey Dance Company was in Baton Rouge, brought there by the Arts Council of Greater Baton Rouge, which I had helped found, to give a performance and master classes. The executive director had been hired the year before during my tenure as president, and he and I had become close friends. Kyle invited me to everything that came along, trying to keep my spirits up as well as demonstrating to people that despite anything my ex-husband said, I was still me. He invited me to the party honoring the dancers after their performance. A small band played, and when they swung into a song perfect for jitterbugging, one of the Alvin Ailey dancers asked me what sort of step went with that beat.

"Jitterbugging."

"Do you know how to do that?"

"Absolutely."

"Will you teach us?"

"Sure."

They formed up behind me, and I led them through the steps. They caught on quickly, and in no time we each had a partner and tore up the floor until the set ended. As I walked away, a board member came up to me and said, "Beth, do you realize you were the only nonprofessional dancer out there?"

"But the only one who knew the steps." I have many memories connected with dancing, and it's among the things I miss.

***

Crop festivals and church fairs are part of an Acadiana fall. Not only is it harvest time, but weather more amenable to being outdoors has arrived, if not consistently, at least enough to end summer's oppressive heat. The first cool front is anticipated for weeks before a morning comes when one steps outdoors and feels, instead of a blanket of humid heat, crisp air that hints of October's brilliant skies and lower temperatures.

Now, there are so many festivals in Louisiana they dot the calendar year-round. When I grew up in Lafayette, I knew only those in the area, beginning with the Sugar Cane Festival in New Iberia, one of the oldest and most notable. It was founded in 1941, and members chose King Sucrose as the king's name. There were also the Cotton Festival in Ville Platte, the Rice Festival in Crowley, as well as the Yam Festival in Opelousas, drawing huge crowds every year, despite the proliferation of festivals in Louisiana that cover the entire state.

By seventh grade, we were considered old enough and reliable enough to be allowed to attend these various festivals in a group. Very much like county fairs in other places, the festivals combined entertainment, food-related competitions, crop judging, vendors selling souvenirs and food, and a carnival that provided everything from a Ferris wheel to the usual booths of games. They were a kaleidoscope of sights and sounds and smells: a young man using his hunting-honed marksmanship to win a trophy for his girl; the sweet scent of cotton candy and the pungent aroma of barbecue ribs; the blare of trumpets and the beat of drums blending with the rhythm of a zydeco band; and, always, casual encounters with boys and girls from other schools, because in this close-knit area, no one could go far without meeting a cousin or a friend of a cousin to perform the introductions.

So, the network of acquaintance grew, forming connections that still appear from time to time all these years later. For instance, the man who built the fence, the screen house for my lap pool, the garage, and the water garden for my home in Prairieville grew up in Franklin, some thirty-five miles from Lafayette. We know many of the same people, and when two friends from Lafayette came to have lunch with me one day when Ron was working here, he came in and had coffee with us, which resulted in the game my friend Helen used to call "playing Lafayette," when her husband and I talked about growing up there, but which on that particular day was "playing Acadiana."

My parents rarely attended any of the festivals, except the Sugar Cane Festival because Uncle Francis was involved in that. But we all attended the fairs put on by the Catholic churches in the small towns circling Lafayette. We did this not because of personal choice, but because my father's transfer to Lafayette had a purpose. Gulf States Utilities wanted to build up a customer base in these towns, so it could afford to run lines out into the lightly populated bayous and swamps. This would require winning local elections to switch from CLECO, an electric cooperative, or from municipal systems. GSU considered my father the ideal person to campaign for the company. Born and reared in Abbeville, the son of a well-known family, and married to the daughter of a family responsible for many educational improvements not only in Acadiana, but the state, he had impeccable personal credentials, as well as the type of personality that earned him trust.

Church fairs featured foods indigenous to not only the area, but also to the cooking style of each little town. Sampling gumbos and jambalayas, and listening to the reactions of the cooks who'd prepared them, taught me an invaluable lesson: the gumbo or jambalaya you're eating is always the best you ever tasted, period.

Since churches scheduled their fairs so as not to conflict with each other, the cooks always knew where my father had been the week before. "*Mais*, Mr. Dubus, I know those women in Duson think they know how to cook gumbo, but *cher*, I bet you had to bite your tongue to keep from telling them how bad it was." Ever the diplomat, my father found ways to compliment these various cooks that neither compromised the truth nor exaggerated reality. I learned, too, that gumbo and potato salad, which is usually served with it in Cajun households, are two of the standards by which a cook is judged. So intense is the rivalry to make the best possible version of these foods that friendships have been broken over dissension as to whether to put tomatoes in gumbo.

Lafayette gumbo did not have tomatoes, nor did it contain much red pepper, relying instead on a mixture of herbs for flavor. A bottle of Tabasco was on every table, allowing diners to heat up their serving or not as they chose. I learned to make the potato salad I still make from Carolyn Littell's mother. The recipe at the end of this chapter gives the "secret" ingredient that makes that little bit of difference.

(One of Aimée's friends, Fran, told her that her mother had stopped speaking to her for three days before Fran learned why. She had made the mistake of telling her mother, not only an excellent cook but the home economics teacher at St. Joseph's Academy, where her girls and mine were students, that Mrs. Michel's potato salad was the best she ever ate.)

Bingo was a fixture at church fairs. I used to watch, wondering how an elderly lady could keep up with as many as five cards. But I spent more time roaming the booths that covered the church and school yard grounds. It would be difficult to think of a type of relish, pickle, jam, jelly, or preserves not present in those booths. If it grew in south Louisiana, it was there. And a beautiful sight those rows of jars made. Some were filled with preserves of many kinds, others with jams and jellies, and others with pickled okra, chow-chow, bread and butter pickles, as well as dill.

The shelves of cakes, pies, cookies, rolls, and bread contained both old favorites and innovative new recipes the baker hoped would attract buyers' attention. The ladies of the church had high standards for the cakes they baked. Layers had to have risen with perfect surfaces. Icing had to be neither too soft nor too hard. And no artificial decorations were allowed.

Normally, anything Mother bought at a church fair lived up to the standards, but I remember one church fair where one didn't. When Mother approached the baked goods booth, one of the ladies pointed at a plate of vanilla cupcakes with caramel icing. "There's something wrong with those cupcakes. Too dry, especially if they were made yesterday."

Another lady chimed in. "She's a new church member, so we don't know her well enough to know if she would cheat and bring cupcakes made in a bakery."

Mother told me later that at that moment, she knew she would have to make a decision that would affect the newcomer's life as long as she lived there.

"So, Mrs. Dubus, could you buy a few, taste one, and see what you think?"

Mother nodded, made her purchase, and bit into a cupcake. Before she could say a word, the lady smiled. "It's dry, yes?"

"Just a little. But maybe it's supposed to be."

"Not if she'd baked them this morning, like she said she did."

"At least she made a contribution.'

"She made an insult," the lady said. "As if no one would notice."

"My husband happens to like slightly dry cupcakes. I'll buy all of them."

"That's a social lie, so it doesn't count," the lady said. I hadn't yet learned the different kinds of lies, but when I did, I learned that there were social lies, meant to save someone's feelings in trivial or harmless manners; jocose lies, meant for a joke and meant to be taken as such; and venial lies, which were near the line dividing them from the worst ones, but not over it. Then came mortal lies, which broke all the virtues the church preached and embraced all the capital sins.

"I do hope you will overlook this woman's mistake. She is new here and must be in need of friends, which church groups usually provide."

Silence, then a series of nods.

"I saved you that cake you like," the lady said. My ears perked up when I heard that.

The cake had three white layers with lemon filling and white Divinity icing on the top and sides. It was Mrs. Mouton's specialty and one of our favorites.

"Now there's a fresh cake," the lady told her. "Mrs. Dubus, the eggs in it were still in the hen eight hours ago."

When I began running a household myself, I realized how much I had picked up from the women I met at these church fairs. I admired the ingenuity they displayed in providing good meals for their families based on what they had available more than I do the expertise of chefs who have a world of luxury ingredients at hand. And I came to understand that, long before recycling and conservation became watchwords, they had been doing this for years: Coffee grounds on roses to keep the aphids down. Bacon fat saved in a jar to use for biscuits or frying. Melting bits of soap and molding a new bar in a muffin cup. And a favorite I taught a grandson: Buddy Burners, which are fire starters made with old newspapers and the wax from used candles. (I had my Girl Scout troop make a box of these for Walker Percy one winter and you'd have thought I'd given him a box of solid gold.)

Rural frugality, combined with a French heritage in which every edible bit of a food source is used and reinforced by the Great Depression and World War II, reveals itself in recipes like Cousin Anna's chicken soup with the chicken's feet providing the flavor and in stocks made from poultry carcasses and beef bones, from turnip, celery, and carrot tops, and from shrimp heads and shells or the fish bones left from filleting. (I will admit that the first time I was served chicken soup with a bright yellow chicken foot in it, I was less than happy.)

When I make stock, I freeze it in ice trays with dividers, and store the cubes in plastic bags. I do the same with the juice from my Meyer lemon tree, guaranteeing a supply until the next crop comes in.

Bread pudding, a Louisiana classic, is a marvelous way to use stale bread. The bits of pastry left from rolling out pie dough can be cut into strips, sprinkled with sugar and cinnamon, and baked along with the pie as an af-ter-school treat for children. Cooks in Acadiana used to turn leftover rice into croquettes, leftover vegetables into omelets or creamed with grated cheese on top. Waste not, want not must have been planted in them at birth.

I grew up knowing that starving children in various places across the world would be very happy to eat the food I wouldn't. Actually, the only foods I really wouldn't eat were liver and fried calves' brains, though the first time I had them, I ate them because I believed Mother when she said they were fried oysters. After I'd finished, she told me the truth. "I just wanted you to see that deciding against a food before you've tasted it might make you miss something really good." They were good. I just couldn't eat them knowing what they were.

When I cooked for my children, I had one simple rule: you were not to announce at the table that you didn't like this or that. The week's menus were posted on the refrigerator, so a child always knew what would be served. If she didn't want to eat a certain item, she would ask if there was something else she could have. There was always something, often peanut butter and jam sandwiches, two staples of any family with children.

An anecdote I read in a *Reader's Digest* entered into our family lore, that store of anecdotes that can smooth rough places and elicit a laugh rather than a groan. It's set in World War II, on a railroad dining car. The waiter approaches a man and asks, "Sir, do you like pork chops?" The man says he doesn't.

"What about creamed spinach?"

"Don't like that either."

"Prune whip?"

"Can't stand it."

"Good day, sir," the waiter says. "You have had your lunch."

This story comes in handy in many situations besides those involving food. To this day, if one sister is driving another mad, she will hear, "Good day, sir. You have had your lunch," which never fails to make them both laugh.

Recipes from Festivals and Church Fairs

Entrées

CHICKEN GUMBO FILÉ

1 large chicken, cut up
1 cup cooking oil
1 cup flour
1 cup chopped celery
2 cups chopped white onions
2 quarts water, heated on the stove, not from the tap
2 teaspoon chopped green onion tops
2 teaspoon chopped parsley
Salt and pepper to taste

Cook chicken in oil until brown, using a cast iron pot. Remove and add flour to oil slowly, making a brown roux. The roux must be cooked over low heat, with frequent stirring, until it is the color of a brown paper grocery bag. Add the white onions and celery and cook until soft. Return the chicken pieces to the pot, and add water slowly, stirring to make a smooth blend. (Note: Using hot water and adding it slowly will keep the roux smooth.) Let cook slowly until chicken is done, checking to make sure the stock is not sticking. If so, add more water and/or lower the heat. When chicken is done, add the parsley and onion tops.

Serve in soup plates over rice. You may either add ½ teaspoon filé to each plate or put it on the table for diners to add their own.

Yield: Serves 6 to 8, depending on appetites.

Note: Filé is made from dried sassafras leaves. The Choctaw taught early settlers how to use it. Filé must *never* be added to gumbo while it is still cooking, as it will result in a gummy soup. Nor must it *ever* be used in okra gumbo, as it will turn that into a stringy mess. But used in a roux-based gumbo, it adds a unique flavor characteristic of gumbos made in Acadiana.

Variations:

Two quarts of drained oysters may be added in the last few minutes of cooking, as they cook quickly. Drained, because the oysters retain enough liquid and any extra will thin your gumbo too much.

Cooked link sausage may be sliced and put in the gumbo once the stock is made. Andouille smoked sausage, which is flavored with anise, is a popular choice, but any firm, tasty sausage may be used.

CHICKEN, HAM, AND SHRIMP JAMBALAYA

1½ lbs. skinless, boneless chicken breasts and thighs, cut into 1-inch cubes
½ lb. cooked ham, cut into 1-inch cubes
2 lb. medium shrimp, peeled and deveined
Oil sufficient to brown the chicken and ham
2 cups chopped yellow onions
1 cup chopped green bell pepper
1 cup chopped celery
Garlic cloves to taste, peeled and minced
3 cups chicken broth (preferably homemade from necks and wings)
1 16-oz can diced tomatoes, liquid reserved
½ cup chopped green onion tops
2 tablespoons chopped parsley leaves
2 cups raw long-grain white rice
Salt, pepper, and cayenne to taste

Mix salt, black, and cayenne pepper and sprinkle over chicken cubes. Brown in oil in heavy pot over medium heat until brown on all sides. Put in a mixing bowl. Now brown the ham cubes, adding them to the chicken. Put chopped onions, bell pepper, and celery in the pot and cook, scraping brown bits from the bottom of the pot. Add the chicken and ham, lower the heat, cover the pot, and cook for 20–25 minutes, stirring occasionally. Mix the chicken broth and tomato juice, add to mixture in the pot, cover, and simmer over low heat for about 45 minutes. Mix the minced garlic into the drained tomatoes and add to the pot, along with the green onions, parsley, and shrimp. Add the rice, cover the pot, and bring to boil before reducing the heat to medium-low. Simmer until rice is tender and fluffy and the liquid is absorbed.

Yield: 6 to 8.

YAM CASSEROLE

3 cups mashed yams, about 4 good-sized ones baked or boiled and peeled
½ cup brown sugar
½ cup butter, softened
2 eggs, beaten
1 teaspoon cinnamon
⅓ cup fresh-squeezed orange juice

Topping:
⅓ cup melted butter
1 cup light brown sugar
1 cup chopped pecans
Chopped marshmallows (optional)

Mix the sugar, the softened butter, eggs, cinnamon, and orange juice into the mashed yams, and put into a greased 9 x 13-inch baking dish. Mix the melted butter, light brown sugar, and pecans and spread on top of the yams. (An alternate topping is to cover the yams with chopped marshmallows.) Bake in a preheated 325° oven for 25 minutes or until topping browns.

Yield: 8 to 10 servings.

Sweet potato casserole made by this recipe entered our family lore when my second daughter, Pamela, moved to Albuquerque. There only a month or so when Thanksgiving arrived, she called to let me know she would not dine alone, that she had been invited to a potluck dinner and was making her favorite sweet potato casserole. She arrived on the street, only to realize she'd left the house address at home. However, seeing numbers that seemed familiar and cars parked in front of a house, she knocked on the door, expecting to see the friend who had invited her. Instead, an elderly woman opened the door, and, realizing her mistake, Pamela asked if she could use the woman's phone. She entered to see a room full of elderly people, all dressed for a festive occasion, all staring at her. Flustered and wishing she were anywhere else, Pamela set down the casserole on the shelf and picked up the phone—and then watched as the casserole slid off the slanted shelf and landed, marshmallow side down, on the hostess's shag rug. A terrible silence followed, which Pamela broke by apologizing, saying she was so sorry, she had never done anything like that in her life, whereupon one old gentleman said, "Oh, sure. I bet you go around knocking on strangers' doors and dropping sweet potato casseroles all over everyone's rugs." Bless her, good sport that she is, she laughs every time we trot out this well-worn tale.

CANDIED YAMS

2–3 large yams
¾ cup granulated sugar, plus 1 tablespoon for soaking
½ cup water
¼ teaspoon salt
½ orange, sliced thin

Peel and cut yams into large chunks. Cover with warm water and 1 table-spoon sugar. Soak for 10 minutes.

Drain yams in a colander. Combine sugar, water, salt, and orange slices in a saucepan, bring to a low boil, then add the yams and cook until the syrup is thick and the yams are done. Just before serving, add 2–3 tablespoons butter.

Yield: Serves 3 to 4.

Note: Sweet potatoes and yams, of course, come from the same botanical family. However, Louisiana's growers prefer to call theirs "yams" because of the richer color and sweeter taste when compared to those grown in the North. Since I have never tested these two vegetables side by side, I have no idea if this is regional pride talking or actual fact.

GREEN RICE

2 cups raw long-grain white rice
⅔ cup green bell pepper, chopped
⅓ cup parsley, minced
1 cup green onions and tops, minced
¼ cup cooking oil
1½ tablespoons Worcestershire sauce
1 teaspoon salt
¼ teaspoon red pepper
4 cups bouillon or chicken stock

Mix all ingredients. Bake without stirring in a tightly covered 2-quart casserole for 45 minutes in a preheated 350° oven, or until the rice has ab-sorbed the liquid and is tender. Remove cover and toss with a fork, as season-ings rise to the top during baking. May be frozen after baking.

Yield: Serves 12.

SPANISH RICE

2 cups cooked long-grain white rice, salted to taste
1 cup sliced white onions
2 tablespoons butter
2⅓ cups canned tomatoes
3 tablespoons diced green pepper
2 whole cloves
1 small bay leaf
2 teaspoons sugar

Cook onions in butter until tender. Add the tomatoes, green pepper, cloves, bay leaf, and sugar and simmer uncovered for 15 minutes. Remove bay leaf and cloves. Add the rice and stir. Turn into a greased 1-quart casserole and bake in a preheated 375° oven for 30 minutes.

Yield: Serves 4.

EXOTIC RICE

2 cups dried apricots
1 cup white raisins
1 cup chopped white onion
½ cup chopped green bell pepper
½ cup butter
6 cups cooked rice (2 cups raw rice)

Chop, then soak raisins and apricots in water to cover for 30 minutes. Drain. Sauté onion and bell pepper in butter; add cooked rice, apricots, and raisins. Turn into a buttered 2-quart casserole and bake in a preheated 350° oven for 40 minutes.

Yield: Serves 12.

Baked Goods

No church fair would be complete without its baked goods booth, where women make the cake or pie they're known for, and a small competition to see whose booth sells out first goes on beneath the watchful eye of the local priests. Here are recipes that appear at these fairs and never fail to sell or please the buyer.

SPICE AND COFFEE CAKE

1 cup dark brown sugar
½ cup butter or margarine
1 cup ground walnuts or pecans
1 teaspoon baking soda
1 cup brewed coffee (lukewarm)
2½ cups all-purpose flour
3 eggs
1 cup raisins
½ cup currants
¼ teaspoon salt
¼ teaspoon allspice
¼ teaspoon cinnamon

Mix baking soda with a little boiling water; make a light paste. Combine sugar, eggs, butter; stir in raisins, currants, soda, salt, and spices. Add the coffee and flour, alternately. Pour into a prepared, regular-size loaf pan and bake one hour in a preheated 350° oven.

Icing
1 cup confectioners' sugar
3 teaspoons dripped coffee (or more if needed)

Mix sugar and coffee, spread on cake.

Note: Sugar planters in Louisiana sometimes keep back some of the unrefined or "raw" sugar, which is close in flavor and appearance to Demerara sugar, named for the colony in Guyana that was its original source. When I lived in a restored Acadian cottage in the country between Port Allen and Maringouin, a friend who had a sugar plantation nearby brought me a supply of his raw sugar, and since he and his wife were also friends of my second husband, he continued to bring some to us at Christmas after we married.

BROWN SUGAR COOKIES

2 sticks butter
1 full cup brown sugar
2 cups cake flour, sifted
1 egg yolk, unbeaten

Cream butter and brown sugar. Add cake flour. Mix in the egg yolk. Drop on ungreased cookie sheet from spoon, a small amount at a time. Bake in a preheated 325° oven for 10–12 minutes.
Yield: 3 dozen.

BEST PECAN PIE

This recipe is from my dear friend Gail Dugal, and it is truly the best I've ever tasted. Browning the butter makes all the difference in the world, and once you've tried it, I doubt you'll ever use another. Boyd Gaines, a famous Broadway actor, gave this pie the name "the wet dream pie," because the first time we met was when my youngest daughter brought him home for Thanksgiving, and a pecan pie along with a number of others was cooling on the kitchen counter. He took one look at it, asked for a taste, and named it on the spot.

1 stick butter
1 cup light corn syrup
1 cup sugar
3 large eggs, beaten
½ teaspoon lemon juice
1 teaspoon vanilla
1 dash of salt
1 cup chopped pecans
8- or 9-inch unbaked pie shell

Brown butter in saucepan until it is golden brown. Do not burn. Let cool. In separate bowl, add ingredients in order listed; stir. Blend in browned butter well. Pour in unbaked pie shell and bake in preheated 425° oven for 10 minutes, then lower to 325° for 40 minutes.
Use either a metal pastry rim or make one with aluminum foil to keep the edges of the pie crust from browning more than the rest of it.

FRESH APPLE CAKE

4½ cups raw apples, peeled and chopped
Lemon juice
1½ cups vegetable oil
2 cups sugar
2 large eggs
2½ cups all-purpose flour
1 teaspoon salt
1 teaspoon baking soda
2 teaspoon baking powder
2 teaspoon vanilla
1½ cup pecans, chopped

Prepare apples: Sprinkle a little lemon juice over them, set aside, and cover. Add sugar and eggs to oil; mix well at low speed until creamy and smooth. Sift flour and measure. Sift again with salt, soda, and baking powder. Add the flour mixture to creamed mixture a little at a time, folding in well after each addition. Add vanilla. When batter is stiff, remove beaters and finish mixing by hand. Fold in apples and nuts. Bake in a prepared 9 x 13 pan or in a tube pan for 55 minutes to an hour in a preheated 350° oven. Let cool and turn out on a platter or cake stand.

This cake may be served plain, with whipped cream, or a scoop of vanilla ice cream. It keeps well and also freezes well.

CHOCOLATE POUND CAKE

2 sticks butter
½ cup solid shortening
3 cups sugar
3 cups flour (sifted before measuring)
½ teaspoon baking powder
½ teaspoon salt
1 cup milk
2 teaspoons vanilla
5 eggs
½ cup cocoa

Cream butter, shortening, and sugar. Add eggs, one at a time. Sift the dry ingredients and add to the creamed mixture, alternating with the milk to which you have added the vanilla. Pour into a greased and floured Bundt cake pan and bake in a preheated 300° oven for 1½ hours or until done. Good served plain or with your choice of icing. Keeps and freezes well.

Lagniappe

ROASTED PECANS

1 quart pecan halves
½ stick butter

Place butter in a cast iron skillet and put in a preheated 300° oven until it melts. Stir in pecans and bake until pecans begin to brown. Stir occasionally. You will have to taste test a pecan to make sure they have reached the proper degree of roasting. Pour out on waxed paper and add salt, stirring to mix it. Cool, then place in an airtight container.

It is pointless to make only one quart of these pecans, unless you live in a very disciplined household. My second husband once offered my youngest daughter fifty dollars if she would tell him where I'd hidden the roasted pecans. She said she knew that wherever they were, they would not be found until I wanted them to be. Not that I'm stingy—but that man could go through a quart of pecans like a famous general went through Georgia.

CHAPTER ELEVEN

At the beginning of seventh grade, we were introduced to two new enterprises, one due to Mother Dolores's zeal to make Mt. Carmel in Lafayette a stellar example of a well-rounded educational institute for girls, and the other due to Sister Veronica's zeal to instill a desire to serve others in girls still young enough to mold. And so, Gail and I, along with about half of our class, found ourselves members of a 4-H Club. Of course, such clubs abounded in the rural schools in the area, but rarely in urban communities, for the excellent reason that many of its activities involved caring for plants and animals and, in general, preparing members for an agricultural career.

I remember learning the pledge and thinking that at least that made a great deal of sense. It included the four words beginning with H that give the organization its name: "I pledge my head to clearer thinking; my heart to greater loyalty; my hands to larger service; and my health to better living for my club, my community, my country, and my world." The motto, "To make the best better," could have been written by Mother Dolores, and we resigned ourselves to devoting ourselves to this new venture, if, as Gail said, all we got out of it was grace to offer up for the poor souls in Purgatory.

I realize that the concept of Purgatory is no longer accepted by the Roman Catholic Church, but being a Jungian, I do believe in a collective unconscious, and I do believe that if we haven't become fully conscious in this world, we're going to have to spend some time in the next getting up to speed.

Mother Dolores enlisted the help of a member of the home economics faculty at SLI. Though she couldn't attend all our meetings, she did furnish Mother Dolores with projects that carried out the 4-H mission, most of these relating to the domestic arts, and did come to the meetings when we presented them, thus validating our club.

Since Mt. Carmel didn't have a home ec. department, when we had sewing projects, we would lay out the pattern pieces on fabric and cut them out at school, pinning and basting together those that we could, and then sewing them by machine at home. Cooking projects moved to the kitchen in the convent, and those were our favorite meetings because not only did we get the cinnamon buns the nun who reigned there had become famous for, but we had glimpses into the mysterious lives of the sisters.

At that time, Mt. Carmel nuns wore the standard white headpiece most orders wear under their veils, but in addition, they wore a frilled piece that framed their faces. One afternoon while we worked in the kitchen, I caught a glimpse of a nun in the laundry room next door standing at an ironing board with a strange looking instrument in her hand. She looked up, saw me watching her, and invited the group in to see how she used that odd tool. It worked like tongs. It had two long, narrow, round pieces of metal that the sister heated on a hot plate. She then crimped the edges of a long piece of damp, starched linen, turning it into the frilled piece that made their habit so distinctive.

Except for the kitchen, until seventh grade, none of us had ever seen the rest of the convent. But in seventh grade, we had a daylong retreat that took place in the nun's chapel upstairs. I remember walking through the hall to the staircase, guarded over by a statue of Our Lady of Mt. Carmel giving the scapular to St. Simon Stock. The chapel overlooked the walled garden in which the nuns took recreation in fair weather. In bad weather, they had a large many-windowed room downstairs that also opened into the garden. The smell of furniture and floor wax, mixed with burning beeswax candles and incense, will forever take me back to that chapel, a place of peace and serenity that I can still revisit.

That year, too, Gail, Lois, Pat Jardell, and I, along with others whose names I don't remember, were invited to wax the hall floors in the school, an invitation that I suppose almost no child today would want to accept, but which we accepted with enthusiasm, recognizing it for the sign of trust it was. Trust, because we worked alongside the nuns, who tucked up their skirts and wore large, blue-and-white-striped aprons over their habits, removed their shoes and black stockings, and like us, wore thick socks that served as polishing rags as we "skated" up and down the halls, first putting down the wax, then, with a fresh pair of socks, polishing it. In this informal atmosphere, we got to know them not as nuns, but as people who had families and had had a life before the convent, lives they shared in bits and pieces, adding information that put together made portraits of young girls who had decided to give their lives to God.

Four members of our class of twenty-three girls did enter the convent: Pat Jardell, Florence Mouton, and Elsie Dupuis entered the Carmelite Order, and Kathleen Miles became a Sister of Mercy, because, when she interviewed orders to see which one suited her best, that order allowed its nuns to travel by themselves, and that liberal view convinced her.

Kathleen had one of the most unusual families of any of my friends. Her father, Dr. John Miles, was a radiologist, but he also served as the doctor for the Southern Pacific Railroad, which gave him and his family free tickets on any train going anywhere on its route. Kathleen had one younger sister and two younger brothers, who were absolute terrors, though to look at their angelic faces—blond, blue-eyed—you'd never have known it. Mrs. Miles was a DeGravelles from Jeanerette, an old and prominent family that has the reputation for a streak of eccentricity that manifests itself occasionally and which, since it has been there for generations, is accepted as being part of who they are.

All of us accepted our friends' parents as being adults we must treat with courtesy and respect and because they maintained a proper distance, not trying to be our friends—which, frankly, would never have entered their minds—but simply being parentis absentia when we were under their roof, I never noticed anything eccentric about Mrs. Miles, or indeed the family. That is, until one Saturday I called Kathleen to see if she'd like to join some of the crowd at a movie, only to be told she'd gone to Houston. "But she'll be back on the five o'clock train," Mrs. Miles said. "She wanted to finish a book and the boys were making so much noise she decided to take the Sunset Limited to Houston and the Argonaut back so she could read in peace." This still strikes me as one of the most civilized solutions to the disruptions of family life I have ever heard of.

I knew from personal experience just how awful Kathleen's brothers could be and I was glad she had such an escape route. My own experience with them still rankles for a number of reasons. One, I was wearing a new peasant blouse that had just become the rage. It had puffed sleeves, lace-edged ruffles around the low, round neckline and, all in all, was an attractive and flattering style. I had also just had my hair cut, washed it, and set it with papilottes to make soft curls that framed my face. (Papilottes are strips of cloth. To use them, you separate a strand of hair, roll it around the cloth, and then tie a knot. They are the devil to sleep on, but they do make very natural looking curls.)

So, I was feeling very pleased with myself as I rode my bike over to Carolyn Littell's, who lived around the corner from Kathleen. We knew without admitting it that some of the neighborhood boys would show up and a pitcher of lemonade and a plate of cookies just happened to be waiting in the kitchen.

Then, Brendan and Terry Miles appeared, carrying a box which, we supposed, held a garter snake or a frog or something equally typical of them. They approached me, and I prepared myself to ward off the reptile when they dumped it on me. But instead, when they tipped the box over my head, dirt rained on me, covering hair, shoulders, blouse. I sat there, unable to move, while Kathleen and Pat took off after them. The boys outran them, and though Carolyn took me inside and we tried to comb the dirt out of my hair and shake it out of my blouse, nothing would do except washing both. I rode home thinking of all the things I would do to those boys if I ever had the chance.

Only two memories remain of my 4-H experience. One is of a parade, part of a day that brought club members from all over Acadiana to Lafayette for a review of projects and an awards ceremony. Mother Dolores had directed our club to construct a house that would somehow incorporate the four aspects of the 4-H pledge. We created a cardboard structure that Gail and I had to carry in the parade, chosen as a reward by Mother Dolores, though neither of us regarded it that way.

Years later, an old schoolmate of my sister's sons, all of whom are exceptionally gifted in anything having to do with engineering, was visiting Dick and me. He told Dick that when Catholic High had a science fair, he would appear with his Styrofoam cup with a bean sprout growing out of it and the Selleck boys would set up their rockets that really worked. The other clubs in that 4-H parade from my childhood had projects so well executed that I knew exactly how he felt.

The second project involved judging crops. When Mother Dolores told Gail and me we would represent our club and our school in this event, I thought that finally, she had overreached. How could Gail and I judge crops? And why did Mother Dolores invariably fix on Gail and me for these projects?

But "ours not to reason why, ours but to do or die," so Gail and I rode our bikes to the SLI Ag Center, where the 4-H district competitions were being held. We entered to see rows of tables with sweet potatoes, ears of corn, and other vegetables laid out. We also saw nothing but boys, and from the way they studied the samples, I knew every one of them brought personal expertise to his task.

"This is ridiculous," I told Gail. "We can't do this."

"Sure we can. All we have to do is pick the boy who looks like the biggest hayseed. Then we follow him around and sneak a peek at his judging sheets. Of course, we won't copy them exactly, everyone would know we cheated. Just enough so we don't come in last."

"But Gail. That's not honest."

"Dubus, do you want Mother Dolores to send us to some stupid class on crop judging?"

"Is there such a thing?"

"Who knows? But I'm not taking a chance. Now come on. Help me pick our boy."

When the judging results were announced, sure enough, Gail and I had not come in last. We were in fourth place. "A respectable effort," Mother Dolores said, "considering neither of you lives on a farm."

I don't know if Gail confessed this deception, but I did. "Was there any material gain involved?" the priest said.

"The first, second, third, and fourth places got ribbons."

"But no monetary awards?"

"No, Father."

A long sigh. "Well, then, I suppose no real harm was done."

"Thank you, Father." He did, however, add two Our Fathers to the usual penance.

***

We had PE the last period of the day on Mondays, Wednesdays, and Fridays. On Tuesdays and Thursdays, we had health class, as boring a class as I have ever taken in my entire life. Perhaps Sister Dorothy felt the same way, because she added lessons in hand-sewing to the curriculum. She would read the day's lesson to us and answer any questions while we learned to make French seams, French knots, the lazy daisy stitch, and other basics of embroidery.

Once we had mastered these techniques to Sister Dorothy's satisfaction, we embarked on our first project, to make an outfit for the statue of the Infant Jesus of Prague. In 1628, a princess, Polyxena of Lobkowicz, brought to Bohemia a wax statue of the Infant Jesus that her mother, Maria Maximiliana Manrique de Lara y Mendoza of Spain, had given her as a wedding gift. She became attached to the Carmelites and gave the statue to the Discalced (meaning they are cloistered) Carmelites in Prague. The princess, when giving the priests the statue, said, "Honor this image and you shall never want." And whether inspired by God or by his own devotion, the Emperor Ferdinand II of the House of Hapsburg sent 2,000 Florins to the Carmelites, followed with a stipend each month.

(The Carmelite Order has three levels: the first order is composed of priests, the second of nuns, and the third of lay people. All Mt. Carmel students at the time I was in school joined the Third Order, and I have a small statue of Our Lady of Mt. Carmel on the prie-dieu my daughters gave me.)

At any rate, a unique feature of the statue of the Infant Jesus of Prague is that it wears real clothes. The statue is forty-eight centimeters, or a little over a foot and a half. It wears a petticoat, then a gown made of some elaborate fabric, such as gold brocade, heavily trimmed with lace and other ornamentation.

Each student had a different task; one might work on a sleeve of the petticoat, another on the body of it. We used French seams, taking tiny, even stitches, which, Sister Dorothy said, were in themselves an act of devotion. Then, Sister Veronica entered the picture.

Learning from Sister Dorothy that we had mastered fine hand-sewing, she spoke to the class, asking for volunteers for a project she wished to begin at Lafayette's Charity Hospital. The project had three goals: to make layettes for babies born there; to visit the children's ward, bringing comic books and candy; and to visit the ward for the elderly. Those volunteering for the project would begin the ward visits that week, but the entire class would work on the layettes. Of course, Gail and I volunteered, as did Lois and Pat and Carolyn. (I know there must have been others, but I don't remember their names.) We collected comic books, got donations of candy bars from the local drug store as well as buying some ourselves, and began this corporal work of mercy without much enthusiasm, but knowing a duty had to be done.

We went first to the children's ward. I still remember the shock of walking into that room lined with beds filled with children with legs in casts elevated over their heads, children recovering from surgery, from burns—even though the air reeked with strong disinfectant, you could still smell infection and urine beneath it, and if Sister Veronica had not been with us, I know I would have bolted. Still, we went from bed to bed, handing out candy and comic books, making conversation when a patient responded to our presence, enduring silence when he or she didn't. And all the while, I thought of what it was like being sick at home, lying in a freshly made-up bed, eating a dainty lunch set on a bed-tray, being read to by Mother when I felt too tired to read—and I knew by looking at my classmates that they thought the same thing.

A subdued group left the children's ward to go upstairs to visit the elderly, and here we had a completely different reception. None of the patients spoke English, so Sister Veronica told us to speak to them in French. We had only begun studying French that year, and our vocabulary as well as our accents caused first consternation, as the patients tried to figure out what we said, and then gales of laughter as they understood we thought we spoke French. A babble of words in the Cajun patois filled the ward, and as we went from bed to bed, we restricted ourselves to "Bonjour, madame," "Bonjour, monsieur," though even that made them laugh.

As we walked down the hall, Sister Veronica congratulated us. "You see, you cheered them up, and that is a very good thing."

"By making them laugh at us," Gail said.

"Gail—humility is a great virtue, as is charity to others. Today, you have learned something about both."

As indeed we had. We continued the visits, gaining more confidence and doing better with our French. When we finished the layettes, Sister Veronica wrapped each set in tissue paper and said she would deliver them to the hospital the next day. We asked if we might go with her. "It is not an appropriate thing for you to do," she said.

"We just want to see the babies," someone said.

"They are human beings, not something for strangers to look at as though they are on display." She waited until this lesson hit home, then said, "There are not many little babies in this world who begin life in layettes with French seams, embroidered flowers, hand-made buttonholes, and French knots, but thanks to your efforts, these babies will. And that should make you very happy."

It did.

***

We hadn't had a dog since Pups, the beagle Dick Hearin gave André and me, disappeared. We had talked about getting one, but, with one thing and another, hadn't followed the talk with action. Then, one weekend in late fall, we were in Baton Rouge for a football game. Mother's youngest brother, Oran, indeed the baby of the family, and his wife Peggy lived in Baton Rouge, where he worked at Standard Oil's chemical plant, which was headed by our Uncle Francis's brother, Alex.

On Sunday, when we went to visit with them, we found Uncle Julian and Aunt Bertha there. Uncle Julian had returned from the war soon after V-E Day, and after a period of R & R, had applied for a job at the Standard Oil plant. He asked us if we had a dog, and when we said no, he suggested he, Daddy, Uncle Oran, and André should go to the local SPCA facility and find one.

The men didn't give Mother time to say no. They piled in a car and drove off, returning later with a yellow mutt. Not only were his looks unprepossessing, he had battle scars that did not bode well. Daddy took one look at Mother's face and assured her that Julian had looked at every dog and had determined that Adam would be perfect. "He has confidence in himself," Daddy said. "Which means he hasn't been mistreated."

"Except by other dogs," Mother said.

"That just means he's courageous," Julian said. "You don't want a coward, do you?"

Mother didn't want this dog at all, but she knew better than to argue. "Has he had his shots?"

"Every one," Julian said.

"One thing," Mother said. "Could he have a new name?"

"But isn't he used to his old one?" I said.

"This is the kind of dog that after you feed him twice, you can call him anything you want, as long as you call him for supper," Daddy said.

"I gathered that," Mother said.

And so, Adam became Mike and more than lived up to Uncle Julian's faith in him. For one thing, besides being housebroken, he had incredibly good manners. He sensed Mother's reluctance to have him in the house, and he treated her with dog courtesy, not even looking as though he might jump on the furniture, not hanging around her heels in the kitchen begging for food, not lying down close enough to her armchair so she could reach down and pet him, something he did the minute Daddy sat down.

We made a bed for him in the basement, though he stayed in the house throughout the day unless André and I took him for a walk or played outside. And after a few weeks, either because we'd gotten accustomed to his looks, or because having a home had boosted his spirits, Mike had a certain style that my parents' friends found charming. They began to make over Mike when they were having a cocktail before dinner, and when someone dropped a peanut on the floor and Mike snapped it up, they began slipping him peanuts and bites of cheese straws without taking their eyes off the person they were talking to. Of course, this operation was about as secret as Kathryn and me slipping under our grandmother's table to ring the bell, but since Mike never begged for a peanut, it met with the same success.

My sister had been bitten by a dog when we lived in Baton Rouge, and because the dog couldn't be found, she had to have the anti-rabies shots, fourteen of them. These are extremely painful shots, given in the abdomen, and it's not surprising that she never liked dogs after that. Mike sensed this. When he entered a room with my sister the only occupant, he did the greatest imitation of "dog entering an empty room" that I have ever seen. I know it was a performance, because I had watched him enter a truly empty room and his behavior was completely different.

That spring, Mother Dolores announced that now the war was over, Mt. Carmel would once more have a May Festival. None of us had heard of this event, but we soon learned all about it. To begin with, a raffle would be held to raise money for a project close to Mother Dolores's heart—a gym. She would get an automobile donated, and since new cars were still not plentiful, people would be happy to buy raffle tickets, which would be sold by students. There would be two courts, one from grades one through six, one from grades seven through twelve. The girls selling the most tickets would reign as queens of the festival; runners-up would serve in their courts. On coronation night, a pageant would be held, consisting of dances put on by various classes. Our class would do a waltz.

Mother Dolores delivered all this information in a tone that brooked no questions and no dissent. To my great relief, she did leave it up to students to choose if they wished to compete for the queen's crown and court. But each of us did have a quota of tickets to sell, which, when achieved, would make a good start for the gym fund.

The Dodge dealer donated an automobile, a 1946 Custom four-door, which, due to the lack of time to retool, was essentially the 1942 model with a new grille. Its list price was $1,389.00, and, as predicted, tickets sold briskly.

Meanwhile, Sister Dorothy had auditions for dancers, choosing twelve girls, including Gail and me. We would dance to Johann Strauss's "Skaters' Waltz," a melody I came to hate as rehearsals dragged on. The waltz step itself isn't difficult; learning the patterns in which we were to move was.

When I saw the design for our dresses, I began to feel better about the whole thing. Made of marquisette, a popular evening dress fabric at the time, they had flowing skirts, sweetheart necklines edged in tiny roses, and puffed sleeves. The dresses would be in six pastel shades: blue, pink, green, yellow, lavender, and aqua, with two girls wearing each shade. Thus, we would create a rainbow effect as we moved through the dance.

One Saturday morning just before I left for rehearsal, the phone rang and Gail's sister, Corinne, gave me the news that Gail had had an emergency appendectomy the night before and was resting comfortably at St. Anne's Infirmary. I bicycled to school as fast as my legs would carry me, bursting in with a breathless announcement, which Sister Dorothy already knew.

"Her mother called to tell me Gail wouldn't be here. But she should be well in time for the pageant. Now, let us begin rehearsal with a prayer of thanks that they got Gail's appendix in time." Before wonder drugs, a burst appendix could be fatal, and all too often was. So, any rise in temperature with no apparent reason, any pain in the right side that persisted, any unex-plained nausea, was taken seriously, and, being a conscientious mother, Mrs. Dugal hadn't waited for more than one symptom to appear before calling their doctor.

I stopped at Borden's to get Gail a cup of vanilla ice cream, since St. Anne's Infirmary was only two more blocks down Jefferson Street. I entered

Gail's room to find her sitting in bed, a jar with her appendix in it on the table at her side. Unfazed as usual, she made light of the whole thing. When I asked her how it felt to take ether, she said she just shut her eyes and took deep breaths like they asked her to, and that's all there was to it.

"You weren't afraid you might not wake up?"

"Dubus, why would I be? If I didn't, I'd never know, so what difference would it make?"

The nurse put the ice cream in the refrigerator until the doctor made rounds and said Gail could eat it. She recovered quickly and in time to be in the pageant. I don't think I have ever known anyone who adjusted to the vicissitudes of life with more pragmatism than Gail. She died of lung cancer a few years ago, but she is one of those people who make such an impression that as long as I have conscious life, in my memory, she still lives.

A man who was quite prosperous won the automobile. Mother Dolores called to tell him, and after he had expressed his pleasure at this good news, she said, "But since you already have a new car, why don't you donate it back to us so we can raffle it again?" Few men in Lafayette could have resisted such a request, and he was not one of them. He donated the car, another raffle was held, and the gym fund got off to an even better start.

Henry Heymann owned a department store in Lafayette, as well as the property that in the 1950s would become the Oil Center. Already wealthy, he gave to many charities, and his family has continued to do the same. Hearing that Mt. Carmel needed a gymnasium, and wanting to honor his mother, Mr. Heymann told Mother Dolores that he would build the gym on the condition that it be named for his mother. Mother Dolores thanked him but said the gym would be named for only one mother, Our Lady of Mt. Carmel.

And then she did something that I still consider a stroke of fundraising genius. She hired a contractor to begin the gym. He put in the foundation and two rows of bricks on top of that. Then, work ceased. Businessmen driving by saw this, and one of them called Mother Dolores to say that if she needed help dealing with her contractor, he and some others would be glad to speak with him.

"I'm not having trouble with him," she said. "We agreed that he would build the gym on a pay-as-you-go basis, and I don't have any money left." Then, she mentioned Mr. Heymann's offer. "But generous as that is, I couldn't let him do it. You do understand?" Her caller understood very well. Mr. Heymann was Jewish and his generosity put Catholic generosity to shame. In a very short time, funds sufficient to build the gym had been raised, and knowing Mother Dolores, I doubt she was surprised.

At one point that spring semester, Sister Dorothy told me Mother Dolores wanted to see me in her office after school. As I walked toward it, I reviewed my recent behavior, wondering what I had done that I would be chided for. Mother Dolores had something entirely different in mind. "The Louisiana Floral Association is having a competition for the best essay about flowers," she said. "I just received the announcement this morning, and it has to be posted by midnight tonight, so there's no time to have a schoolwide contest. You will write the essay for us."

She said she had called my mother to tell her I would be late getting home, and that if I went to the refectory, I could have milk and a cinnamon bun. I returned to her office, took out pen and paper, thought a bit, and began to write. I finished and handed Mother Dolores my work. She read it, crumpled it, dropped it into the wastebasket, and said, "That will not win."

Win? She expected me to win? Of course.

Creative writing included serving as editor of the school newspaper, *Echoes*.
I am seated on the left, in the black vest.

And so, I began again. And again. And again. Finally, it dawned on me that I would sit like a monk chained to his desk until somehow I wrote something that Mother Dolores thought would win. In a rebellious mood, I changed my approach entirely, producing an essay that she read and then said, "This will do."

I gave it no more thought until a few weeks later, when Mother Dolores announced in morning assembly that I had won the local contest, and that an orchid would be delivered to my house. And then, a few weeks after that, she announced that I had won the state competition, and that the prize was $75.00. As I walked to the front of the auditorium to receive my prize, I knew what she would say: "I told you so."

But she didn't. Instead, she looked into my eyes and said, "Beth, a teacher has two responsibilities. One is to instill knowledge in her students' minds. The other is to bring out what the student doesn't know is there. You are a writer."

As it turned out, I was.

***

The summer of 1946 marked my last one before I entered my teens in October. I was one of the youngest in our crowd and still hadn't started menstruating or developing breasts. Many of the girls, including Gail, had gotten their first period, and many were also developing breasts. Thus, the summer made a transition between childhood and adolescence, and the nature of our activities began to change.

We had dancing classes that summer, from a Mr. Jack Lamont, a true five-by-five, who, nevertheless, was one of the lightest dancers I've ever encountered. He held his classes in the Oak Room at the Evangeline Hotel, and when Gail and I entered the room, we saw that his students were a mixture of boys from Cathedral, girls from Mt. Carmel, and boys and girls from Lafayette Junior High. He played records, selecting music that made matching our steps to the beat relatively easy. He used "Whispering" for the foxtrot, and though I rarely hear it, when I do I am instantly transported back to that room, paneled in oak, lights dim, moving to the beat while held by a boy who more often than not stared at his feet—forbidden—and counted—also forbidden.

Mr. Lamont proved to be a strong taskmaster, and any boy with mischief on his mind soon forgot about it when Mr. Lamont threatened a public spanking to anyone who disrupted his class. One night, Tommy LeBlanc purposely dropped Sally Somebody-or-Other while doing the shag to punish her for refusing him a kiss. (I doubt anyone still does the shag, but at one point, the boy bends his knees, the girl sits on them, and he then takes hold of her and slides her over his head to his back.) Mr. Lamont ordered Tommy to lie on his knees and spanked him ten times before releasing him. Sally wasn't hurt, but Tommy's pride suffered greatly, and after that, decorum reigned.

And no, Tommy's parents not only did not sue Mr. Lamont, his mother called him to thank him for giving Tommy a lesson he well-deserved.

Mr. Lamont also insisted that we learn to converse while dancing. He suggested we talk about movies we'd seen or wanted to see, and other events in our lives our partners might be interested in. If anything is guaranteed to tie the tongues of people at that awkward age, being ordered to engage in conversation will do it.

As usual, Gail had no trouble doing this. Any boy who danced with her talked until the dance ended, while the other girls struggled with partners who seemed to have lost their vocal cords. When I asked Gail why her partners talked nonstop, she looked at me with that mild amazement such questions usually evinced. "Dubus, these boys aren't interested in anything but having class end so they can go home. So, I ask them about their dogs."

"What if they don't have one?"

"Dubus. Have you ever met a male of any age around here who doesn't have a dog?"

Good advice.

When my second daughter's husband, who grew up in Albuquerque, asked me how I knew so much about sports, I told him that any woman growing up in south Louisiana knew she had to be able to talk about hunting, fishing, and football, and that though the only two college teams I have any interest in are Tulane and Ole Miss, I make sure I am sufficiently informed about LSU and the Saints to at least ask the right questions.

***

Farm families needed drivers for farm equipment, so driver's licenses could be obtained at age fifteen. Since the boys who were beginning to be part of our crowd were two years older than we, a good number of them had driver's licenses, and Sunday afternoon outings began.

After years of gasoline rationing, people took to the roads on weekends, sometimes driving for the sake of driving with no destination in mind. Louise's brother Louis, two years older, had a driver's license, as did Laurie Richard, the boy who lived behind us. Another boy, Brice Francez, formed the third in this trio, and on Sunday afternoons, they would appear at my house with Louise and Mary Alice Blanchet already in the car, and we would be off for an afternoon that would end at the White Hut, a local drive-in.

Brice's father was a partner in the local Cadillac dealership, and we often used his convertible. He got a new one every year but had no interest in them. He reserved that for his palomino stallion, a splendid horse that he allowed no one to ride. He kept the horse at a ranch his father owned near their home in Carencro and spent as much time out there as he could, thus earning him the nickname "Tex."

Henri Bendel, the designer and founder of the New York store, had been born in Louisiana and lived in Lafayette as a child. In his later years, he built a Spanish-style house with arches and a red tile roof set on a large piece of walled property bordered by the Vermilion River. Yet Bendel spent most of his time in New York, and after he died in 1936, the house stood empty for years. Eventually, the property became a subdivision named Bendel Gardens, and a number of my friends live there.

At the time, we believed a more romantic (though inaccurate) version of the story: a story of Bendel as a young groom, building a house for his bride and then, devastated by his bride's early death, leaving the house forever. This tale appealed to our imaginations, and we would occasionally drive by on Sundays, hoping to find the wrought-iron gates open. And one Sunday, we did. Louis was at the wheel, and though Louise, Mary Alice, and I said we thought we shouldn't go in, of course the boys disagreed.

So, we drove in, following the drive until it reached the house. It did indeed look mysterious, the perfect setting for one of the Nancy Drew mysteries I loved. The boys got out and tried to peer through windows, but heavy shutters covered them, and they gave up.

As we approached the gate, we saw it had been closed, and then a man stepped out and confronted us. Louis stopped the car, and the man came up to his window and asked what he thought he was doing, trespassing on private property. Louis faked what he thought was a Virginia accent and said we were tourists and seeing the gate open, mistook it for a historic site we wanted to see. "Well," the man said, "I see you have Louisiana license plates and I imagine if I asked for your license, I'd see a Lafayette address, so if I were you, son, I'd get out of here thanking my lucky stars I let you off."

Such a mild prank, and yet, knowing what Mr. Cornay would have said to his son, we all vowed never to breathe a word to anyone and drove away determined to never trespass anywhere again.

Around the same time, groups of boys and girls began meeting at the Jefferson Theatre, the town's biggest and best, for the Sunday matinee. I don't remember anyone arranging this, it just came about, and before long there might be as many as sixteen of us, sitting together and then walking to Borden's for ice cream. We saw *Sister Kenny*, in which Rosalind Russell portrays Elizabeth Kenny, an Australian nurse whose method of helping polio victims regain the use of their limbs made medical history, though not without creating controversy. The movie reminded us of a constant summertime threat—a polio epidemic—during which movie theaters and swimming pools closed, and parents were advised not to take their children to any place a crowd gathered, not even church.

I can remember summers from my childhood when, for weeks at a time, we barely left home. When Dr. Jonas Salk's vaccine became available, and I took my children to Dr. Louis Tyler's office to receive it, the prayers of thanks I gave came not just from the fact that the dreadful disease had been conquered, but from the knowledge of what it could do.

One of my closest friends, Jeannie Maraist, whose father retired from the army as a brigadier general after a career in which he led one of the armies that met the Russians at the River Elbe in World War II, had polio at age ten. It left her crippled, so that she had to use two hand canes to walk, and though she had a tough spirit and determination, as well as a family that encouraged her in every way, I can only imagine how she felt when she watched her friends walk and dance with ease and grace.

We saw *Anna and the King of Siam* that summer, and later, when my cousin Walter married Barbara Jean Perkins, whose father, after serving as president of Jefferson Medical College in Philadelphia, took his family to Siam where he served as a medical missionary, she told me of watching the King of Siam play golf, accompanied by a servant who held a seven-pagoda parasol over the royal head.

Esther Williams, who gained her first fame by winning swimming competitions—she would have represented the United States in the 1940 Olympics had they not been canceled due to the war—had become a movie star, with her first big film, *Easy to Wed*, appearing in 1946 with Van Johnson, Lucille Ball (in her first comedic role), and Keenan Wynn. Before that, Williams had starred in Billy Rose's *Aquacade*, replacing Eleanor Holms. Williams's movies, musicals with aquatic performances, brought swimming to the fore, and her glamorous bathing suits, caps, and cover-ups gave a lift to female bathing attire, something very much to be desired. When these movies came out, Gail—who else?—got a group of us to practice routines from Williams's movies in the municipal pool, and under her tutelage we learned enough to put on a short show.

Seventeen magazine had begun publication in 1944, and now we began reading it, getting together to try out hairstyles and giving each other manicures and pedicures, using either a clear gloss or the palest pink polish, but still feeling very grown-up when we went to Begnaud's Drug Store and headed for the cosmetic counter.

Evening in Paris was a popular line of perfume and powder sold in drug stores. Its signature color, cobalt blue, made its products stand out, and the shape of the bottles, the silver tops with blue tassels, accounted for its popularity as much, probably, as did its scent. Of course, we weren't old enough to use perfume, not even eau de toilette, but we could sniff the sample bottles, and even touch a scent to our wrist, trying to determine what might work on our skin when the magic day we could use it came.

On my thirteenth birthday, my Aunt Florine gave me a set of five colognes, each a floral scent, each bottle with a white wooden top with the appropriate flower painted on it. When I was old enough to use a more sophisticated perfume, Faberge's ACT IV became my favorite, though in my naivete, it was a while before I realized to what act the name referred.

Maureen Daly's *Seventeenth Summer*, published in 1943 and considered the first young adult novel—at least the first written at that time—had gained a must-read standing, and I still remember a classic line from that book: "Men are like streetcars. There's always another one coming." And time after time, I've learned how true that is.

That summer our crowd began to have Coke parties, at which we played the newest records and also turned the pages of our parents' magazines looking for automobile ads, not with any idea of buying a car, but because it had become essential to be able to identify them by sight, because automobiles had taken over the top spot on the boys' interest list.

On one of those afternoons, someone suggested we form a club. "What kind of club?" someone asked.

"A secret club."

"Why?" Gail, naturally.

"Well, because there'll be secrets we don't want anyone else to know, and if we have a club, we can have an initiation where we all have to promise never to tell one thing another club member tells us." I thought it a fine idea, not only because of the assurance that my secrets would be safe, but because adolescence seemed scary, to say the least, and if I belonged to a club, I would feel braver.

There happened to be seven girls present at Louise's that day. Louise, Gail, Lois, Patsy, Kathleen, Carolyn, and me. So, we called ourselves the Secret Seven. Later, we would become the Elegant Eight, the Notorious Nine— we hadn't seen that movie, but we knew it dealt with secrets and spies—the Terrific Ten, and on up to the Fabulous Fifteen.

A late summer watermelon party serves as a metaphor for that transition summer. As usual, it took place in Girard Park and also as usual, we ate watermelon and prepared for the race afterward. But this time, the boys seemed charged with a different kind of energy, and when they ran after us, it seemed clear they had more than catching us and rubbing watermelon all over us in mind. When one of them caught me, a boy I had danced with quite a bit at dancing class, he rubbed watermelon with the fruit still on the rind all over me, soaking my blouse and shorts with juice, making a mess of my face and hair. I felt his hands on me, not stopping and really feeling me, but still, with strength I hadn't noticed before. When he let me go, we looked at each other. And then he jumped up and ran away.

A group of us went to Elia (nicknamed Tootsie) Torian's for supper and to spend the night. She had just arrived in Lafayette. Her father had a high position in the Southern Pacific Railroad, they had family in the area, and she became the member who first changed our club's name. Mrs. Torian told us to shower and put on our pajamas and robes, and she would immediately wash our stained clothes.

After supper, we sat in a circle on the floor of the Torian's living room, and Gail suggested we each say what kind of husband we'd like to marry. Most of the descriptions blended movie stars and a real live boy, though no one used anyone's name. Gail's description of what she wanted stayed with me: "I want to marry a doctor because the man stays out and the money comes in." As always, she was way ahead of us, already realizing that we are formed by our early lives, and that since she had seen the polite distance between her parents, she had decided that she might as well accept marriage's limitations and plan her life in spite of them.

As for me, I entered my teens with the idea that a husband and wife could be deeply in love with each other for years after their wedding day, that they could enjoy the same music, the same books, the same friends—in a word, that with love came compatibility. And though that has proved true many times in my life, that belief blinded me to one significant flaw: if the other person only pretends to enjoy the same people and the same things, then the whole edifice is built on a falsehood, and like any weak structure, will eventually give way.

One morning shortly before my thirteenth birthday, my father told me he was going out to inspect the new Gulf States line that ran from Henderson Bay in the Atchafalaya Basin back into the bayous, and asked if I'd like to go with him. Of course I did. He picked me up at school and we drove to Henderson Point, where a crewman waited in a pirogue with the GSU symbol on the bow.

As he helped me step down from the dock, he said, "*Mais*, Miss Beth, don't bother that turtle, no. He's my supper." Since snapping turtles are very aggressive when out of water, and since they can amputate a finger with one snap of their jaws, I had no intention of getting anywhere near it.

As we followed the line, and reached the first dock, a woman came out to meet us, carrying a jar of fig preserves in her hand. "*Mais*, Mr. Dubus," she said, handing him the jar, "thank you for the lights. Now my baby's milk, it don't spoil anymore."

This scene with little variation was repeated at every dock. And no matter how much my father protested that he had not achieved electrifying the swamps and bayous without a great deal of help, Cajun logic said differently.

"*Mais*, Mr. Dubus. Before you come, we not got lights. Then you come and we have them."

I have never forgotten that afternoon, nor the expression on my father's face as he watched the lights come on in cabin after cabin as dusk came on. These were his people, and though his French roots were different from theirs, both the Acadians and the French Royalists had been exiled for political reasons, the Acadians because they wouldn't give up their religion to take an oath to the English king—which would have meant becoming, like all his subjects, Anglicans—and the French Royalists when Maximilien Robespierre, after Louis XVI died in 1793, began what came to be called the Reign of Terror, in order to save their heads.

Coming to a territory still under Spanish rule, they brought with them the customs, mores, religious beliefs, and ethnic history that had been part of their people's lives for centuries. Those two heritages met in the area around Lafayette: the formality of the Royalists balanced by the exuberance of the Acadians; the education of one extended by the other's knowledge of nature and her ways. The culture created by these two migrations is still unique, still strong in its belief in family, in character, and in God. It has withstood natural disasters like Hurricane Katrina, and man-made ones like the BP oil spill, with courage, perseverance, and hope. After Katrina, many people thought New Orleans was dead, buried, and past resurrection. These people didn't understand that cities with a soul never die.

New Orleans has a soul, one composed of descendants of French Royalists, enslaved Africans and free people of color, descendants of soldiers who fought in the War of 1812, descendants of Lafitte's pirates, artists of all kinds, and families who were among the first twenty French families to enter New Orleans.

Acadiana is derived from Acadia, which is what the French called Nova Scotia when they settled there. Acadia means "Happy Land," and I will be forever thankful that I was privileged to spend the formative years of my life in such a place.

Traditional Recipes

Beverages

HOT EGGNOG

1 quart whole milk
4 tablespoons sugar
4 eggs separated, with whites beaten
Nutmeg
Bourbon whiskey

Cream egg yolks and sugar until light in color. Heat milk just to the boiling point (do not let boil) and add a little to the creamed mixture, stirring. Blend creamed mixture into the pot of hot milk. Fold beaten egg whites into this mixture. Add desired amount of whiskey and serve with nutmeg sprinkled on top.
Yield: Serves 4 to 8.

CAFÉ BRULOT

16 lumps sugar
24 whole cloves
12 jiggers cognac
4 large twists orange peel
4 sticks cinnamon
10 demitasse cups of strong coffee
2 twists of lemon peel

Allow all ingredients except coffee to muddle 1 hour before serving. Blaze all for 1–2 minutes. Add coffee slowly. Using a slotted spoon, take the cinnamon sticks, whole cloves, and lemon and orange peel from the brew. Serve in demitasse cups.

Appetizers

PICKLED BLACK-EYED PEAS

4 cups cooked black-eyes peas, drained
1 cup salad oil
¼ cup wine vinegar
1 cup garlic buds (yes, 1 cup), tied into cheesecloth
1 medium onion, sliced thinly
½ teaspoon salt
Freshly ground black pepper

Mix ingredients. Store in a covered container in the refrigerator. Remove garlic after one day.

May be kept refrigerated for as long as two weeks. Serve with king-size Frito chips or the equivalent.

MUSHROOMS IN BURGUNDY WINE

1 cup burgundy wine
1 clove garlic
1 scallion
¼ teaspoon black pepper
⅓ cup butter
8-ounce box fresh mushrooms
1 teaspoon minced parsley

Crush the garlic and chop the scallion fine. Put in a saucepan with the burgundy. Simmer until liquid is reduced to half volume. Cool and blend in pepper, minced garlic, and melted butter. Pan-broil mushrooms and cover with wine butter. Serve hot in a chafing dish.

Multiply recipe as needed.

Eggs and Cheese

EGGS DIJON

1 teaspoon prepared Dijon mustard
¼ teaspoon salt
1 cup sour cream
3 tablespoons grated Gruyère cheese
1 tablespoon dry white wine
6 eggs
Buttered breadcrumbs

Mix together the Dijon mustard, salt, sour cream, grated cheese, and wine. Break eggs into a greased shallow baking dish or two eggs in each of three ramekins. Cover eggs with sauce and sprinkle buttered breadcrumbs over top. Place in a pan of hot water and bake in a preheated 350° oven for 15 minutes.

Yield: Serves 3.

CHEESE GRITS

1½ cups grits
7 cups water
1 teaspoon salt
1 lb. sharp cheese, grated
2 eggs
1 tablespoon Worcestershire sauce
1 garlic bud, pressed
1 stick butter
Tabasco sauce

Cook grits in salted water until thick. Add remaining ingredients, mix well, put in a buttered casserole and bake in a preheated 450° oven for 45 minutes.

Yield: Serves 6.

Seafood

CRAWFISH ÉTOUFFÉE

1 cup vegetable oil
1 cup chopped celery
½ cup chopped bell pepper
2 tablespoons chopped parsley
2 tablespoons chopped green onion tops
2 cups chopped white onion
Salt and pepper to taste
1 cup water
6 lb. crawfish tails with fat

Cook vegetables in oil until sautéed. Add the crawfish fat and let cook well. Add the water, then the boiled, peeled, and deveined crawfish tails. Cook about 15 minutes. Make the day before so the flavors can set. Reheat very carefully or the tails will cook too much. Do not reheat in a microwave.
Serve over rice.
Yield: Serves 12 generously.

REMOULADE SAUCE

1 pint homemade mayonnaise
½ cup Creole mustard
2 tablespoons salad mustard
Salt to taste
1 tablespoon horseradish
1 teaspoon Worcestershire sauce
Juice of ½ lemon
1 clove garlic, grated or pressed
Dash Tabasco sauce

Optional:
½ cup finely chopped celery
½ cup finely chopped bell pepper
½ cup finely chopped onion

Mix all the ingredients together, blending well. Keep in a well-covered jar in the refrigerator. Serve over boiled shrimp and shredded lettuce.
Yield: 6 to 8 servings.

CHOCOLATE FUDGE

3 cups sugar
3 squares Baker's unsweetened chocolate
3 tablespoons white corn syrup
1 tablespoon butter
1 cup pecans
2 teaspoons vanilla extract
1 small can evaporated milk

Cook sugar, milk, chocolate, and syrup in a saucepan on low fire until soft ball stage. Add butter and take off the stove. Cool by putting the pot into the sink with water up to where the fudge in the pot stops. Beat until thick; add pecans and vanilla extract. The entire process takes about 20 minutes. Pour out in a buttered pan or dish.

Note: A soft ball stage is tested as followed: Put ice-cold water in a cup. Drop a half teaspoon of fudge into the water. If it immediately makes a soft ball, it is at the right stage.

Lagniappe

CHESS PIE

1 unbaked pie shell
3 whole eggs
¾ stick butter, melted
1½ cups sugar
1 teaspoon vanilla
1 tablespoon corn meal
1 tablespoon vinegar or lemon juice

Mix all ingredients well in order listed. Pour into an unbaked pie shell. Bake for 35 minutes in a 350° oven.

Note: This may be made in a square or rectangular pan. The result is then cut into squares and served at coffees or teas. There are recipes that call for vinegar instead of lemon juice.

The Southwestern Louisiana Institute Debate Team (I am located top row, center)

EPILOGUE

After four happy years in high school, I graduated in May 1951 and entered what was then Southwestern Louisiana Institute in September. I majored in English, Speech, and Theater. I had been on an award-winning debate team in high school and joined the one at SLI with a close friend as my partner. Those debate trips were highlights of the year, and because we had a superb coach in Professor Murphy, we placed first most of the time.

The summer of 1954, the *Brown v. Board of Education* case was settled in favor of integration, a decision that was not welcome in southern states. SLI stood out among the schools in those states by opening its doors to African American students that fall. President Joel Fletcher, Dean of Men Glynn Abel, and Dean of Women Miss Agnes Edwards contacted alums across the state, as well as African American leaders, to help recruit students. Believing that the first year of college is difficult enough, they encouraged transfer students who would have that first year behind them.

At the time, every new female student, freshman or transfer, had a Big Sister who would serve as a mentor the first semester. The earlier weeks were the most important, as new students needed information about the campus, ranging from the locations of buildings to the personalities of professors.

I was a junior, well-known on campus, and decided to offer to take one of the transfer students as my Little Sister because no one would make trouble when she was with me. I went to Miss Edwards's office and made my request. To my great surprise, she burst into tears.

When I asked her what was wrong, she said, "These are tears of joy. Every female cheerleader, every beauty queen, every officer of every sorority, every member of the homecoming court, and every member of the ROTC auxiliary has said the same thing. There aren't any transfer students left, so you'll have to settle for someone else."

That same week, a local student called a meeting in the auditorium in the Speech and Music building. He was pompous and thought well of himself, though few people shared that assessment. He watched students come in until every seat was filled, then called for silence.

"We can't keep them out of the dorms, or the classrooms, or the library, or the dining hall, but we paid for the Union, and we can keep them from it."

Someone in the back row stood up. "Hey, Julian. Where do you drink your coffee?"

"The Union."

"If we let the likes of you in there, who would we not allow?"

Whereupon we all got up and left.

More proof of the students' attitude to the transfer students came when my roommate, Barbara, and I and one of the African American transfers, Raymond, were in line at the dining hall. Raymond was a skilled radio technician, and he was going to work the board for a rather challenging radio show Barbara and I were in charge of.

We were discussing how to meet the challenges when a large boy, bully written all over him, came up to Raymond and made a vicious slur. Barbara, who was what was called a "Pocket Venus," reached out her right hand. The bully took it, thinking she was congratulating him. Instead, she flipped him over her shoulder, and he landed on his back. She wore shoes with Baby Louis heels and planted one foot in the middle of his chest.

"Apologize." The bully murmured something.

"Louder."

The bully looked to the crowd for support but met only cold faces. He apologized, and Barbara let him up. "If I ever hear of you bullying someone again, you'll deal with my boyfriend, and I don't think you'd enjoy that, because he's a champion welterweight boxer."

As an alumna of UL Lafayette, I receive news weekly, and it's clear that students' welfare is a top priority. Recent examples include UL being the first university in the country to provide a "Quiet Room" after hearing one had been created in California, where rape victims can talk in a home-like room rather than in a police office. Earlier examples are the administration's response to the 2016 flood. Deadlines for tuition were extended, people could pay tuition in installments, and when students arrived at the campus before the dorms were open, townspeople were asked to take them in.

The town also welcomes newcomers, those who arrive separately and those who arrive as a group, as did employees of every major oil company in the country when the oil boom began in the mid-1950s. Town and gown join to welcome newcomers not from a sense of duty, but with joie de vivre that results in Lafayette being chosen the happiest town in the country by *USA Today* every year. How very fortunate I was to spend my formative years there!

RECIPE INDEX

ABOUT THE AUTHOR

Elizabeth Nell Dubus published four Louisiana-based historical novels—*Cajun, Where Love Rules, To Love and To Dream*, and *Twilight of the Dawn*—in the United States, Canada, Great Britain, Australia, and France, as well as a contemporary novel, *Marguerite Tanner*, published in the United States and Denmark. Her numerous award-winning plays, including *Slow Fugue Before Dying, Jazz at Midnight*, and *Wages*, have been produced in theaters across the nation, including Los Angeles, Chicago, Washington, DC, New York City, and New Orleans. Two additional plays, *Power Point* and *Welcome Party*, were published in whole and as part of an anthology, respectively.

For more than a decade, Ms. Dubus penned a popular local newspaper column, "Conversations Over Coffee," which ultimately led to the publication of her parenting book, *When a Parent Imposes Limits: Discipline, Authority, and Freedom in Today's Family*.

Ms. Dubus taught writing at Louisiana State University, Southern University, and what is now the University of Louisiana at Lafayette, her alma mater. With a colleague, she also created and taught a drama program at the Louisiana State Penitentiary (known locally as Angola) that continues today.

Memories of a Louisiana Girlhood, her final work, was published posthumously.

Printed in the USA
CPSIA information can be obtained
at www.ICGtesting.com
CBHW021532070124
3206CB00003B/17